Policing and Minority Communities
Bridging the Gap

❖

DELORES D. JONES-BROWN

John Jay College of Criminal Justice
City University of New York

KAREN J. TERRY

John Jay College of Criminal Justice
City University of New York

Editors

M. L. DANTZKER

Series Editor

PEARSON

Prentice
Hall

Upper Saddle River, New Jersey 07458

Library of Congress Cataloging-in-Publication Data
Policing and minority communities: bridging the gap / Delores Jones-Brown, Karen
Terry, editors.
    p. cm.—(Prentice Hall's policing and ... series)
  Includes bibliographical references.
  ISBN 0-13-027017-2
    1. Police—United States. 2. Minorities—United States. 3. Police-community
relations—United States. I. Jones-Brown, Delores D. II. Terry, Karen. III. Series.

HV8139.P65 2004
363.2'0973—dc21

2002038119

Editor-in-Chief: Stephen Helba
Executive Editor: Frank Mortimer, Jr.
Assistant Editor: Sarah Holle
Production Editor: Emily Bush, Carlisle Publishers Services
Production Liaison: Barbara Marttine Cappuccio
Director of Production & Manufacturing: Bruce Johnson
Managing Editor: Mary Carnis
Manufacturing Buyer: Cathleen Petersen
Creative Director: Cheryl Asherman
Cover Design Coordinator: Miguel Ortiz
Cover Designer: Miguel Ortiz
Cover Image: Rich Meyer, Corbis/Stock Market
Editorial Assistant: Barbara Rosenberg
Composition: Carlisle Communications, Ltd.
Printing and Binding: R. R. Donnelley & Sons

Pearson Education LTD., *London*
Pearson Education Australia PTY. Limited, *Sydney*
Pearson Education Singapore, Pte. Ltd.
Pearson Education North Asia Ltd., *Hong Kong*
Pearson Education Canada, Ltd., *Toronto*
Pearson Educacíon de Mexico, S.A. de C.V.
Pearson Education-Japan, *Tokyo*
Pearson Education Malaysia, Pte. Ltd.

10 9 8 7 6 5 4 3 2 1
ISBN 0-13-027017-2

Dedication

This volume is dedicated to the memory of Sergeant Cornel Young, Jr.
and
To his father, Major Cornel Young, Sr.
May the tragedy of his loss never be repeated or forgotten.

Contents

❖

Preface

❖

Although policing in minority communities has been scrutinized for decades, there were two specific incidents that prompted the conception of this book. One was the shooting death of Amadou Diallo by four New York City police officers in 1999. Amadou, an African immigrant, was standing in the vestibule of his Bronx apartment building, unarmed, when the four plainclothes officers mistook him for a rapist they we ᵕ seeking. The exact details of what happened that night are unclear, but through a series of miscommunications the police fired 41 shots at Amadou, hitting him 19 times. This created outrage in the community and prompted a number of departmental changes (e.g., putting plainclothes officers back into uniforms). These changes were not systemic, were hastily implemented, and eventually most were repealed. Though the officers involved in the incident were criminally charged, they were eventually acquitted—an action that further dissociated minority communities from the police.

The other incident, which actually preceded the Diallo shooting (having occurred during the Spring of 1998) was, in a subtle way, even more striking given that it occurred at a school of criminal justice. Each year, John Jay College publishes an annual compilation of short essays written by its students. These essays are submitted by professors who received the work in class. One particular submission, written by a Latino student, was titled "Dead Cops Make Me Smile." In the essay, the student described how he was profoundly affected by a single humiliating encounter with a White police officer who, for no apparent reason, approached him on his stoop, addressed him using racial slurs, and was otherwise verbally abusive to him in front of his younger brother. In the essay, the student, who was in his mid-teens at the time of the encounter, goes on to note that continuing into young adulthood, the first encounter was followed by others less traumatic but equally unpleasant. While the later encounters involved other officers, he notes that it was the initial encounter with "Blondie" that crystallized into anger toward all police; so much so that, when he hears that a police officer has been shot, he can't help but smile at the fate of the cop who, in the essay author's opinion, received the fate he deserved.

Although this essay was inflammatory in its language against police officers, it highlighted a persistent problem in policing minority communities: the everyday interactions between police officers and residents of the communities. It is these interactions that create negative feelings between the two groups and allow for the most serious incidents–such as the shooting death of Amadou Diallo–to occur. Unfortunately, it is only the serious incidents of deadly force or systemic misconduct that come to the attention of the general public. However, the everyday interactions that lead to such abuses are the incidents that first must be examined and changed.

The purpose of this book is to analyze the everyday interactions between the police and minority communities as well as those incidents that come to public attention. Admittedly, the book's title is somewhat a misnomer because the pages which follow do not specifically address the relationship between the police and all of the various groups that are designated "minorities" within American society. The majority of the chapters focus on the plight of racial minorities (e.g., African Americans) as opposed to ethnic minorities (e.g., Hispanics, Asians, or persons from the Middle East). Nor does the book directly address issues related to persons whose minority status (and consequent treatment by the police) is as a result of their religion, sexual orientation, or physical abilities. However, many of the lessons learned from the chapters regarding police and their relations with racial minorities can easily be extended to other minority groups as well.

How the perception of differentness affects the social interaction between the police and residents of various neighborhoods is an important focus of the book. This book also looks at the actions that have been taken to alleviate the negative interactions that occur in these neighborhoods and why they are or are not effective at changing the attitudes of both the police and the community being policed. The reader will find that the onus of change is not on the police alone; rather, it is dependent upon a number of factors in the criminal justice system—such as consistent prosecution for police misconduct, implementation of changes recommended by investigative commissions, and increased accountability to both management and the community.

There are no easy answers on how to improve police-community relations in minority neighborhoods. However, by recognizing the issues that create conflicts we hope that it will be possible to more effectively reduce or eliminate these problems.

Acknowledgments

Our sincere appreciation for their patience and support goes to Mark Dantzker, the *Policing And...* series editor, and to Kim Davies, former Criminal Justice editor. We thank them both for making this opportunity possible. Many thanks to our contributors for their hard work and patience in bringing this project to fruition. A special thanks is extended to Robert McCrie, chair of the Department of Law and Police Science at John Jay College, who in the midst of controversy was willing to encourage meaningful dialogue and academic expression regarding this very important subject. We also wish to acknowledge and thank those members of the Department of Law and Police Science who took time out from their busy schedules to attend and provide meaningful input during the 1998 Anti-Police Bias meetings and the Better Teaching Seminar on Handling Anti-Police Bias in the Criminal Justice Classroom. We thank John Jay College President Gerald Lynch, Provost Basil Wilson, and Faculty Senate President Karen Kaplowitz for sponsoring the seminar in recognition of the importance of open dialogue in an academic setting. Finally, we are particularly indebted to Peter Diaz, a former John Jay student, for having the courage to share his pain; and to his English professor, Lee Jenkins, for recognizing the terrible profundity of the five shocking words that began Peter's essay.

Contributors'
Biographical Information

❖

Geoffrey P. Alpert is professor of Criminal Justice and Director of Research for the College of Criminal Justice at the University of South Carolina. For the past twenty years Dr. Alpert has concentrated his research and training on the evaluation of high-risk police activities, including the use of force, deadly force and pursuit driving, and accountability systems including Early Warning Systems. Dr. Alpert is currently working on two studies concerning police use of force to control suspects and Early Warning Systems. He has authored numerous books and monographs including *The Force Factor: Measuring Police Use of Force Relative to Suspect Resistance* (with R. Dunham), and *Police Pursuits: What We Know* (with R. Dunham, D. Kenney, and W. Smith). Dr. Alpert has also written more than 125 articles on topics including the use of force, pursuit driving, and accountability systems.

Christopher Cooper is an associate professor at Saint Xavier University in Chicago. He teaches in the Department of Sociology, Anthropology, & Criminal Justice. A former Washington, D.C. police officer, he holds a Ph.D. and is a licensed attorney. In 1996, he served as postdoctoral Fulbright Scholar and Lecturer at the University of Copenhagen, Denmark. He lectured on and conducted research into patrol police interpersonal conflict resolution methodologies. Dr. Cooper is one of the twelve authors of the book *Twelve Black Men Speak Out on Law, Justice and Life* (2002) published under the Amistad imprint of Harper & Collins.

Roger G. Dunham is a professor of Sociology at the University of Miami, Florida. He has coauthored four books on policing with Geoffrey Alpert and has published numerous professional papers and chapters. Recent coauthored books include *Critical Issues in Policing, 4th edition* (2001), *Policing Urban America, 3rd edition* (1997), and *Crime and Justice in America, 2nd edition* (2002). In addition, he has coauthored several research monographs with the Police Executive Research Forum, including *The Force Factor: Measuring Police Use of Force Relative to Suspect Resistance* (1997).

Mary F. Gibbons is an attorney with extensive experience in federal trial and appellate practice. She has served as an adjunct professor within the Department of Law and Police Science and currently instructs members of the NYPD in a special leadership program at John Jay College.

Heath Grant has seven years of experience working with law enforcement/community partnerships across the country analyzing problems, developing strategies, and creating systemwide changes through collaboration. He is currently working on a Bureau of Justice Assistance (BJA) sponsored project to assess national training and departmental needs related to cultural diversity and policing. He is a doctoral candidate and member of the faculty in the Department of Law and Police Science at John Jay College.

Anthony Harriott is a lecturer in the Department of Government at the University of the West Indies, Mona Campus. He has written several articles and reports on policing and crime control in the Caribbean and is the author of the recently published book *Policing and Crime Control in Jamaica: Problems of Reforming Ex-Colonial Constabularies.*

Delores D. Jones-Brown is an Associate Professor in the Department of Law, Police Science and Criminal Justice Administration at John Jay College, City University of New York. Her recent publications include *The System in Black and White: Exploring the Connects between Race, Crime and Justice*, coedited with Michael Markowitz (Praeger, 2000), *Race, Crime, and Punishment* (Chelsea House, 2000), and "Debunking the Myth of Officer Friendly: How African American Males Experience Community Policing," *Journal of Contemporary Criminal Justice* (May, 2000). She is a former postdoctoral fellow with the National Development and Research Institutes, Inc., and Teachers College, Columbia University. She holds both a Juris Doctor and Doctorate in Criminal Justice from Rutgers University, and is a former assistant prosecutor in Monmouth County, New Jersey.

John Kleinig is professor of philosophy in the Department of Law and Police Science, John Jay College of Criminal Justice, City University of New York, and director of the Institute for Criminal Justice Ethics. He is the editor of the *Journal of Criminal Justice Ethics.* Among his publications are *Punishment and Desert* (1973), *Paternalism* (1984), *Valuing Life* (1991), *Professional Law Enforcement Codes: A Documentary Collection* (with Yurong Zhang, 1993), and *The Ethics of Policing* (1996). He is currently writing a book on loyalty.

Raymond Manus is an adjunct professor of Police Science at John Jay College of Criminal Justice. He has retired as a lieutenant in the New York City Police Department where he undertook many evaluation projects.

James E. McCabe is a 15-year veteran of the New York City Police Department. He currently holds the rank of Deputy Inspector and is assigned as the Executive Officer of the Police Commissioner's Office. As the Executive Officer to the Police Commissioner, Deputy Inspector McCabe advises the Police Commissioner on operational and policy issues and oversees a reinvigorated Community Relations Program within the Department. He holds a Bachelor of Arts degree in Psychology from Queens College, a Master of Arts degree in Labor and Policy Studies from Empire State College, and is currently a Doctoral Candidate at the City University of New York Graduate School specializing in Criminal Justice.

Robert P. McNamara is Associate Professor of Sociology and the Director of the Center for Social Research at Furman University. He is also the Director of the Greenville Social Services Training Institute in Greenville, South Carolina. He has written numerous articles on a variety of topics and is the author of ten books: *Perspectives on Social Problems; Crossing the Line: Interracial Couples in the South* with Maria Tempenis and Beth Walton; *Crime Displacement: The Other Side of Prevention; The Times Square Hustler: Male Prostitution in New York City; Sex, Scams and Street Life: The Sociology of New York*

City's Times Square; Beating the Odds: Crime, Poverty, and Life in the Inner City; Police and Policing with Dr. Dennis Kenney; *The Urban Landscape: Selected Readings* with Dr. Kristy McNamara; *Social Gerontology* with Dr. David Redburn; and *Managing a Deviant Status: Field Research and the Labeling Perspective* with Deanna Ramey and Linda Henry. Dr. McNamara is a Senior Research Fellow for the National Strategy Information Center, the Policy Lab, and the Police Executive Research Forum in Washington, D.C. He is currently working with the Regional Community Policing Institute at Eastern Kentucky University to study school safety in eight high schools across the state. In addition, he is working with the Mexican government and the National Strategy Information Center to develop an anticorruption curriculum in their public schools. His Ph.D. in Sociology is from Yale University.

T. Kenneth Moran is a professor of Police Science at John Jay College of Criminal Justice. His main research interest is in police personnel and criminal justice policy. He has completed several research projects on police and criminal justice agencies.

Eugene O'Donnell is an attorney and teaches in the Departments of Law and Police Science and Special Programs at John Jay College of Criminal Justice. He has served as a New York City police officer, in the offices of the Queens and Brooklyn (New York) District Attorney, and as unit chief at the New York City Commission on Human Rights.

Eli B. Silverman, Ph.D., is a Professor in the Department of Law, Police Science and Criminal Justice Administration at John Jay College of Criminal Justice, City University of New York. He has previously served with the U.S. Department of Justice and the National Academy of Public Administration in Washington, D.C. and was a Visiting Exchange Professor at the Police Staff College in Bramshill, England. He has served as head of the Section on Public Budgeting and Finance of the American Society for Public Administration and as a consultant to numerous criminal justice agencies. Most recently, he is the author of a book *NYPD Battles Crime: Innovative Strategies in Policing* (Northeastern University Press, 1999) and several articles, including "Urban Policing and the Fear of Crime," in *Urban Studies,* Vol. 38, Nos. 5–6, May 2001; "William Bratton's Perspective on Democratic Policing," in *Policing, Security and Democracy: Theory and Practice*, M. Amir and S. Einstein (eds.) (Office of International Criminal Justice, 2001); and "Reigning in the Police," *Criminal Justice Ethics*, Vol. 17, No.2 Summer/Fall 1998. He has published numerous other chapters and articles related to his areas of interest, which include community policing, police management, comparative policing, policy analysis, compstat, and crime mapping.

Karen J. Terry is a criminologist at John Jay College in the Department of Law, Police Science and Criminal Justice Administration. She is currently carrying out research on sex offenders, focusing on issues of treatment efficacy, supervision of offenders, and management of offenders in prison and the community. She has also conducted research on internal versus external systems of review for police officers.

1

Policing and Minority Communities

An Introduction to the Exploration

M. L. Dantzker and Delores Jones-Brown

Harmony is a word not easily found in the lexicon of police and community interaction, especially with respect to minority communities. Since its modern beginning, the relationship between the police and minority communities has been anything but harmonious. From enforcing slavery and "Jim Crow" laws to the segregation of police power, where Black officers could only police Blacks—unless a White officer was around—yet the White officers could police everyone, the interactions between the police and minority communities have been strained at their best, and hostile and violent at their worst (Barlow & Barlow, 2000; Shusta, Levine, Harris, & Wong, 2002).

As this book was being created, one of the most controversial issues regarding policing and minorities was racial profiling. "Few issues in society today generate as much controversy as the issue of racial profiling" (Schott, 2001, p. 24). Racial profiling for the sake of this chapter refers to the actions taken by police officers against or toward an individual simply based on the person's race or ethnicity. The concern for this type of action had become so great that many states took decisive action to address the issue. For example, a Texas law that went into effect January 1, 2002, required that every police agency in the state take steps toward combating racial profiling. Such steps included mounting video cameras in all police units, keeping statistics for all traffic stops, and the training of all sworn officers against racial profiling.

The general consensus appears to be that racial profiling is a negative action by the police. Yet, as it has been suggested, "Profiling is an essential element of law enforcement, as necessary to preventing crimes and solving them as a badge and a gun. It is the head and the heart of intelligent policing" (Eisner, 2002, p. 1). Furthermore, "race can be a legitimate consideration for police officers" (Schott, 2001, p. 30). Therefore, one would assume that racial profiling would be an acceptable practice and it is, but only when there is reason to establish race as a prerequisite to an investigation (Huntington, 2001; Schott, 2001). The problem is that race is more often used as an excuse to make a stop or conduct an investigation as opposed to simply being an element of the stop or investigation. Regardless of how it is used, race has become a predominant issue in the area of policing, which is why this book has been developed.

The interesting aspect of problems pertaining to policing and minority communities is the question of perceptions. It is well documented in the study of psychology that how a person perceives an event, encounter, or activity will weigh heavily on how it is interpreted. Because everyone has a different perception, and thus many perceptions of the same event are inevitable, it is difficult to offer just one view of a particular situation. With this in mind, the remainder of this text should be thought of as a collection of perceptions regarding policing and minority communities where no one perception is either wrong or right but simply a matter of how each author perceives the particular area of discussion.

Beginning with Chapter 2, *Revering Some, Reviling Others*, McNamara examines how and why the police treat minority group members differently than nonminority group members. He suggests that there is evidence to substantiate differential treatment through a variety of indicators. For example, with respect to violent crime, the evidence suggests that both the race of the victim and the race of the offender plays a role in how the police will respond. Regarding the use of force and deadly force (by the police), although the number of incidents has declined, members of minority groups are still the greatest number of victims. He notes that minority officers may be guilty of being abusive toward minorities, too. Pertaining to arrests, the evidence indicates that the race of the victim and the offender plays an important role in the decision to make a formal arrest. Finally, in terms of other forms of abuse (for example, verbal or psychological), although these incidents generally leave no tangible proof of harm, McNamara notes that several studies conducted by both private and government agencies, along with plentiful personal anecdotal evidence, support the notion that in some locations race does appear to play a significant role in determining who is most likely to be the subject of verbal abuse, frisks, and other negative police action.

McNamara continues by noting that in its most basic form, the discussion of how the police treat minorities is essentially one involving police discretion. He then focuses on neighborhood and situational factors regarding use of discretion. He continues with a discussion of how the police subculture and its influence plays a major role in how police officers treat minorities.

Ultimately, McNamara suggests that many of the problems and tensions between the police and minorities are based largely on both groups' attitudes and perceptions of each other. He concludes by suggesting possible ways of improving the relationships, which include more training, improving recruitment and selection, and the establishment of clearly defined policies.

As previously noted, there is a long history of racial injustice in this country, with the criminal justice system, policing in particular, being a principal tool. This position is explored further in Chapter 3 by Harriott who uses the specific case of Amadou Diallo to examine *Presumed Criminality, Racial Profiling, and Policing in America*.

Harriott begins by noting that as the issue of crime becomes heavily racialized in the United States, policing tends to become a major conflict point and battleground. Using the Diallo case, he further illuminates the general problem of racial bias in the criminal justice system. This exploration begins with an examination of the literature on bias in criminal justice. His stance is that bias, especially racial profiling, has not yet been adequately addressed in mainstream literature.

The discussion continues with an explanation of how criminal profiling degenerates into racial profiling. Harriott's perception is that criminal profiling becomes racial profiling when it elevates race to the primary principle for predicting criminality and no longer serves as an investigative aid to case solving but instead serves as a tool for race differential surveillance and investigative detentions. His discussion continues with a look at the presumption of criminality, a condition where normal legitimate actions are taken out of context and given meaning that unreasonably imputes criminality. It is this condition he suggests that is most evident in racial profiling.

Harriott continues by noting that the evidence seems to suggest that a basic dualism of style exists. That is, he perceives that Whites tend to experience a protective professional and civil law enforcement while Blacks tend to experience a repressive and more militarized style associated with security policing. This chapter concludes with the perception that racialized injustice remains a major problem in the United States and that an end to the racial dualism is necessary.

Because racial profiling was one of the most popular areas of contention during the writing of this text, it was inevitable that at least one chapter would be devoted to a legal discussion of this specific topic. Chapter 4, *Profiling—More Than a Euphemism for Discrimination: Legitimate Use of a Maligned Investigative Tool,* by Gibbons is that chapter. Gibbons explores the use of profiling as a legitimate investigative tool and its concomitant acceptance by the courts. She begins with a discussion on profiling itself, noting that profiling has long been recognized as identifying general characteristics as a sign of a crime. She explains that the profiling established by the Federal Aviation Administration (FAA) and Drug Enforcement Administration (DEA) (hijackers and drug couriers) has passed muster in the courts. The courts have accepted profiles as an investigative tool as long as the stop was not made solely because of the race or ethnicity of the subject. She concludes that the courts have established the propriety of police reliance on broad descriptive categorizations of personal characteristics and that such conduct is acceptable.

Gibbons continues that race as an element of the reasonable suspicion necessary to initiate an investigative detention is a reasonable and acceptable practice as long as it is not the sole reason for the investigation. She indicates that an investigation where race is part of a direct description of the suspect is allowable, but that blanket stops are not. Furthermore, she discusses how disparate enforcement of the law can lead to the abuse of profiling. Overall, she suggests that while the practice of racial profiling has been maligned, profiling itself is recognized as a legitimate investigative tool. She concludes that profiling in and of itself is good, but using only or primarily race is not.

In Chapter 5, Kleinig presents an interesting perspective regarding the application of police ethics to police and minority community relations. In the chapter titled, *Police Ethics and Minority Communities,* he attempts to expand the understanding of police ethics by examining some of the contextual underpinnings of policing and the implications that these have for a police ethic.

Kleinig begins by developing what he terms an ethic of police professionalism. He is concerned with identifying the ways in which such an ethic can address minority concerns in police-citizen encounters. He discusses how the granting of power and discretion to police officers, in conjuction with issues of accountability, officer culture, and management culture all play a role in the police ethic. Furthermore, he argues that the police should be encouraged to develop an ethic of professionalism, that is, an ethic grounded in the socially sanctioned purpose of policing. To accomplish this task he suggests that there exists:

1. an appropriateness to quality of services and how they are provided,
2. an avoidance of unfortunate assumptions that police lack moral sensibility and need, somehow, to be initiated into the moral community,
3. a comportment that will be compatible with the outlook of those who have chosen to make policing their career,
4. a cultural base for effective self-policing, and
5. a reminder of the high calling to which police have committed themselves.

Kleinig continues with an in-depth discussion of ethics in a diverse culture. He notes that in diverse cultural settings the police, who are typically drawn from the dominant culture, may lack personal empathy for those policed. At the same time, they may be called upon to act in matters that express deep societal divisions and to respond to the nontraditional practices of marginalized or newly immigrant groups. Given these circumstances, he suggests that the development of a professional ethic among police means that there must be a recognition of constraints (legal and otherwise). There must be attempts to respond to social divisions in ways that reflect a commitment to peacekeeping rather than taking sides. And, in some instances the police are required to enforce the social status quo as inferred from existing statutes, despite the conflict with individual (or group) cultural practices and beliefs. In general, Kleinig advocates that the development of an ethic of professionalism in policing goes beyond just general ethics, but is also an attempt to explicate the implications of good character for a specific occupational role, the development of which would assist in major strides toward alleviating problems in relating to minority communities.

One of the longer lasting theories about criminality and a police approach to addressing it has been Wilson and Kelling's Broken Windows theory. In Chapter 6, *Fixing Broken Windows or Fracturing Fragile Relationships?* O'Donnell revisits this long-standing theory, advocating that there is nothing new about the Broken Windows approach. He argues that Broken Windows not only deliberately ignored the often painful lessons learned by law enforcement, particularly in the 1960s and 1970s, but was offered as a political decoy to divert attention from more serious and more enduring societal problems such as discrimination and poverty.

O'Donnell suggests that police activity, particularly that which involves aggressive tactics, falls disproportionately upon minorities and minority communities. To support his perception he uses the example of New York City's "zero-tolerance" policing and how it tended to overwhelmingly involve minorities. In closing, he offers how Broken Windows is an insightful philosophy but in order to be successful in application, it must not be disproportionately applied in minority communities.

Often left out of discussions about how the police deal with minorities is the role of police management. In their chapter, *Managing Ambiguity: The Role of the Police Middle Manager in Brokering Police-Minority Community Relations* (Chapter 7), Moran and Manus address this shortcoming. They begin by contending that the police will be most effective when they operate with the full cooperation and consent of the community.

The purpose of their chapter is examining the institutional forces that lead to the differing needs of the police department, the community, and the political system, using the Diallo tragedy as a prime example of what occurs when the police-community partnership breaks down. In particular, Moran and Manus's focus is on middle managers because of the belief that they are the key conduits of policy making from the police hierarchy to the community.

Moran and Manus offer five recommendations to assist police middle managers to better supervise their officers.

1. Recognize that the real problem goes beyond race to routine police management practices.
2. Reduce pressures to employ extra-legal tactics to "fight crime."
3. Relax the rhetoric, facilitate understanding, and avoid the diversions of blame and denial.
4. Restore the hierarchical chain of accountability.
5. Establish criteria to reward meritorious community policing.

They conclude that blame goes beyond the individual officer and that improvement is possible with community interaction.

Although racial profiling has moved to the forefront of the media, the use of force remains a very close second. The standard perception is that there exists a long line of use-of-force incidents against minority group members with the cases of Diallo, King and McDuffie being implicated as common practices by police officers. However, in Chapter 8, *The Effects of Officer and Suspect Ethnicity in Use-of-Force Incidents: Miami-Dade County, Florida*, Dunham and Alpert examine this perception.

To begin, Dunham and Alpert suggest that the use of force by police officers against minorities is an infrequent event. They suggest that recognition of this fact requires study of all known uses of police force against citizens and an assessment of the differences between force used on minorities and nonminorities. Therefore, the purpose of this chapter is to assess patterns of force by police for different levels of resistance by suspects while accounting for the ethnicity of officers and suspects. This was accomplished through a multiyear study of use of force in a large metropolitan police department in Miami-Dade County, Florida.

Dunham and Alpert's findings include that the use of force by police officers against suspects during arrest situations showed remarkably similar levels of force used against suspects of different racial and ethnic backgrounds. Furthermore, they conclude that there are some minor indications that the amount of force used against suspects varies based on officers' race or ethnicity—where minority officers may use higher levels of force against minority suspects than against Anglos, while Anglo police officers use about the same level of force against all suspects, regardless of race or ethnicity.

Despite their findings, Dunham and Alpert caution generalizing their findings because of the progressiveness of the Miami-Dade Police Department (MDPD), its data collection techniques, and training and supervision. Other agencies may not be equal to MDPD and thus their findings should not be generalized. However, Dunham and Alpert do conclude that it should not be accepted that race or ethnicity is not a factor in use of force, however, under certain circumstances it is not.

Continuing with the topic of police brutality, Cooper in Chapter 9, *Prosecuting Police Officers for Police Brutality From a Minority Perspective,* discusses and provides evidence that police brutality against minorities is more common than perceived, especially by Whites. He suggests that part of the issue is the failure to prosecute such actions.

According to Cooper, part of the problem regarding prosecuting police officers for brutality involves the fact that many prosecutors are White. However, he advises that prosecutors must realize that some White officers do commit brutality out of racial animus, but may not overtly display these racist tendencies. He suggests that failing to truly address this phenomenon makes it very difficult to improve the manner in which police officers (in particular, White officers) act toward minorities. Cooper concludes that although prosecuting police officers is a formidable challenge, it is not impossible, and it begins with open-minded prosecutors.

In recent years it has been strongly suggested that to address problems between the police and minority communities, cities should develop civilian review boards and actually implement their findings and recommendations. The exploration of this solution is the focus of Chapter 10, *The Roads Not Taken: Improving the Use of Civilian Complaint Review Boards and Implementation of the Recommendations From Investigative Commissions.* In this chapter, Terry and Grant analyze the root of the problems between the police and minorities within the context of the history of investigative commissions in the United States.

They begin their discussion by identifying problems encountered in policing minority communities, such as understanding the nature and quality of police-community interactions, discretion as an underlying issue, and the cycle of misunderstanding leading to the development of an "us versus them" mentality for both police and the community. The discussion continues with an examination of the cyclical nature of policing investigative commissions, examining the findings of such commissions as Wickersham, Kerner, Knapp, New York State Deadly Force Task Force, Mollen, and Christopher. They note that all cited poor police-community relations (PCR) as an underlying factor in the cases the commissions investigated and all gave recommendations for improvement.

Terry and Grant continue by identifying the outcomes of the commissions and how their implementation could help improve PCR. Among the recommendations were:

- improvements in recruitment and selection
- improving accountability mechanisms
- experiments with civilian oversight
- early citizen advisory boards
- the ombudsman model
- linking internal review processes with civilian review
- nationally implemented civilian review boards

Additionally, they noted that almost every commission has recognized the need for increased accountability, both hierarchically and democratically, and the need to resist "quick fix" options. They conclude that the key is not only to employ an adequate police complaint system and increase communication between the police and the community, but also to reduce the number of complaints to begin with. Ultimately, the focus should be on everyday interaction not just high-profile incidents.

Undoubtedly, every police department should be recognized for its efforts to combat crime. For the New York City Police Department (NYPD) the city's diversity offers a myriad of issues that cannot be addressed through a single vision. The last chapter of this text, *Policing a Diverse Community: A Case Study*, by Silverman and McCabe offers some insight into how an effort by one of NYPD's 76 precincts addressed the concept of community policing. In this chapter, Silverman and McCabe discuss the 110th Precinct's efforts to simultaneously focus on crime reduction and order maintenance while gaining citizens' confidence in the police.

The foundation of the 110th's efforts is the provision of visibility in highly traveled areas, responding back to crime scenes, aggressively attacking disorder and crime conditions, listening to the needs of the community and responding immediately, and working closely with both precinct and community members. Overall, Silverman and McCabe found that community policing was alive and well in the 110th Precinct.

Reality requires acknowledging that problems do exist regarding the police and minority communities. However, it should also be recognized that part of the problem results from perceptions formed by both police officers and community members. This text in no way is able to address all the problems nor does it offer all the answers, but it does attempt to offer varying perspectives as to the problems between police and minority communities. If nothing else, this text offers a place to begin seriously discussing a problem that cannot be ignored—policing and minority communities.

REFERENCES

Barlow, D. E. & Barlow, M. H. (2000). *Police in a multicultural society: An American story.* Prospect Heights, IL: Waveland Press.

Eisner, J. R. (2002). Use behavior, not skin color, to catch criminals. *The McAllen Monitor,* p. 1.

Huntington, R. (2001). Profiling: Suddenly politically correct? *Police, 25*(12), 18–20.

Schott, R. G. (2001). The role of race in law enforcement: Racial profiling or legitimate use? *The FBI Law Enforcement Bulletin, 70*(11), 24–32.

Shusta, R. M., Levine, D. R., Harris, P. R., & Wong, H. Z. (2002). *Multicultural law enforcement* (2nd ed.). Upper Saddle River, NJ: Prentice Hall.

2

Revering Some, Reviling Others

Robert P. McNamara

Early on the morning of February 4, 1999, a young immigrant from Guinea named Amadou Diallo was returning to his Bronx apartment when he was approached by four plainclothes New York City police officers. According to some accounts, Mr. Diallo fit the description of a serial rapist who had assaulted some 40 women in areas around Manhattan. What happened as the officers approached Mr. Diallo is unclear. The officers contend they identified themselves and said Mr. Diallo's behavior led them to believe he was reaching for a weapon. Others present at the time disagree with this interpretation of events. What *is* known is that officers drew their weapons and fired a total of 41 shots, resulting in the unarmed Mr. Diallo's death ("Only a Minority," 1997).

In 1997, Abner Louima, a 30-year-old immigrant from Haiti, was arrested when he tried to intervene in a fight outside a Brooklyn nightclub. When Mr. Louima arrived at the police station, he was dragged into a restroom and sodomized by officers with the handle of a toilet plunger, which was then forced into his mouth. Eventually, he was taken to the hospital after having been charged with resisting arrest and disorderly conduct. Mr. Louima was critically injured, suffering a perforated colon, a lacerated bladder, several missing teeth, and an assortment of other injuries (Puddington, 1999).

Recent studies in Maryland and New Jersey have confirmed profiling by police agencies that target African Americans. In April 1999, the Attorney General of New Jersey issued a report stating that state troopers had engaged in racial profiling along the New Jersey Turnpike. The data used in this report showed that people of color constituted nearly 41% of the stops made on the turnpike and although few stops resulted in searches, 77% of those searched were people of color. This is in contrast to searches of Whites, which constituted approximately 11% of the total searches (Farmer & Zoubek, 1999).

In New York City, a report issued by the New York Attorney General also indicated that racial profiling occurred with regard to stop and frisk practices. After reviewing

175,000 incidents in which citizens were stopped by the police over a 15-month period in 1999, African Americans were stopped six times more often than Whites, and Latinos were stopped four times as often. African Americans make up 25% of the city's population but 50% of the people stopped (Spitzer, 1999).

On almost any given day, we hear of instances like the ones just described. These dramatic episodes raise questions about the role of the police in our society, particularly in their interactions with minority groups. Some minority leaders, as well as others, have asserted that the police, and to some extent the entire criminal justice system, are prejudiced and racist. These individuals argue that situations like the ones described above are indicators that the police single out minorities and treat them differently. Is there any truth to these assertions? Are the police racist? Do they treat minorities differently? This chapter reviews the information available about how and why the police treat minorities differently. Part of the explanation is found in the socialization of police officers as well as the labeling theory of deviance.

PUBLIC OPINION AND THE POLICE

According to a 1997 Justice Department report, an estimated 45 million people in this country—about 20% of the population—have some form of face-to-face contact with the police every year. In a review of the literature on the public's attitudes toward the police, Decker (1981) found that while race and ethnicity are the most important factors in shaping attitudes toward the police, the vast majority of Whites have very favorable attitudes toward the police. More recently, according to the 1998 *Sourcebook of Criminal Justice Statistics,* 85% of the people surveyed by the Department of Justice said they were very satisfied with the police who served their neighborhoods. Whites expressed the most satisfaction, with 90% being very satisfied or satisfied, while only 76% of African Americans felt that way.

There is also a difference in the way people feel about how the police treat other groups. According to the 1998 *Sourcebook of Criminal Justice Statistics,* in response to the question "Do you think the police in your community treat all races fairly or do they tend to treat one or more of these groups unfairly?", 59% felt the police treat all groups fairly, 33% felt they treated one or more groups unfairly, and 7% did not know. When the race of the respondent is included however, a dramatically different picture emerges. Sixty-seven percent of Whites felt the police treat all races fairly, while only 48% of Hispanics and only 30% of African Americans felt that way.

These figures show that in general, a significant proportion of the population thinks the police are doing a good job. Problems become clearer when other variables are accounted for. Minorities generally feel less confident in the police and are generally less satisfied with police services. Another important factor is the characteristic of the neighborhood. As Smith and Visher (1981) have found, people living in high-crime neighborhoods and low-income communities tend to have more contact with the police and report less overall satisfaction with them. Furthermore, because minorities tend to live in low-income and high-crime neighborhoods, it is not surprising that the confidence in the police is lower than that of Whites.

Why do police officers have more contact with low-income and minority neighborhoods? Part of the answer is that this group makes greater use of police services than other groups. As Walker, Spohn, and Delone (1996) describe, police departments assign more patrol officers to these neighborhoods because of greater calls for service and because there are higher crime rates in these areas. Another reason cited by Walker, Spohn, and De-lone (1996) is that minorities and low-income people are more likely to call the police to solve a variety of noncriminal matters. Compared with middle-class Americans, for instance, people in the low-income category are more likely to call the police for assistance for things like medical emergencies and family problems. This means that the police are more actively and intrusively involved in the daily lives of people from these areas. This greater contact also means that the decisions made by officers may not be what the members of these neighborhoods prefer, resulting in lower levels of satisfaction.

Judging from the evidence, and while these topics remain controversial, there appears to be evidence to substantiate a differential treatment of minorities on a variety of indicators: violent crime, deadly force, arrests, and other less serious forms of abuse.

VIOLENT CRIME

Many people, including the police, believe that minorities are more involved in violent crime than Whites. Moreover, this perception affects how officers respond to violent crimes. For instance, using data from the *National Crime Victimization Survey* from 1987 to 1992, Bachman (1996) examined the relationship between the victim's and the offender's race on three police responses to robbery and aggravated assault: the response time to the scene, the amount of effort made by officers to investigate these crimes at the scene, and the likelihood of arrest.

With regard to arrest, officers were quicker to respond and invested more effort in the investigation (i.e., searches) when the incident consisted of African American offenders and White victims. This relationship held even when variables such as poverty, victim's gender, and whether or not the victim was injured were taken into account. With regard to aggravated assault, particularly involving strangers, officers were more likely to be more thorough at the scene if it involved a White victim and an African American offender. Officers were also much more likely, all other things being equal, to respond more quickly and to put forth a more determined effort if there was an injury to the White victim.

Thus, the evidence suggests that the race of the victim and the offender plays a role in how the police respond to violent crime. If the crime involves a White victim and African American offender, officers seem to respond more quickly to the scene of the crime, investigate it more thoroughly, and arrests are more likely to occur.

ARRESTS

Is race a factor in the arrest of a suspect? It seems fairly clear that minorities are arrested out of proportion to their representation in the population. According to the *Uniform Crime Reports* in 1998, African Americans represented about 12% of the population but 34% of all arrests, with 41% of those arrests for violent crimes. However, there is a great deal of controversy surrounding this issue. What are the reasons for this apparent differential treatment? Do police officers arrest minorities more frequently due to racial bias or because minorities commit more crimes? What variables are considered in the decision to arrest?

Almost 30 years ago, Black (1971), in his famous article "The Social Organization of Arrest," found that the decision to arrest was usually predicated on a number of factors.

These include the strength of the evidence, the seriousness of the crime, whether or not the complainant or victim wanted the suspect arrested, and whether the suspect was disrespectful toward the officer. The decision to arrest was also based on the relationship between the victim and the offender. If the suspect was a stranger to the victim, the officers were more likely to arrest him or her.

Interestingly, Black found that race was not a factor in the decision to arrest. He did find that African Americans were arrested more often than Whites, but this was mainly because they were less likely to show deference to the officer. As he describes, this creates a vicious cycle, where the African American men who are arrested more often have negative feelings toward the police. When these feelings are demonstrated, these men are more likely to be arrested. This, in turn, increases the hostility felt by African Americans.

Although Black did not find that race was a factor in the decision to arrest, since that time a great deal of research (e.g., Bachman, 1996 mentioned previously) has found that it does matter. In the 1980s, for instance, race was considered in terms of the decision to arrest. Smith, Visher, and Davidson (1984) found that in those instances where the suspect was African American and the victim was White, officers were much more likely to make an arrest. Similar to Black's (1971) findings, in these situations officers were also more likely to arrest the suspect when the victim requested it.

In 1983, Petersilia found that African Americans and Hispanics were more likely to be arrested on less evidence than Whites. She also found that they were more likely to be released without the case going to the prosecutor. Although at first glance this may appear to be advantageous, arrest still represents a form of punishment even though formal charges may not be filed.

From another point of view, Son, Davis, and Rome (1998) studied 718 police officers in Ohio and examined the extent to which a suspect's race influenced an officer's behavior. The results of the study showed that officers did not feel race was a significant factor in determining their behavior. However, like the findings by Black in 1971, what was significant (as reported by these officers) was the suspect's demeanor—how he or she acted toward the officer.

In summary, the evidence seems to suggest that race does play an important role in the decision to arrest, albeit, perhaps indirectly. Namely, African Americans who are accused of committing crimes against White victims and/or who (in the perception of the responding officer or officers) do not show sufficient deference to the officers' authority, are more likely to be arrested—particularly if the victims request the arrests. For historical reasons (e.g. the role of police in the enforcement of discriminatory laws), and/or because of prior personal or indirect negative experiences with the police, African American suspects may come to the police encounter with unfavorable attitudes toward law enforcement agents. The police, in turn, respond to the expression (or perceived expression) of these attitudes by finding a reason to make a formal arrest.

USE OF FORCE

While the Rodney King example is perhaps the most visible and memorable reminder of the excessive use of force by police officers, there had been considerable interest in the topic prior to the King incident (Friedrich, 1980; Cohen, 1986; Adams, 1995). One area of study on this topic that has been overlooked involves Hispanics. Although the subject of police treatment of minorities has been discussed in a variety of ways, such as the aforementioned arrest rates

(Sampson, 1986; Smith & Visher, 1981), abusive practices (Reiss, 1971; Westley, 1970), and the use of deadly force (Fyfe, 1982; Sorensen, Marquart, & Brock, 1993), most of these have overlooked Hispanics, an increasingly large segment of our society. In one of the few studies on the subject, Holmes (1998) compared perceptions of police abuse of minorities by Whites and Hispanics in a U.S.-Mexico border community. He found that young, male Hispanics and those living in the barrio were more likely to report having seen abusive practices.

Similarly, the police in these communities were more likely to view individuals in the communities with suspicion and rely on stereotypes to explain their behaviors. Other research supports this finding. For instance, Maguire, Pastore, and Flanagan (1998) found that a higher proportion of Hispanics, compared with others, believed the police use excessive force. Thus, it appears that like their African American counterparts, Hispanics are more likely to be perceived as threatening to the police, and this creates a climate of fear, suspicion, and hostility from both groups.

DEADLY FORCE

Generally speaking, despite the notoriety when such events occur, there has been a general decline in the incidence of deadly force by the police (Walker, Spohn, & Delone, 1996). However, a great deal of attention has been given to the frequency with which police officers use deadly force against minorities (Shoop, 1998; Fyfe, 1988; Dunham & Alpert, 1993; Westley, 1970). As Fyfe (1988) and Geller and Scott (1992) found, African Americans are disproportionately killed by the police when compared with their numbers in the population. However, the findings of these studies also suggest that when compared with rates of police-citizen contacts, arrest rates, and resistance to or attacks upon the police, there is no apparent racial disparity in the use of deadly force by the police.

As Walker, Spohn, and Delone (1996) point out, by the mid-1980s when many departments adopted a defense of life rule, the number of persons shot and killed by the police decreased significantly. Part of the reason for the general decline in the use of deadly force has come from more restrictive policies at the departmental level as well as from the United States Supreme Court's decisions. Sherman and Cohn (1986), for instance, found that between 1970 and 1984 the police use of deadly force declined substantially, particularly against African Americans. More recently, the data indicate that the racial disparity in the number of people shot and killed by the police has decreased from about seven African Americans for every White to about three to one (Walker, Spohn, & Delone, 1996).

By the 1980s, a number of departments had changed their use of deadly force policy to one using a "defense of life" criteria. These are situations in which the officer is justified in using deadly force if the officer's or another person's life is in jeopardy. Another situation in which deadly force is justified occurs when the officer prevents the escape of a person who is extremely dangerous (Roberg & Kuykendall, 1993). One of the most significant changes in the use of deadly force came as a result of a Supreme Court decision.

In *Tennessee v. Garner*, two officers used deadly force against an African American juvenile who was fleeing the scene of a burglary. At that time, the officers were justified in using deadly physical force against a fleeing felon, defined as someone who had committed a felony and was attempting to elude the police. However, the Court ruled that this was no longer acceptable. As a result, many departments were required to modify their policies concerning use of force against fleeing felons. Thus, although there was a time when officers were given wide latitude in using deadly force, since 1985 departments all over the country have changed their policies regarding the use of force, and the number of incidents has declined considerably.

MINORITY POLICE OFFICERS: ABUSERS, TOO?

Although the study of the relationship between minorities and arrests is fairly well documented, another area that has not been examined in as much detail is how minority officers interact with people who live in low-income neighborhoods.

According to Carter (1995), minority police officers are in an extremely difficult position. He contends that African American officers feel that there is a subtle distinction in the decision-making process between White and minority officers. Black officers believe that minority officers will be disciplined or fired if they use unnecessary force against a White or affluent person. Until only recently, White officers knew no such fear when they acted similarly in poor or minority neighborhoods. Carter (1995) also argues that an increasing number of minority officers have never lived in inner-city neighborhoods, and this lack of exposure may explain why some African American officers react too harshly—similar to their White counterparts. Additionally, the nature of policing contains within it a pervasive cultural influence: fitting in is an important part of being a police officer. Carter believes that as a consequence, some minority officers overreact in their treatment of minorities because they want to fit in with their White colleagues.

There is an added problem for minority officers, however, which adversely affects minority recruiting. Many minority officers are accused of "selling out" or being a traitor to their race by entering law enforcement. Because of the suspicion and tension between minorities and the police in neighborhoods around the country, and because many of these sentiments are confirmed in interactions with the police and others, many minorities, particularly African Americans, dislike and mistrust other African Americans who enter the profession.

Moreover, as Peak (1993) contends, many African American officers feel as though they experience a double dose of marginality as police officers. Not only must they perform their duties at a high level, but oftentimes they are perceived by other officers as well as community members to be representatives of the feelings of their race. To complicate matters further, because many urban minority communities have high crime rates and other problems, minority officers may also be prevailed upon by their superiors to maintain control in those communities.

OTHER FORMS OF ABUSE

The issue surrounding discriminatory treatment extends beyond serious offenses however. In fact, one might argue that it is the less serious forms of abuse that create a climate of fear and hostility between the police and minorities. These indignities, or what Liebow (1999) has referred to as the "little murders of everyday life," characterize the attitudes the police have toward minorities in some circumstances. The difference between this type of abuse and the others discussed, however, is that there is no tangible reminder that the incident occurred.

Unlike the use of force or arrest, verbal abuse, profanity, stop and frisk searches, or profiling usually end with the interaction. These incidents usually occur on the street and typically involve no witnesses. This makes sustaining allegations very difficult and results in continued tension between the police and minorities.

For instance, the New Jersey State Police are under investigation for allegedly ordering officers to concentrate on stopping Black drivers. Three state troopers have stated they were instructed by their superiors to single out African American drivers for traffic stops. The Justice Department is currently investigating these allegations. Additionally, a 1992 study of traffic stops in Florida found that while 5% of the drivers on the road were African American or Hispanic, nearly 70% of those stopped and 80% of those searched were African American or Hispanic.

Further, according to Cole (1999), from January 1993 to August 1995 almost 90% of the individuals subjected to search and seizure operations on buses and trains were people of color. Another study of all reported federal decisions from 1993 to 1995 involving bus and train sweeps found that nearly 90% of those targeted were minorities.

Another example of stopping and searching minorities occurred in Los Angeles in 1988, known as Operation Hammer. The purpose of Operation Hammer was to identify potential offenders in certain neighborhoods and to decrease fear among residents. For two years, African American and Hispanic youth who were found in middle-class neighborhoods were very likely to be stopped and searched and, subsequently, very likely to be arrested (Crank, 1998). More than 1,400 minority youths were arrested; many of them were released later for lack of any charges.

Browning et al. (1994) explored the extent to which there are racial differences in getting hassled by the police, which they defined as the frequency with which Whites and Blacks are stopped or watched by the police when they have done nothing wrong. They also explored the extent to which there are racial differences in getting hassled—which they defined as being stopped or watched by the police as well as what they identified as *vicarious hassling* (knowing someone who has experienced this type of treatment by the police).

Their main argument is that African Americans are more likely to perceive that they are hassled by the police personally and vicariously. Nearly one-half of African Americans in their study had experienced a negative police interaction and two-thirds knew someone who had a similar experience. This compared with the 10% of Whites who experienced this type of treatment in the same way. Although they do recognize that it could be a result of different patrol practices, which focus on minority neighborhoods, they also recognize that some of these perceptions may be a result of frequent police contact. A third explanation may be that there exists a perception by officers that African Americans and other minorities are more likely to commit crimes and thus are potential offenders that warrant their attention.

Finally, there is verbal abuse. Many complaints are filed each year against officers who verbally abuse citizens. The Christopher Commission, created to investigate allegations of abuse in Los Angeles following the beating of Rodney King by White officers, found that officers frequently use abusive language. This may occur during the interaction with citizens or it may happen between officers. For instance, the commission discovered computer messages were sent between officers that contained racially offensive comments.

Research on police behavior suggests that derogatory comments and the stigmatizing labeling of people are ways for officers to control suspects. As White, Cox, and Basehart (1991) note, profanity serves several functions: to gain the individual's attention when interacting with officers, to keep them at a social distance while the interaction occurs, and to psychologically dominate the individual.

What does all this tell us? It should remind us that the relationship between the police and minorities is a complex one. And while minorities are arrested disproportionately, it may be due in part to the greater involvement in criminal activities, and it may also have to do with the way they respond to police contact. Structural issues such as poverty and overcrowding in urban areas may contribute to greater police contact, in that the problems experienced in those areas require more frequent police presence. Minority involvement with the police may also have something to do with the attitudes of police officers—some officers believe minorities are more likely to become involved in criminal activities so they merit greater police attention. Finally, minority overrepresentation may also have something to do with the perceptions of the police by the public, particularly minority groups, and this tends to inflame the nature of the interaction between the two groups. What must be remembered, however, is that while there may be an overrepresentation of minorities in arrests and criminal activity, this still represents only a small proportion of the overall minority population.

FACTORS THAT CONTRIBUTE TO POLICE DECISION MAKING

In its most basic form, the discussion of how the police treat minorities is essentially one involving police discretion. The topic of police discretion has been studied at length (Goldstein, 1991; LaFave, 1965; Mastrofski, Ritti, & Hoffmaster, 1987; Powell, 1981). Brooks (1993) does an excellent job of conceptualizing the factors that contribute to police decision making. While there are a set of organizational factors that contribute to police discretion, such as the degree of bureaucracy, size of the department, and the supervisors' span of control of officers, and while individual officer variables such as age of the officer, years of experience, and education level are significant, perhaps most important are what Brooks describes as neighborhood and situational variables.

Neighborhood variables include the racial composition of an area. As was mentioned, generally speaking, the higher the proportion of African Americans in a neighborhood, the greater the likelihood of the police being called to that area. Also, officers tend to conclude that when they are called to such an area, there is a greater likelihood that an arrest will be made, that someone involved in that situation will resist, and the potential risk to officer safety is higher. Thus, the anxiety level for officers is higher and they will react more quickly to threats that they perceive as a danger to their safety (Eisenman, 1995).

Situational variables affect police discretion in that the decisions of officers are based not so much on structural characteristics, such as the racial composition of a neighborhood, but on what a person does in the course of the interaction with that officer. Examples of situational variables include demeanor, age, gender, preference of the complainant, visibility of the encounter, and the presence of others. Van Maanen (1978), in his seminal paper on the perceptions and attitudes of the police, found that the police tend to focus not on suspects, but on individuals who, in their behavior, displayed a resentment about the intrusion of the police into their lives. He referred to these individuals as *assholes*. In response to the presence of people like this, the police feel that they exist, in part, to protect the world from assholes.

According to Van Maanen (1978), the asshole isn't easily identified. Labeling someone an asshole involves an interaction between the person and the police. In other words, the process of labeling the person has more to do with what the individual does in the encounter with the police than with any characteristic or trait they possess.

Finally, the officer's attitude about minorities, which is generally a function of the police subculture, is an essential ingredient to how and in what way the officer responds to the situation and the individuals in it. Because understanding the behavior of officers is, in part, a function of their attitudes, it is important to examine how those attitudes are shaped and influenced.

Some contend that police officers have very different personalities from people in other occupations (Crank, 1998). Others maintain that there is a cultural distinction that separates law enforcement from other occupations (Putti, Aryee, & Kang, 1988). Still others contend that officers have neither personality nor cultural differences from other occupations. In sum, what we know about the police culture and personality is dependent on how one views police behavior. Although no single perspective provides a complete understanding of the varieties of police behavior, there is a long history of debate as to whether they have unique personalities or whether socialization and subcultures play a significant part in the behavior of police officers (Adlam, 1982).

What can be said with some confidence is that the roles and functions of the police set officers apart from other members of society (Radelet, 1986). The remainder of the chapter will focus on what some researchers refer to as the police "subculture." Certain of these subcultural aspects play an important role in understanding officers' attitudes, values, and beliefs, as well as their behavior with regard to minorities.

THE SOCIALIZATION OF POLICE OFFICERS

A number of researchers argue that personality is subject to change based on different personal experiences and socialization (Kornblum, 2000; Adlam, 1982). This school of thought focuses on the role of the police in society and how professionalization, training, and socialization influence an individual's personality and behavior. Researchers operating from this paradigm study how the work environment, peers, and academy training shape and affect a police officer's personality and behavior.

A somewhat different approach contends that socialization occurs, but it is more of a group experience than an individual one (Stoddard, 1968; Van Maanen, 1973). For example, Van Maanen (1973) disagrees with the idea that police officers have certain personality characteristics, such as authoritarianism. He argues instead for a perspective based on both group socialization and professionalism. The latter is the process by which norms and values are internalized as an individual begins his or her new occupation. In this way, just as attorneys and physicians learn the values endemic to their profession, so too do police officers.

The socialization perspective assumes that police officers learn their "social" personality from training and through exposure to the demands of police work. It follows then that if police officers become cynical or rigid, it is not because of their existing personality or individual experience, but because of the demands of the job and the shared experiences of others. Some research supports this idea (Crank, 1998; Kenney & McNamara, 1999).

For instance, Bennett (1984) found that while probationary officers' values are affected by the training process, little evidence was available that officers' personalities were shaped by their peers in the department. Other studies, such as Putti, Aryee, and Kang (1988), find socialization into the subculture of police may occur at different points in officers' careers. There is little evidence concerning the extent of how reference groups affect the personality of older officers, but it seems that in the beginning of his or her career, the officer's occupational values are shaped during the training and probationary process.

To deal with the social isolation that is derived from their use of authority (some of it self-imposed), officers use other members of the profession to cope with social rejection. As a result, many, perhaps most, police officers become part of a closely knit subculture that is protective and supportive of its members while sharing similar attitudes, values, understandings, and views of the world. The idea of the police being a subculture is not new and has been well documented (see for instance Westley, 1970; Rokeach et al., 1971; Kirkham, 1976; Bittner, 1970). Entry into this subculture begins with a process of socialization whereby recruits learn the values and behavior patterns characteristic of experienced officers. The development and maintenance of negative attitudes and values by police officers has many implications.

Skolnick (1966) as well as Westley (1970) were among the first researchers to examine the influence of the police culture. In a study of two cities he called Eastville and Westville, Skolnick (1966) noted that police officers displayed prejudicial views toward African Americans. He distinguished, however, between prejudice and racist behavior. Although negative attitudes toward African Americans were common, these feelings were not often acted upon—racist behavior was uncommon. While there was no training conducted that told officers to treat African Americans differently, Skolnick states "from the point of view of the African American or the White who is generally sympathetic to the plight of the Black in America, most police officers—Westville and Eastville alike, would be regarded as highly racially biased" (p. 80). The essential question for Skolnick was not whether officers were racially prejudiced but whether racial prejudice influenced their judgment in the use of discretion.

Skolnick's work has made a significant contribution to our understanding of police-minority relations. Police attitudes toward minorities, as they are toward citizens in general, are filtered through a subcultural lens that has a significant impact on an officer's behavior. The attitudes, values, and beliefs that are strongly encouraged by the subculture have a major impact on how individuals will encounter and interact with all members of the community.

CONCLUSION: MAKING SENSE OF POLICE-MINORITY RELATIONS

It seems that police officers discriminate against minorities and it seems that they learn this in the context of being socialized as police officers. As Van Maanen (1978) has described, officers generally appear to have strong convictions about their assessment of these groups. This is similar in some ways to how most people in our culture understand things around them. In general, it seems that once we learn something in society, whatever its source, it is often very difficult for us to consider another way of understanding that phenomenon. We all have what Leon Festinger (1954) called a fundamental "need to know" or understand the physical and social world around us. As such, we seek answers to questions around us and sometimes use stereotypes to answer those questions.

We tend to take cues from people and things and when enough cues emerge, we tend to categorize the person. If a person acts in a particular way, he or she must be *that* type of a person. If a person looks or dresses unconventionally, then sweeping generalizations about who that person is and what he or she believes are often made by other people. This simplistic understanding of the world around us and the people in it leads to what phenomenologists call *typifications*. We put people and things into categories so that we are able to understand where they fit into our world, and, conversely, we understand our place in it as well. We label people and these labels can be negative ones—such as stereotypes about minorities. This categorizing is what Fritz Heider (1958) referred to as a *naive psychology* in that we all do this, and for the most part it is harmless. But is it? Does it reflect a myopic view of the world in which everyone and everything must fit someplace into some category?

The reasons why we use a naive psychology lie in part in people's perception. They tend to take their social world for granted, accepting their society and customs as unquestioningly as they do the physical world around them. Thus, while people want to understand their world, they do not want to understand too much of it.

Since people see the world narrowly because they do not transcend their own experiences, many have very firm but erroneous beliefs about "how things ought to be." They have not taken that next step in understanding, and, for the most part, they do not want to. Because many people in our society take such a position, it changes the influence of the larger social order on people's behavior. It also helps to explain how and in what ways stereotypes are created and perpetuated. In fact, one might argue that stereotypes are little more than typifications that have been used to explain people's attitudes, values, beliefs, and behaviors over time.

This naive psychology along with the "need to know" also affect police officers. They, like the rest of us, seek answers to questions in part because of their safety needs and in part because they are expected to solve the problems our society faces. Perhaps nowhere is this naive psychology better understood than with the way the police perceive minority groups.

One of the primary cues police officers use to identify and typify a person, as well as their attitudes, behaviors, values, and beliefs, is race. It is the most visible indicator, it is the easiest to identify, and, in policing, where the officer must make an assessment of the person quickly, it is often the only one used. But that initial assessment may lead the officer to draw a host of conclusions, which, in turn, influence the officer's behavior. This behavior will be interpreted by the minority and he or she will react accordingly. Thus, if the officer concludes that African Americans or Hispanics are more likely to commit crimes, are more likely to pose a threat to the officer's physical safety, and are more likely to challenge the officer's authority, the officer will inevitably begin the interaction with these thoughts in mind. The minority member will respond to what he or she perceives as threatening behavior, creating a self-fulfilling prophecy. The behavior of the minority will confirm what the officer thinks he or she already knows: minorities are potential trouble. When in reality, what may have happened is that the officer created the circumstances in which that outcome was derived.

Thus, many of the problems and tensions between the police and minorities are based largely on the attitudes and perceptions of both groups about each other. These attitudes, values, and beliefs are reflected in the negative labels applied by each group. For many police officers, these attitudes and overall treatment of minorities are derived largely from the way officers are socialized and conform to the standards of the police subculture. While not all officers adopt these values, given the nature of policing and the significant influence of the subculture on its members, many officers adopt views that contribute to the long-standing tensions between the two groups.

WHAT TO DO?

Obviously, this is a complex problem that will not be solved with a single strategy or a simple solution. However, there are some things that departments can do to begin addressing the problem more effectively. For many criminal justice practitioners, the obvious answer is more training. This is sometimes coupled with collecting data in a given community to determine the extent of racial tensions and to use that information to educate officers about the deleterious effects of stereotyping, racial profiling, and biased policing. Still others will call for improved recruitment and selection procedures to screen out those officers who would be more likely to treat minorities differently. In a recent article in the *FBI Law Enforcement Bulletin,* the author discusses the three ingredients necessary to implement nonbiased traffic stops (Carrick, 2000). Those three ingredients are a clearly defined organizational policy prohibiting unfair treatment of minorities (e.g., profiling); officer training, which involves diversity and profiling discussions in refresher and recruit training courses, and the collection of data to demonstrate to the public that mistreatment of minorities is not a widespread practice in the department. These are said to strengthen the bonds of trust with the community as well as demonstrating an air of professionalism within the department.

Although all of these suggestions are important and deserve mention, it is important for administrators to take a step back even farther from the immediacy of the problem. Rather than simply providing more training or to begin collecting data on the topic, it is important for police chiefs to ask a more fundamental question: What type of officer do I need to hire? As was mentioned, perhaps the problem is embedded in the characteristics of existing police officers. These, of course, stem from the personality traits of officers as well as the environment in which they are socialized. Perhaps what is needed is a new breed of officer who will understand and avoid the traps to which such practices can lead.

REFERENCES

Adams, K. (1995). Measuring the prevalence of police abuse of force. In W. Geller & H. Toch (Eds.), *And justice for all.* Washington, DC: The Police Executive Research Forum.

Adlam, R. K. (1982). The police personality: Psychological consequences of becoming a police officer. *Journal of Police Science and Administration, 10*(3), 344–349.

Bachman, R. (1996). Victims' perceptions of initial police responses to robbery and aggravated assault: Does race matter? *Journal of Quantitative Criminology, 12*(4), 363–390.

Bennett, R. R. (1984). Becoming blue: A longitudinal study of police recruit occupational socialization. *Journal of Police Science and Administration, 12*(1), 47–57.

Bittner, E. (1970). *The functions of police in modern society.* Chevy Chase, MD: National Clearinghouse for Mental Health.

Black, D. (1971). The social organization of arrest. *Stanford Law Review, 23,* 1087–1111.

Brooks, L. W. (1993). Police discretionary behavior: A study of style. In R. G. Dunham & G. P. Alpert (Eds.), *Critical issues in policing: Contemporary readings* (pp. 140–164). Prospect Heights, IL: Waveland Press.

Browning, S. L., Cullen, F. T., Cao, L., Kopache, R., & Stevenson, T. J. (1994). Race and getting hassled by the police: A research note. *Police Studies, 17*(1), 1–11.

Carrick, G. (2000). Professional police traffic stops: Strategies to address racial profiling. *FBI Law Enforcement Bulletin, 69*(11), 8–10.

Carter, R. A. (1995). Improving minority relations. *FBI Law Enforcement Bulletin, 64*, 14–17.

Cohen, H. (1986, Summer/Fall). Exploiting police authority. *Criminal Justice Ethics,* 23–31.

Cole, D. (1999). When the reason is race. *The Nation, 268*(10), 22.

Crank, J. P. (1998). *Understanding police culture.* Cincinnati, OH: Anderson.

Decker, S. H. (1981). Citizen attitudes toward the police: A review of past findings and suggestions for future policy. *Journal of Police Science and Administration, 9*, 80–87.

Dunham, R., & Alpert, G. (Eds.). (1993). Critical issues in policing: Contemporary readings (2nd ed.). Prospect Heights, IL: Waveland Press.

Eisenman, R. (1995). Is there bias in U.S. law enforcement? *Journal of Social, Political, and Economic Studies, 20*, 229–240.

Farmer, J., & Zoubek, P. (1999). *Final report of the state police review team.* Trenton, NJ: Office of the Attorney General.

Festinger, L. (1954). Theory of social comparison. *Human Relations, 7*, 117–140.

Friedrich, R. J. (1980). Police use of force: Individuals, situations, and organizations. *Annals of the American Academy of Political and Social Science, 452*, 82–97.

Fyfe, J. J. (1982). Blind justice: Police shootings in Memphis. *Journal of Criminal Law and Criminology, 73*, 707–722.

Fyfe, J. J. (1988). Police use of deadly force: Research and reform. *Justice Quarterly, 5*, 165–205.

Geller, W. A., & Scott, M. S. (1992). *Deadly force: What we know.* Washington, DC: Police Executive Research Forum.

Goldstein, H. (1991). Controlling and reviewing police-citizen contacts. In T. Barker & D. L. Carter (Eds.), *Police deviance* (2nd ed.). Cincinnati, OH: Anderson.

Heider, F. (1958). *The psychology of human relations.* New York: John Wiley and Sons.

Holmes, M. D. (1998). Perceptions of abusive police practices in a U.S.-Mexico border community. *Social Science Journal, 35*(1), 107–118.

Kappler, V. E., Blumberg, M., & Potter, G. W. (1993). *The mythology of crime and criminal justice.* Prospect Heights, IL: Waveland Press.

Kenney, D. J., & McNamara, R. P. (Eds.) (1999). *Police and policing: Contemporary issues* (2nd ed.). Westport, CT: Praeger.

Kirkham, G. (1976). *Signal zero.* New York: Ballantine.

Kornblum, W. (2000). *Sociology in a changing world* (5th ed.). Belmont, CA: Wadsworth.

LaFave, W. (1965). *The decision to take a suspect into custody.* Boston, MA: Little, Brown and Company.

Liebow, E. (1999). *Tell them who I am.* Chicago: University of Chicago Press.

Maguire, K., Pastore, A. L., & Flanagan, T. J. (Eds.). (1998). *Sourcebook of criminal justice statistics.* Washington, DC: U.S. Government Printing Office.

Mastrofski, S., Ritti, R., & Hoffmaster, D. (1987). Organizational determinants of police discretion: The case of drinking and driving. *Journal of Criminal Justice, 15*, 387–401.

Only a minority: Police brutality. (1997, August 23). *The Economist, 344*(8031), 19.

Peak, K. J. (1993). *Policing American methods, issues and challenges.* Englewood Cliffs, NJ: Prentice-Hall.

Petersilia, J. (1983). *Racial disparities in the criminal justice system.* Santa Monica, CA: RAND.

Powell, D. (1981). Race, rank and police discretion. *Journal of Police Science and Administration, 9*, 383–389.

Puddington, A. (1999). The war on the war on crime. *Commentary, 107*(5), 25.

Putti, J., Aryee, S., & Kang, T. S. (1988). Personal values of recruits and officers in law enforcement agency: An exploratory study. *Journal of Police Science and Administration, 16*(4), 245–249.

Radelet, L. (1986). *The police and the community* (4th ed.). New York: Macmillan.

Reiss, A. J., Jr. (1971). *The police and the public.* New Haven, CT: Yale University Press.

Roberg, R. R., & Kuykendall, J. (1993). *Police and society.* Belmont, CA: Wadsworth.

Rokeach, M., Miller, M., & Snyder, H. (1971). The value gap between police and policed. *Journal of Social Issues, 27,* 155–171.

Sampson, R. J. (1986). Effects of socioeconomic context on official reaction to juvenile delinquency. *American Sociological Review, 51,* 876–885.

Sherman, L., & Cohn, E. (1986). *Citizens killed by big city police, 1970–1984.* Washington, DC: Crime Control Institute.

Shoop, J. G. (1998). National survey suggests racial disparity in police use of force. *Trial, 34*(1), 97.

Skolnick, J. (1966). *Justice without trial: Law enforcement in a democratic society.* New York: John Wiley and Sons.

Smith, D. A., & Visher, C. (1981). Street level justice: Situational determinants of police arrest decisions. *Social Problems, 29,* 167–177.

Smith, D. A., Visher, C., & Davidson, L. A. (1984). Equity and discretionary justice: The influence of race on police arrest decisions. *Journal of Criminal Law and Criminology, 75,* 234–249.

Son, I. S., Davis, M., & Rome, D. M. (1998). Race and its effect on police officers' perceptions of misconduct. *Journal of Criminal Justice, 26*(1), 21–28.

Sorensen, J. R., Marquart, J. W., & Brock, E. (1993). Factors related to killings of felons by police officers: A test of community violence and conflict hypotheses. *Justice Quarterly, 10,* 417–440.

Spitzer, E. (1999). *The New York City Police Department's "stop and frisk" practices: A report to the people of the State of New York from the Office of the Attorney General.* New York: Civil Rights Bureau, Office of the Attorney General.

Stoddard, E. R. (1968). The informal code of police deviancy: A group approach to blue-collar crime. *Journal of Criminal Law, Criminology, and Police Science, 59*(2), 201–203.

Tennessee v. Garner, 471 U.S. 1 (1985).

U.S. Department of Justice: Bureau of Justice Statistics. (1998). *Sourcebook of criminal justice statistics.* Washington, DC: U.S. Government Printing Office.

Van Maanen, J. (1973). Observations on the making of policemen. *Human Organization, 32,* 407–418.

Van Maanen, J. (1978). The asshole. In P. Manning & J. Van Maanen (Eds.), *Policing: A view from the street.* Santa Monica, CA: Goodyear.

Walker, S., Spohn, C., & Delone, M. (1996). *The color of justice: Race, ethnicity, and crime in America.* Belmont, CA: Wadsworth.

Westley, W. (1970). *Violence and the police: A sociological study of law, custom, and morality.* Cambridge, MA: MIT Press.

White, M. F., Cox, T. C., & Basehart, J. (1991). Theoretical considerations of officer profanity and obscenity in formal contacts with citizens. In T. Barker & D. L. Carter (Eds.), *Police deviance* (2nd ed., pp. 275–297). Cincinnati, OH: Anderson.

3

Presumed Criminality, Racial Profiling, and Policing in America—with Special Reference to the Diallo Case

Anthony Harriott

Two defining features of a democracy and important markers of a civilized society are the equal protection of all citizens from arbitrary and repressive state violence, and the respect for the rule of law by the institutions charged with the enforcement of the law. In such societies, breeches of these principles may and do occur, but not in a systematic pattern of abuse of particular subpopulations. Moreover, in such societies the commitment to justice requires that when breeches of these principles do occur, authoritative institutions provide ample avenues for material and symbolic redress. Sadly, the historical experiences of subordinate groups in the United States, particularly the experiences of African Americans, cast doubts on the commitment of the society and state to these principles—as *universals* rather than as *in-group prerogatives.*

The United States has had a long history of racial injustice—with its criminal justice system and police services in particular being principal instruments of repression (and at times social advances) (Higginbotham, 1978; Staples, 1999). Being a highly politicized system, it has always been influenced by the prejudices (racial and otherwise) as well as the resistance movements that reflect the positive ideas of its people. But this problem of racial injustice is not peculiar to the United States; racism is a truly global phenomenon. Thus Canada (Wortley, 1999), England (Holdaway, 1996; Keith, 1993; MacPherson, 1999; Webster, 1997), France (Tournier, 1997), and other countries of Europe (Tonry, 1998), Australia (Purdy, 1996), Latin America (Moffett, 2000), and the Caribbean (Chadee, 1998; Deosaran, 1985), which also have highly visible Black and other non-White populations, tend to suffer similar problems of institutionalized racism in their police services. The intensity of this form of racial oppression varies with the level of permissiveness or tolerance of racist practices in these societies. In America, racism has been a profound social movement that has historically been in decline but still waxes and wanes and has helped to shape the behaviour of important American institutions—particularly the control institutions of the state. The present attitude in the United States is largely shaped by a conservative social movement with a strong racial subtext—mobilized to put an end to the perceived pandering to subordinate groups and Blacks in particular—to dismantle affirmative action, repatriate illegal non-White immigrants, get tough on petty criminal offending, and protect the claims of Whites to privileged access to social goods (Block, 1987). While this movement has been broadly contested, it has largely succeeded in setting the agenda for public policy debates and in forcing many concessions to its programme. These get-tough-on-crime policies, or rather the excesses of police abuse associated with them, which are rightly seen in the current context as part of the inherent logic of this policy, serve to sharpen racial tensions and the conflicts between the police and minorities. As the issue of crime becomes heavily racialized, policing tends to become a major conflict point and battleground on which the contestation of the social construction of the racialized criminal and the racialized responses of the state to this criminality takes place.

This was the context in which the Diallo case occurred and was publicly debated. On February 4,1999, Amadou Diallo, a young, Black immigrant from Guinea, West Africa, was shot to death at the door of his apartment in the Bronx borough of New York City. His assailants were four White police officers, all of whom were members of a special Street Crimes Unit of the New York City Police Department (NYPD) who, in sum, fired 41 shots at him, 19 of which hit their mark. At the time of the shooting, the victim was unarmed, had no previous criminal record or reputation, and by all reports was a law-abiding, productive, and responsible "resident alien." He was neither a discredited nor a discreditable person—which, as will be seen later, is usually treated as a matter of considerable importance in such cases. Yet the police officers responsible for killing him were acquitted of all the criminal charges that were brought against them.

Such cases are extreme in the severity of their consequences (lethal violence is used in only a very small proportion of the incidents of police brutality) and perhaps in the vulgarity of the injustice, but they resonate with the wider populations of subordinated "minorities" because in their extremity they highlight the systematic abuse and the difficulties of claiming justice in these racist systems. The extreme nature of the incident, the seemingly blatant injustice, and the rebuffing of the efforts of the victimized to claim redress, served to bring into sharp relief the contrast between the legitimacy rhetoric of the system and its practices. In their essence, instances such as the Diallo case capture the problems of racialized interaction between lower-class Blacks and the control agents of these powerful countries where they are treated as racialized others, strangers regardless of their nationality and the value of their contribution to national life.

The Diallo incident and the subsequent trial of the accused officers raises a number of troubling issues about the character of policing and criminal justice in America and the problem of racialized notions of criminal suspicion. Earlier, the similarly celebrated cases of Rodney King and O. J. Simpson highlighted the problem of the divergent perceptions of the criminal justice system among Blacks and Whites; that is, "Why can't we see eye to eye?" In the King case, despite the presentation of videotaped evidence of the crimes of the police officers, the judgment of the Simi Valley jury and the integrity of the system was not called into question—except by the rioting Black population. However, in the Simpson case, after his acquittal, the judgment of Black jurors was called into question and the generalizations and proposals for systemic reengineering came with great speed and fury. The debate was kept focused on possible structural solutions. It was suggested that if the judgment of Black jurors could be so racially distorted (that they could not see the "mountain of evidence" and "obvious" guilt of Simpson), perhaps it was time to abolish the jury system. The discussion of possible systemic imperfections was restricted to criticisms of the jury system, which was perversely seen as allowing minority misperceptions of justice and erroneous ideas about the imperfections of the system to enter its deliberations and thereby to infect and corrupt it. Unlike in the Diallo case, as noted earlier, the central thrust of popular (media) concern in the King and Simpson cases seemed to have been with the differing racialized *perceptions* of the Black and White populations, rather than with the legitimacy or illegitimacy of the *claim,* of the U.S. criminal justice system, that it is based on universal notions of justice and uniform application of similar standards of justice, regardless of the status of the defendant. There was also no consideration given to the dangers posed to subordinate racial groups by state police violence and racially motivated corruption of the processes of criminal investigation and adjudication. In this chapter an attempt is made to further illuminate the general problem of racial bias in the criminal justice system in America. It tries to do this by using the Diallo case to explore the problem of racial profiling and to illustrate the problem of the presumed criminality of Blacks. Here it is argued that the targeting of Amadou Diallo by the police and the facility with which the justification for the killing was accepted by the courts and promoted in the electronic media, is best explained by this presumption of criminality—which is grounded in judgments about the intrinsic moral character of Blacks. (That groups have intrinsic moral qualities is quite a dubious claim, but exploring this would be too much of a digression.)

Of course to argue that there is systematic racial bias in the American criminal justice system is in effect to argue that it is not a just system. After all, the essence of justice is fairness. This perhaps explains the intellectual gymnastics and incredible efforts to deny the evidence of an existing (not just historical) racial bias in the system (Wilbanks, 1987). Much of the discussion is on the operative ideas that were played out in the tragic killing of Amadou Diallo and during the processing of this event in the court and the media. However, racism is not simply ideational in its sources. There are real interests and issues of institutionalized socioeconomic and political power that condition these attitudinal orientations and belief structures. Nevertheless, in an effort to stay close to the actors, this chapter focuses on an interpretation of the interactions and how they are informed by beliefs about Black criminality.

BIAS IN THE CRIMINAL JUSTICE SYSTEM

In its generality, as racial bias in the criminal justice system, this is an old and highly controversial issue that has generated a considerable literature (Markowitz & Jones-Brown, 2000; Mhlanga, 1997; Hood, 1992; Wilbanks, 1987; Christianson, 1986; Barkan & Cohn, 1998; Culliver & Sigler, 1995; Smith, et al, 1984). Yet in its specificity—as racial profiling—this problem remains a terribly neglected topic. A survey of six of the major criminology and criminal justice journals put out by the main professional organizations representing academic researchers and practitioners in the United States, Canada, and England, where this problem is most evident and has been a topic of popular debate for some time, revealed the following: Of the 103 articles published in *Criminology* during the period 1995–1999 (excluding 1998, which was inaccessible to the author), none were on this issue. Similarly, of the 129 articles published in *Justice Quarterly* during this period, while 9% (11) were concerned with issues of race, none engaged the particular issue of racial profiling. This issue was completely absent from the *Canadian Journal of Criminology and Offender Therapy* and the *British Journal of Criminology,* although in the case of the latter, of the 157 articles, three were concerned with the problem of race and criminality or race and justice. The *Journal of Contemporary Criminal Justice,* like *Justice Quarterly,* was fairly attuned to issues of race and crime and dedicated an entire volume to a discussion of hate crimes, but of the 96 articles only one approximated a discussion of this theme by exploring police use of deadly force with respect to race. Perhaps this problem could be viewed as a narrow sociolegal issue. But then even the *International Journal of the Sociology of Law,* which carried 91 articles, published only one article that was directly related to this issue. Despite the centrality of race in much of the popular discussions about crime and criminal justice in America, during the period under review, none of the articles in these journals explicitly discussed, as a focal issue, the problem of racial profiling in America or even the more general issue of racism in the American police services. The mainstream journals have clearly ignored this mainstream issue.[1] In 1993, Barbara Hudson characterized mainstream criminology as having little concern

> with the part played by social reactions in producing criminal identities and an absence of any appreciation of crime and criminal justice as contingent outcomes of social-political configurations. With regard to race issues, it remains focused on questions of race and criminality and explaining the differences in black and white patterns of offending. (Hudson, 1993, p. 3)

This characterization still remains quite accurate. With regard to racial profiling, the more general published works have been largely devoted to measuring and empirically exploring the problem in order to better inform the debate on the biases in the system. This author is unaware of any attempt to elaborate the problem of racial profiling conceptually.

Racial Profiling

Before attempting to develop the analysis, it may be useful to try to clarify the concept of racial profiling. Such clarification may best begin with an understanding of criminal profiling, as racial profiling is essentially a perversion of this idea. Bartol suggests the following definition of criminal profiling:

> It is a technique for identifying the major personality, behavioral, and demographic characteristics of offenders based on an analysis of the crimes they committed. (cited in Cook & Hinman, 1999, p. 231)

---

[1] Since the writing of this chapter, three articles on racial profiling have appeared in mainstream criminology journals: "Race and Place: The Ecology of Racial Profiling African-American Motorists" by A. Meehan and M. Ponder and "Theory and Racial Profiling: Shortcomings and Future Directions in Research" by R. Engel, J. Calnon, and T. Bernard. Both were published in *Justice Quarterly*. A third, "Perceptions of Racial Profiling: Race, Class, and Personal Experience," by R. Weitzer and S. Tuch was published in *Criminology*.

Criminal profiling begins with data from the scene of a specific crime, from which a profile of the offender is developed in order to focus the investigation of the particular crime. Such profiles, which are highly speculative, may include attributes such as race, sex, and age (which are fairly general in that they are *group attributes),* possible relationship to the victim (which may be inferred from, for example, the intensity with which the harm was inflicted on a murder victim—signs of intense anger may suggest a close emotional relationship to the victim), the psychological state of the offender, and so forth (Cook & Hinman, 1999). It is the multiplicity of attributes that allows the police to narrow their focus and to match the speculations of the profiler with other sources of information and data, thereby even further narrowing their investigations. The profiler helps to develop a theory of the event and thus to guide further investigation. This is clearly useful—if its limitations are understood and taken into account. It however has great potential for abuse, as is evidenced by its degeneration into racial profiling.

Criminal profiling becomes racial profiling:

- When it elevates race to the primary principle for predicting criminality. Good predictor variables differentiate between criminals and noncriminals. For as complicated a phenomenon as criminality, prediction, to the extent that it may have any real value, must be based on a dynamic interaction of the relevant predictor variables. To highlight a single factor, as is the case in racial profiling, simply does not differentiate between the likely criminal and the noncriminal.
- When it no longer serves as an investigative aid to case solving—but instead as a tool for race differential surveillance and investigative arrests.

When criminal profiling becomes racial profiling, the focus on the individual offender and its use as an aid to case solving is lost. To fail to differentiate at the individual level and to simply focus on people *as members of a group,* suggests a shift from its use as an investigative tool to a tool for control and repression (Verna, 1997). As racial profiling, it becomes intrusive and discriminating, while violating the right of the individual involved. It is a presumed "Black criminality."

The Presumption of Criminality

The Diallo case, if nothing else, expressly made evident the operation of a racialized presumption of criminality in police encounters with young "minority" and particularly Black males. A presumption of criminality refers to a condition where normal legitimate actions are taken out of context and given meanings that unreasonably impute criminality, such as looking down the street becomes "behaving furtively," admiring a Ferrari becomes "perhaps he is considering how to steal the Ferrari," window-shopping makes one a suspected shoplifter, a wallet in the hand of an adult male becomes a gun in the hands of a dangerous person, a candy bar in the hand of a child becomes a gun in the hand of a threatening delinquent, and so forth. In my personal experience, simply sitting in the international airport in Miami reading a newspaper while awaiting an outgoing flight to Costa Rica was enough to excite the imagination of DEA agents (ironically, I was en route to an international conference on drug trafficking in the hemisphere). *Normal* activity evokes *criminal* suspicion.

These ideas may be further illuminated by contrast. The opposite of the presumption of criminality may roughly be regarded as the presumption of innocence. However, the latter only applies when one is already a suspect: it applies to the process of moving a case through the criminal justice system and the treatment of the accused during this process by the police and courts. The former, that is, the presumption of criminality, applies in the first instance to the process of becoming a suspect—by virtue of social categorization, of belonging to a social group, in the case of African Americans, by their racialized existence. This presumption of criminality then persists throughout all subsequent stages of the process, thereby setting in train a complex of injustices. Because of the systematic bias in the system, once set in motion by the initial injustice (at the point of contact with the police), it becomes extremely difficult for the other institutions of the system to correct the initial injustice. This is evident in the current public debate on how death row prisoners who may be innocent ought to be treated (Cannon, 2000; "Dead Man," 2000). Official responses seem to be guided by a crude utilitarian logic that objectifies these convicts and makes re-trials and the admission of system-induced miscarriages of injustice difficult. In this regard, the American criminal justice system truly acts as a system.

The presumption of criminality is perhaps most evident in racial profiling. Racial profiling is no more than the codification of racial prejudice—as a guideline for the selective surveillance and investigation of the members of designated racial groups without much regard for their behaviour as individuals. With racial profiling, the presumption of Black criminality is shaped by the police into codes or guidelines for occupational conduct. Prejudice and discrimination is thereby masked and legitimized as "professional" conduct; becoming less visible to the unprejudiced police officer who sees his enforcement of the guidelines as simply "doing his job." Prejudiced police officers may, with greater facility and institutional support, zealously overpolice and underprotect Blacks without fear of reference to their prejudice. The logic associated with overpolicing of the Black population is similar and related to the justification for underprotecting this population: as Blacks who are not criminally implicated tend to be viewed as being supportive of their criminal kin, they are viewed as not being worthy of proper police protection. This is an extension of the argument associated with racial profiling.

Unprejudiced and normally reluctant discriminators, to borrow Merton's (1949) terminology, may now engage in discriminatory behavior while considering themselves to be good officers simply doing their duty.[2] Criminality is racialized and blackness criminalized—in institutionally authoritative ways. With Blacks criminality is anticipated, and subsequent conduct, particularly conduct that rightly questions the judgment of the officer(s) and the police department, is in turn taken as an indicator of hostility to law and law enforcement and thus a purported predisposition to criminality. After all, from the perspective of the police and the White population, why would anyone resent being stopped by the police if they are honest, law-abiding citizens? So even if criminality is not confirmed in the particular stop, that is, no incriminating evidence is found during the stop, this criminality is nevertheless affirmed by the (rightly) uncooperative behaviour of the Black target/victim. The outcome of most involuntary contact between Blacks and the police therefore tends to confirm this presumption of criminality.

---

[2] See *Discrimination and the American Creed* by Robert Merton (1949). In *Discrimination and National Welfare*, edited by Robert MacIver, New York: Harper and Row.

The low threshold of reasonable suspicion in the case of Blacks is perhaps most apparent from data on police-initiated stops of citizens in different public settings. In a report recently published by the Attorney General of New York State, considerable data is given on stop-and-frisk by the NYPD. For the period 1997–1998, the New York City Police Department (NYPD) reported 35,000 stops conducted by its officers. It is estimated that this represents approximately 10% of the number of true stops; that is, only 10% of all stops are really reported by the police. Of some 15,000 police stops that were analyzed, 62% of all persons stopped were African American—even though this group accounts for only 25% of the population of the city. Blacks were 2.5 times more likely to be stopped by the general police than Whites (and 4 times more likely to be stopped by the Street Crimes Unit than Whites) (Spitzer, 1999).

Of course, it may be argued that Blacks are disproportionately stopped because they account for a disproportionately large number of the crimes that are committed—a central argument made by spokespeople for the NYPD, including its chief. The data however does not support this claim. Regression analysis of the data indicates that the difference in stop rates for Blacks and Whites was not sufficiently explained by differences in crime rates in the areas where the stops occurred (Spitzer, 1999, p. 121). Moreover, such unequally intense surveillance would be expected to yield a disproportionate arrest rate even if the rate of offending across the races was uniform. Any honest discussion of this issue should take this into account. Nevertheless, the records on the activity of the more zealous Street Crimes Unit of the NYPD indicate that the arrest yield from these stops in the case of Black suspects was 1 in every 16.3 stops. These data suggest that in relation to African Americans, at minimum, a very low standard of suspicion is being employed by the NYPD. Further analyses of these data are needed in order to better probe how racialized notions of criminal suspicion operate.

If the primary objective of policing in Black neighborhoods is indeed crime control, then one would expect that even if the police operate with crude racialized profiles of the criminal offender based on high rates of Black offending, this would still be mediated by sex, age, and class. Data from Toronto suggest that while age offers Blacks some protection from police harassment, it offers them much less than their White counterparts (Wortley, 1999). If in the United States the probability of being stopped if one is a young Black male is little different from that of a middle-aged Black male (there are no significant age effects), this would indicate a particularly virulent form of racist policing. There is considerable anecdotal evidence in support of this. In fact, with respect to high occupational status, while this is believed to protect Whites, the opposite is true for Blacks. In the case of Blacks, it is felt that to the extent that they display the material markers of high occupational status, such as ownership of expensive cars, this tends to place them under police suspicion rather than protect them. Their race remains their master status. This problem needs to be analyzed statistically. There are a number of important implications that would follow from any conclusive supporting evidence. For example, one would have to question whether policing in Black communities is primarily about law enforcement or rather about intimidation and the control of an entire subpopulation—a style that approximates the security policing that typifies much of Latin America and which contrasts sharply with the styles of policing typically experienced by White America. The evidence seems to suggest that a basic dualism of style exists.

Whites tend to experience a protective professional and civil *law enforcement* while Blacks tend to experience a repressive and more militarized style associated with *security policing.*[3]

In a study of traffic stops conducted in the New Jersey area in 1993, it was found that African Americans made up 13.5% of the driving population in the research site and 15% of the traffic violators. Nonetheless, they represented 35% of those stopped for speeding. In this case Blacks were 4.85 times more likely to be stopped than members of other racial groups (Lamberth, 2000, p. 241).

Even more revealing are the data on stops and searches at international airports. Summarizing a report by the General Accounting Office of the U.S. government, Loven writes:

> Only a fraction of 1% of the 71.5 million passengers entering the United States on international flights in fiscal year 1998 were singled out for searches, the report said. And the majority of those 52,455 searched passengers were subjected to simple pat-downs.
>
> Black women were selected for more intrusive searches—strip searches or X-rays—more than any other group. Whites also had a high likelihood of being strip-searched, and black men were chosen more often than most other passengers to be X-rayed. (Loven, 2000, p. 1)

Both the selection and the intensity of the scrutiny are racially disproportionate. But what is interesting here is that the pattern of searches bears no relationship to the real pattern of arrests for international drug trafficking offences. It is well known among specialists in narcotics policing that international traffickers tend to use White females as drug mules and to avoid the use of Blacks, precisely to exploit the notions of White innocence and to avoid the scrutiny to which Blacks are usually subjected (Personal correspondence, 2000).

A similar pattern occurs with regard to the policing of drug users. Thus, while Blacks reportedly account for 13% of all drug users in the United States (which closely approximates their proportion of the population), they account for 55% of all drug convictions and 74% of all incarcerations (Johnson, 2000, p. 93). In the United States, less than 40% of all victimizations are reported to or are detected by the police (Schmalleger, 1999, p. 80). It follows from this that intensive scrutiny and effective investigation of *any group* would considerably increase its arrest and conviction rates. This is especially true for groups that are currently subjected to relatively low levels of police scrutiny. To use the city of New York as an example, in sharp contrast to Blacks who comprise 26% of the population, but account for 51% of all persons stopped by the police, Whites comprise 43% of the population but account for only 13% of all stops (Spitzer, 1999, pp. 94–95). Indeed, there is some limited evidence that suggests that were Whites similarly subjected to the intensive surveillance and investigation that Blacks are subjected to, their arrest and conviction rates would perhaps exceed the rates recorded for Blacks. In this regard, data provided by the NYPD on its stop-and-frisk activity indicate that while 1 in 9.5 stops of Blacks resulted in arrests, the arrest yield when Whites were stopped was 1 in 7.9 (Spitzer, 1999, p. 111). Based on these data, the logic of efficiency

---

[3] For an elaboration of the distinction between ordinary law enforcement and security policing, see *Police and Crime Control in Jamaica: Problems of Reforming Ex-Colonial Constabularies,* by A. Harriott (2000). Kingston, Jamaica: University of the West Indies Press.

would suggest the increased surveillance and investigation of Whites, but the fixations of the NYPD are such that instead Blacks were six times more likely to be stopped than Whites.

As noted earlier, one of the interesting things about racial profiling is that racial prejudice and discrimination are institutionalized so that these acts are masked and legitimized in the form of a professional code. Racism is masked in an occupational idiom. Attempts to unmask the institutionalized effects of race, to show its unconscious workings, thus become readily viewed as "playing the race card," and being unfair to people who are really not prejudiced and who are simply being professional (but who may from time to time err in their professional judgment as allegedly occurred in the Diallo case).

Given these influences, it was not surprising that in the case of the killing of Mr. Diallo, the courts ruled that the officers acted reasonably and properly. One difficulty here is that if Mr. Diallo also acted properly, we would be left at a loss to explain how after proper and reasonable conduct on all sides, the body of one of these reasonable actors was left lying on the ground. Clearly, if the rules are appropriate, some of the participants in the drama must have acted improperly. The argument, roughly but hopefully not inaccurately, is as follows. By sitting on the steps of his apartment (in a dangerous neighbourhood) late in the night, and looking up and down the street (at a slowly approaching and thus conspicuously suspicious unmarked car and perhaps if other such cars were approaching from the opposite direction), Mr. Diallo put himself under suspicion. By subsequently attempting to evade the armed males who alighted from the car and who overtly displayed an interest in him, Mr. Diallo thereby confirmed that this suspicion was justified.

His perceived criminality was confirmed with a curiously remarkable facility and specificity. According to the officers responsible for killing Diallo, he *became* (was treated as if he was) the rape suspect who was believed to have been preying on females in that area of the city. That Diallo was treated as a suspect because of this rapist at large is a concrete expression of presumed Black criminality. His ordinary and rational behavior (taking evasive action when aggressively approached late in the night by four armed men) was taken to confirm his dangerousness. His possession of a beeper and a wallet—common and ordinary possessions held by so many New Yorkers at any time of day—in the setting of his area of residence, which was regarded by the police as having a high crime rate, was quickly transformed into a gun and his evasive actions a threat to the lives of the police officers and the occupants of the building.

Goffman's (1963) idea of stigma helps to further illuminate this problem. He notes that social status is usually taken as holding clues to social identity, meaning that, from a group's location in the social structure, assumptions are made about the moral attributes of its members. In the case of African Americans, their status in American society carries a presumption of criminality (social identity). Given the level of residential segregation in America, Black places are likely to have a similar status because the setting establishes what kind of person is likely to be encountered there. In a red-light district, for instance, one is likely to encounter prostitutes. In a predominantly Black inner-city area with a high rate of violent crime, what is to be expected? From the viewpoint of the police, dangerous types—drug pushers, rapists, other forms of "low life" and "trash," and their collaborators.

"Black places," therefore, are considered to be dangerous places. Perhaps some law-abiding citizens may also be encountered there, but even these persons are still likely to be considered somewhat tainted by their social proximity to the criminal offenders who operate in their communities. Prolonged interaction with the stigmatized, even if involuntary, is always stigmatizing. This type of setting may be believed to filter out the Black middle class (indeed, the Black middle class tends to avoid these settings and close association with the Black poor, thereby cutting their social ties with them precisely to avoid stigmatization and possibly being the victim of Diallo-type experiences). According to Goffman, a match between social identity and the setting "allows us to deal with anticipated others *without special attention and thought*" (Goffman, 1963, p. 2). The anticipations based upon social identity and the setting are transformed into normative expectations. Thus, for police officers subjected to these expectations (codified as racial profiling), it is easy to become aggressive and confrontational in encounters with the morally and criminally suspect as signified by Blackness—especially but not exclusively in settings associated with high crime rates. This may perhaps partly explain why in the inner-city setting, some of the more zealous police tend to adopt an aggressive normative predisposition. Here, a self-awareness of direct racialized targeting is no longer necessary. It simply will happen and it may happen to any Black person caught in the inner-city setting. This is because, as Goffman observes, stigmatization usually entails objectification (treating people as members of a category rather than as distinctive individuals). Such categories of persons are thus usually considered to be *interchangeable*—especially in the inner-city setting where normative assumptions are easily made. This is the logic that *made* Mr. Diallo *the* dangerous rape suspect that the police officers were allegedly searching for. In this sense, Amadou Diallo is a symbol of the interchangeability of all Blacks. This is indeed a major source of Black outrage at the treatment of the case—which finds expression in the popular view that "it could have happened to any one of us."

The objectification of African-Americans and the derived principle of the interchangeability of Blacks was perhaps most evident in the past practice of lynching. Lynchings involved execution for alleged breeches of established *norms, not just laws,* without proof of guilt and the niceties of law—the essence of which (from the viewpoint of the Black experience) was the objectification of the lynch victim. The victim's real innocence or guilt was irrelevant; what mattered was the victim's social identity. This altered characterization is important because before the law the person ought to be *deobjectified,* that is, treated as an individual suspect, whose actual guilt ought to be proven "beyond a reasonable doubt." Of course, historically many Blacks were convicted by court systems that objectified them much in the manner of lynch mobs—but with more flair and ritual and perhaps less shame. In a recent article entitled "Lynching Victim Is Cleared of Rape," Emily Yellin reports on a court hearing of the lynching of Ed Johnson in 1906 after his conviction in a Tennessee court for allegedly raping a White woman. Judge Douglas Myers after setting aside Johnson's conviction noted:

> Something I don't believe the white community really understands is that especially at that time, the object was to bring in a black body, not necessarily the person who had committed the crime. (Yellin, 2000, p. L24)

The objectification of African Americans still remains a painful reality in American policing.

THE SOURCES OF THE PRESUMPTION OF CRIMINALITY

The idea of presumed criminality for Blacks may be painfully evident in policing, but it enjoys a more pervasive presence in American society. It could hardly be otherwise. The police are not so unrepresentative of the society. American society has had a long history of racism and racialized notions of justice (Jones-Brown, 2000; Kennedy, 1997; Mann, 1993; McIntyre 1993; & Higginbotham, 1978).

The idea of a special Black propensity to criminality has its origins in the presumed morality deficit of Blacks. While these ideas were fairly prevalent in America during the early colonial period (Higginbotham Jr., 1978), they were not systematized and given a pseudoscientific veneer until the 19th century. Deeply influenced by Darwinian evolutionary biology, 19th-century researchers sought, with considerable zeal, to explore the difference between the races. These efforts focused on physiological differences such as skull size. From this an evolutionary argument about the savagery and proximity of the non-White races to animals was made. On this logic, the lower in the evolutionary ranking that a racial group was placed, the lower its moral capability was believed to be.

This debate and methodology no doubt deeply influenced the search for the criminal type and the work of the positive school of criminology. Cesare Lombroso, the leader of the school, was 24 years old at the time of the publication of Darwin's *Origin of Species* (1859). The positive school adopted this methodology—comparing criminals and noncriminals in terms of their head size, ear size, lip size (if fleshy and protruding, then the subject would "naturally" tend to criminality), length of arms (indicative of evolutionary proximity to the apes), and so forth (see Vold & Bernard, 1986, pp. 50–51). From flawed research designs and the associated erroneous evidence, it was concluded that the criminal was a poorly evolved type. It is not an overindulgent speculation to suggest that this was transposed to Blacks. Applying the method of 19th-century scientific racism, North American scholars such as Herrnstein and Murray (1994) and Rushton (1999) have reinvigorated these ideas. Black intellectual inferiority, impulsiveness, and aggressiveness and, thus, a special Black predisposition to criminality is inferred from similar Lombrosian measurements of brain size, penis size, and so forth, in addition to the earlier ideas such as those of Franz Gall, who associated criminality with the so-called lower propensities of destructiveness, low self-esteem, and intellectual frailty (Rushton 1999). None of this is new; attempts are always made to recast old prejudices in the new paradigms of the day. This tends to give them a new vitality and acceptance, especially among those already predisposed to racial prejudice.

The prevalence of these ideas in contemporary America, especially in racially diverse cities such as New York and Los Angeles where many police still harbour very negative views of the African American and other so-called minority populations that they are required to serve, is particularly problematic. For example, many NYPD officers are known to freely refer to Blacks as "trash" and to promote the practice of harassing and falsely arresting such "trash" "for cash," that is, arbitrarily arresting Blacks who might be in view at the end of the officers' shifts so that the officers may be paid overtime for processing them (John Jay College, 2000). Such self-interested acts of injustice are accepted because they originate in and exploit racial prejudice and are perpetuated against "trash," that is, people who are seen as deserving of such treatment and who are not powerful enough to prevent it in its more routine and less physically harmful expressions. Democratic policing is inconsistent with and indeed is impossible where such attitudes and practices remain with such intensity and prevalence within the police service.

CONCLUSION

The extent and severity of the problem in terms of the consequences for its victims should not be underestimated. Racialized injustice remains a major problem in the United States.

Racialized justice is certainly inconsistent with democracy—especially where such views inform public policy and the behaviour of state institutions as instanced by racial profiling. The logic of a stigmatized social identity is that it will tend to subject such subpopulations to unequal treatment and repressive state violence. For example, the representation of the violent and dangerous Black male serves as justification for the kind of repressive control and style of policing practiced in Black neighbourhoods—it serves to legitimize (among the White majority) repressive state violence and further entrench exclusionary practices in the labour market, which in turn contribute handsomely to some of the problems of drug abuse and criminality among the subordinate subpopulations. The cycle is a vicious one.

But the negative consequences of racial profiling extend well beyond the suffering of the individual victims. Racial profiling serves to profoundly delegitimize the police services among their main targets—the Black and Latino populations. From the viewpoint of these subordinate groups, the system cannot be trusted to treat their members fairly regardless of whether they are implicated in criminality or not. In fact, it is seen as being particularly unfair to those who are criminally implicated. Such distrust has its consequences in terms of periodic collective actions of resistance that may take very destructive forms as evidenced by the Los Angeles riots of April 1992.

There are also implications for transnational policing—which has become so important for investigating transnational organized crime. Countries such as those of the Caribbean with predominantly Black (and in some cases East Indian) populations may become increasingly doubtful of extradition treaties that subject their citizens to investigation and trial by a system that responds to the race of a suspect. These implications and costs of a persistent institutionalized racism are of some significance even for a rich and powerful country.

The treatment of Blacks may be taken as a measure of the democratic maturity of the United States. It was only in the late 1960s that the right to vote became universal. To complete the process of democratization, the United States must end the racial dualism in the treatment of its citizens and the repressive style of policing to which non-Whites are subjected. It must truly democratize its policing.

REFERENCES

Barkan, S., & Cohn, S. (1998). Racial prejudice and the support by Whites for police use of force: A research note. *Justice Quarterly, 15*(4), 743–753.

Block, F. (1987). *The mean season: The attack on the welfare state.* New York: Pantheon Books.

Cannon, C. (2000). The problem with the chair—A conservative case against capital punishment. *National Review, 52*(11),1.

Chadee, D. (1998). Drug trafficking and trial by jury in Trinidad and Tobago. *Caribbean Journal of Criminology and Social Psychology, 3* (1-2).

Christianson, S. (1986). Our Black prisons. In K. Hass & G. Alpert (Eds.), *The dilemmas of punishment. Readings in contemporary corrections.* (pp. 64–76) Prospect Heights, IL: Waveland Press.

Cook, P., & Hinman, D. (1999). Criminal profiling: Science and Art. *Journal of Contemporary Criminal Justice, 15* (3), 230–241.

Culliver, C., & Sigler, R. (1995). Police use of deadly force in Tennessee following *Tennessee v. Garner. Journal of Contemporary Criminal Justice, 11*(3) 187–195.

Dead man walking out. (2000). *The Economist, 355* (8174), pp. 21–23.

Deosaran, R. (1985). *Trial by jury: Social and psychological dynamics.* Trinidad: Institute of Social and Economic Research. UWI, St. Augustine Campus.

Goffman, E. (1963). *Stigma. Notes on the management of spoiled identity.* Englewood Cliffs, NJ: Prentice Hall.

Harriott, A. (2000). *Police and crime control in Jamaica: Problems of reforming ex-colonial constabularies.* Kingston, Jamaica: University of the West Indies Press.

Herrnstein, R., & Murray, C. (1994). *The Bell Curve: Intelligence and class structure in American life.* New York: The Free Press.

Higginbotham, L. (1978). *In the matter of colour—Race and the American legal process: The Colonial period.* New York: Oxford University Press.

Holdaway, S. (1996). *The racialisation of British policing.* London: MacMillan Press.

Hood, R. (1992). *Race and sentencing.* Oxford: Clarendon Press.

Hudson, B. (1993). Racism and criminology: Concepts and controversies. In Dee Cook & Barbara Hudson (Eds.), *Racism and criminology.* London: Sage.

John Jay College. (2000). Presentation by a former detective of the NYPD.

Johnson, S. (2000). The self-fulfilling prophecy of police profiles. In M. Markowitz & D. Jones-Brown (Eds.), *The system in black and white—Exploring the connections between race, crime and justice,* pp. 93–108. Westport, CT: Praeger.

Jones-Brown, D. (2000). Race as a social construct: Implications for American justice. In M. Markowitz & D. Jones-Brown (Eds.), *The system in black and white—Exploring the Connections between race, crime and justice* (pp. 137–152). Westport, CT: Praeger.

Keith, M. 1993. *Race, riots and policing: Lore and disorder in a multi-racist society.* London: University College London Press.

Kennedy, R. (1997). *Race, crime and the law.* New York: Pantheon.

Lamberth, J. (2000). Driving while Black. In K. Rosenblum & T. Travis (Eds.), *The meaning of difference. American constructions of race, sex and gender, and sexual orientation* (2nd ed.). Boston: McGraw-Hill.

Loven, J. (2000, April 10). *Black women searched more often.* Associated Press. http://news.excite.com/news/ap/00410/02/news-customs-searches

MacPherson, W. (1999). *The Stephen Lawrence inquiry. Report of and inquiry by Sir William MacPherson on CLUNY.* London: Home Office.

Mann, C. (1993). *Unequal justice a question of color.* Bloomington: Indiana University Press.

Markowitz, M., & Jones-Brown, D. (Eds.). (2000). *The system in black and white—Exploring the connections between race, crime and justice.* Westport, CT: Praeger.

McIntyre, C. (1993). *Criminalizing a race: Free blacks during slavery.* Queens, NY: Kayode.

Merton, R. (1949). Discrimination and the American creed. In R. MacIver, (Ed.), *Discrimination and national welfare.* New York: Harper and Row.

Mhlanga, B. (1997). *The colour of English justice.* London: Ashgate.

Moffett, M. (2000, July 18). Suits of armor: Guatemalans begin to seek war redress by marching to court. *The Wall Street Journal,* p.1.

Purdy, J. (1996). Racism and the law in Australia and Trinidad. *Caribbean Quarterly, 42* (2-3).

Rushton, P. (1999). *Race, evolution and behaviour.* New Brunswick, NJ: Transaction Books.

Schmalleger, F. (1999). *Criminology today.* Upper Saddle River, NJ: Prentice Hall.

Smith, D., Visher, C., & Davidson, L. (1984). Equity and discretionary justice: The influence of race on police arrest decisions. *Journal of Criminal Law and Criminology 75*(1), 234–249.

Spitzer, E. (1999). *The New York Police Department's stop and frisk practices: A report to the people of New York from the Office of the Attorney General, Civil Rights Bureau.* New York: Office of the Attorney General.

Staples, B. (1999, December 19). Unearthing a riot. *The New York Times,* pp. 64–69.

Tonry, M. (1998). A comparative perspective on minority groups, crime and criminal justice. *European Journal of Crime, Criminal Law and Criminal Justice, 6* (1), 60–73.

Tournier, P. (1997). Nationality, crime and criminal justice in France. In M. Tonry (Ed.), *Ethnicity, crime and immigration: Comparative and cross national perspective* (pp. 523–551). Chicago: University of Chicago Press.

Verna, A. (1997). Construction of offender profile using fuzzy logic. *Policing: An International Journal of Police Strategy and Management, 20* (2), 408–418.

Vold, G., & Bernard, T. (1986). *Theoretical criminology* (3rd ed.). New York: Oxford University Press.

Webster, C. (1997). The construction of British "Asian" criminality. *International Journal of the Sociology of Law, 25*(1) 65–86.

Wilbanks, W. (1987). *The myth of a racist criminal justice system.* Belmont, CA: Wadsworth.

Wortley, S. (1999). *The unusual suspects: Police and crown discretion and the over-representation of Black people in the Ontario criminal justice system.* Paper presented at the International Conference on Crime and Criminal Justice in the Caribbean, Barbados.

Yellin, E. (2000, February 27). Lynching victim is cleared of rape, 100 years later. *The New York Times,* p. L24.

4

Profiling—More Than a Euphemism for Discrimination

Legitimate Use of a Maligned Investigative Tool

Mary Gibbons

Effective policing in minority communities calls for critical analysis and understanding of the uses—both proper and improper—of race as a factor in the exercise of discretion by police agencies. The purported selection of members of the minority community for enhanced investigative scrutiny has come to be known as "racial profiling"—a shorthand term for the use of race and ethnicity as a clue to criminality (Wilgoren, 1999). Charges of disparate treatment of people of color have focused on the targeting of minorities for investigative detentions. There is no more divisive issue in the minority community than the charge, widely made and commonly accepted, that such targeting has created a *de facto* offense of DWB (i.e., "driving while Black"). An American Civil Liberties Union Special Report (1999) pointed out that

> On our nation's highways today, police ostensibly looking for drug criminals routinely stop drivers based on the color of their skin. This practice is so common that the minority community has given it the derisive term, "driving while black or brown"—a play on the real offense of "driving while intoxicated." (Harris, 1999, p. 3)

Claims of disparate treatment of members of the minority community are not confined to the highway; the profiling controversy has called into question a full panoply of police activities. The U.S. General Accounting Office (March, 2000) has studied the efficacy of the use of invasive search techniques by U.S. Customs in airports, while state and local authorities, such as the New York State Attorney General, have been called upon to investigate the use of the "stop and frisk" by large metropolitan police forces. Such targeting has become the focus of civil rights litigation in several jurisdictions, and in New Jersey (State v. Soto, 1996), Maryland (Wilkins v. Maryland State Police, 1995), and Colorado (Whitfield v. Board of County Commissioners, 1993) it has resulted in liability of police agencies for damages. Other sites of successful racial profiling suits have included Tinicum County, Pennsylvania, and Chicago, Illinois, while allegations of such profiling reach as far as Los Angeles, Beverly Hills, and Hollywood, California. In New Jersey, litigation concerning racial profiling by the state police has resulted in the imposition of court-ordered supervision and monitoring (United States v. State of New Jersey and Division of State Police of the New Jersey Department of Law and Public Safety, 1999).

Notwithstanding the connotation of "profiling" as a euphemism for police discrimination, this investigative methodology has a history of acceptance by the courts as a legitimate tool in the detection and prevention of crime. Although any tool can, of course, be misused to become an instrument of discrimination and bias, the current debate on profiling largely ignores the legitimate use of this tool.

This chapter explores the use of profiling as a legitimate investigative tool and its concomitant acceptance by the courts as such. The profiling considered here, which identifies certain characteristics as correlative with criminal involvement, should be distinguished from behavioral profiling, in which specific crimes are studied for the purpose of developing a psychological profile of a suspect who would be likely to have committed a particular crime (Ingram, 1998, p. 239). Focusing on the current "racial profiling" controversy, the use of race as a profile element must be examined to identify whether any such use of this factor can ever be appropriate, whether within the minority community or the larger society. Only after establishing the appropriate parameters of profile use can we identify and distinguish the abuses of this investigative tool, which have led to the current controversy, and explore the likely response of the courts to such abuses. This analysis is directed toward achieving an understanding of the legal limitations of profiling, which, together with strict adherence to those limitations, can allow police to utilize this investigative tool to serve an appropriate police function.

PROFILING—GENERAL CHARACTERISTICS AS A SIGN OF THE CRIME?

Widespread profiling of travelers began its incarnation as a tool of contemporary policing with passenger screening profiles developed under the auspices of the Federal Aviation Administration (FAA) to identify potential terrorists who posed a threat to the security of airline travel (Smith, 1998, p. 167). A joint Task Force combining expertise in psychology, law, engineering, and administration developed these initial profiles in the late 1960s. Smith (1998) details the inception of the airport profiles: "[I]n response to the hijacking dilemma, the FAA and other federal agencies collected and examined information on the characteristics of **known** [emphasis added] terrorists and hijackers. Researchers used this information to list distinguishing characteristics that would differentiate a terrorist for identification purposes" (pp. 171–172). Examining this profile, a federal court in New York detailed the careful process that went into the development of the profile:

> After studying known hijackers, the task force compiled twenty-five to thirty characteristics in which hijackers differed **significantly** [emphasis added] from the air-traveling public. By putting only a few of them together they could obtain a reliable combination differentiating potential hijackers from non-hijackers. During the testing period and shortly thereafter in 1969 the task force studied an additional sample of 30 new hijackers and found that over **90%** [emphasis added] of that group would have met the profile. There has been a continuous process of reevaluation in light of new hijackings and changes in trends of hijacking. Thus far the original profile has retained validity. Those characteristics selected can be easily observed without exercising judgment. They do not discriminate against any group on the basis of religion, origin, political views, or race. They are precisely designed to select **only** [emphasis added] those who present a high probability of being dangerous. Thus, they violate none of the traditional equal protection standards. (*United States v. Lopez,* 1971, pp. 1086–1087)

Based on this careful review, the *Lopez* Court concluded "that studies underlying the profile were thorough. Procedures followed in developing it were adequate. Appropriate statistical, sociological and psychological data and techniques were utilized. The profile is a highly effective procedure for isolating potential hijackers" (p. 1086).

In contrast to the thorough, scientific process used to develop the FAA hijacking profile, the "drug courier profile" was developed informally in the mid-1970s, largely by DEA Agent Paul Markonni, then of the Detroit office of the DEA. This profile was a listing of various characteristics which he and other agents thought, based upon their experience and anecdotal evidence, to be common to drug couriers carrying controlled substances through airports. The "drug courier profile" has been characterized as "chameleon-like" in that there are no essential, defined elements to it; rather the profile varies case-by-case to the point of including diametrically opposed elements (e.g., round-trip ticket, one-way ticket; appearing "cool," calm demeanor, quivering voice, perspiring profusely; walking quickly, walking slowly, etc.) (Becton, 1987, p. 474). The subjectivity of these elements requires that the application of the profile be based upon the interpretation and experience of the particular agent utilizing it. Social science research suggests that such subjective determinations are made through a filter of racial stereotypes, thus resulting in different conclusions being drawn from the same behavior exhibited by persons of different racial groups (Thompson, 1999). With the advent of the so-called war on drugs, the use of these "drug courier profiles" became widespread (Harris, 1999; Wisotsky Statement, 1988, pp. 410–454).

Beginning in the early 1980s, the DEA began a cooperative effort with New Mexico and New Jersey, called Operation Pipeline, which was born from the seizures of controlled substances during highway stops, in part along the I-95 corridor from Florida to the northeast (Becton, 1987; Greene and Wice, 1981; Hall, 1993). Operation Pipeline, a nationwide highway interdiction program that focuses on private motor vehicles, is acknowledged by the DEA as one of its most effective operations, characterized by cooperation between the DEA and state and local police agencies in three areas: training, real-time communication, and analytic support. Although the DEA now asserts in its Web-site description of Operation Pipeline that it "does not advocate profiling by race or ethnic background," it is noteworthy that New Jersey, one of the two states in which the DEA "drug courier profile" was first developed and utilized, has been at the center of the "racial profiling" controversy with regard to the use of drug interdiction programs on the highway. Along with others noted previously, the program utilized by the New Jersey State Police has been the subject of civil rights litigation, and at the time of this writing, was being operated under a consent decree with the Department of Justice in an effort to resolve a federal lawsuit claiming racially discriminatory policing.

Notwithstanding the vagaries of the DEA's profiling program, it has withstood a barrage of legal challenges and remains an accepted policing tool. The continued viability of this tool requires an understanding of its legal basis and parameters of its proper use. Absent a clear view of the appropriate limitations of profiling, combined with explicit restrictions on its use in keeping with fundamental constitutional principles, the abuses of this valuable investigative tool may very well lead to its wholesale rejection by the courts.

COURTS HAVE ACCEPTED PROFILES AS AN INVESTIGATIVE TOOL

The Supreme Court has considered cases involving the investigative use of profiles as a part of its effort to define and establish that quantum of "specific and articulable facts which, taken together with rational inferences from those facts, reasonably warrant [the] intrusion" (p. 21) of an investigative detention—the standard articulated in *Terry v. Ohio* (1968). Since *Terry* accepted the principle of a seizure of the person based upon less than probable cause—historically required by the Fourth Amendment—both police and courts have sought some definitive formulation of the quantum of knowledge, filtered by training and tempered by experience, which would justify the lesser intrusion of a "brief investigative detention in contrast to an arrest." Falling between an impermissible "hunch" and the more rigorous standard of probable cause necessary to support an arrest, the standard of sufficiency for a factual showing of "reasonable suspicion" has been elusive.

The consideration of ethnicity by police as the *sole* factor to justify the limited intrusion of an investigative detention was first broached in *United States v. Brignoni-Ponce* (1975). In that case, the issue concerned the authority of the Border Patrol to stop automobiles near the Mexican border to question occupants about their citizenship and immigration status. In *Brignoni-Ponce,* the Court noted that, "The only issue presented for decision is whether a roving patrol may stop a vehicle in an area near the border and question its occupants when the only ground for suspicion is that the occupants *appear* to be of Mexican ancestry" (p. 876) (emphasis supplied). This critical policing decision—to stop a vehicle for questioning of the occupants—is likewise fundamental to the DEA's Operation Pipeline. According to the DEA, sometime after the early 1980s, "Highway law enforcement officers began to ask key questions to help determine whether or not motorists they had stopped for traffic violations were also carrying drugs. These interview techniques proved extremely effective," netting more than a million and a half kilograms of drugs and $704 million between January 1986 and December 2001 (U.S. Department of Justice, 2002). Thus, the law enforcement effort in the drug profile stops was directed, at least initially, to simply stopping the vehicle and questioning the occupants, just as in the case of the Border Patrol stops at issue in *Brignoni-Ponce.* A subsequent search of the vehicle would necessarily require separate justification.

Recognizing the significance of the public interest at stake in enforcing the immigration laws, the *Brignoni-Ponce* Court nonetheless pointed out that "[i]n the context of border area stops, the reasonableness requirement of the Fourth Amendment demands something more than the broad and unlimited discretion sought by the Government. Roads near the border carry not only aliens seeking to enter the country illegally, but a large volume of legitimate traffic as well" (1975, p. 882). With particular relevance to "racial profiling," the Court stated:

> In this case, the officers relied on a single factor to justify stopping respondent's car: the apparent Mexican ancestry of the occupants. We cannot conclude that this furnished reasonable grounds to believe that the three occupants were aliens. At best, the officers had only a fleeting glimpse of the persons in the moving car, illuminated by headlights. Even if they saw enough to think that the occupants were of Mexican descent, this factor alone would justify neither a reasonable belief that they were aliens, nor a reasonable belief that the car concealed other aliens who were illegally in the country. Large numbers of native born and naturalized citizens have the physical characteristics identified with Mexican ancestry, and, even in the border area, a relatively small proportion of them are aliens. The likelihood that any given person of Mexican ancestry is an alien is high enough to make Mexican appearance a relevant factor, but, standing alone, it does not justify stopping all Mexican-Americans to ask if they are aliens. (*Brignoni-Ponce,* 1975, pp. 886–887)

Thus, over 25 years ago, the Fourth Amendment was held to prohibit the use of ethnicity as the sole basis for an investigative detention of the occupants of a vehicle, the same issue presented in contemporary "racial profiling" cases.

Considering further the Fourth Amendment status of vehicle stops, in *Delaware v. Prouse* (1979), the Supreme Court rejected a program of spot checks of drivers' license and registration documents, carried out by wholly discretionary vehicle stops unsupported by any *individualized* suspicion, much less probable cause. Focusing on the lack of any articulable basis for any particular stop, the Court reasoned:

> When there is not probable cause to believe that a driver is violating any one of the multitude of applicable traffic and equipment regulations—or other articulable basis amounting to reasonable suspicion that the driver is unlicensed or his vehicle unregistered—we cannot conceive of any legitimate basis upon which a patrolman could decide that stopping a particular driver for a spot check would be more productive than stopping any other driver. This kind of standardless and unconstrained discretion is the evil the Court has discerned when, in previous cases, it has insisted that the discretion of the official in the field be circumscribed, at least to some extent. (*Brignoni-Ponce,* 1975, p. 661)

Having made these two prior decisions, ruling out the legality of ethnicity-based and totally random stops, in 1980, the Supreme Court decided a pair of cases that specifically examined the adequacy of the DEA's "drug courier profiles" as the basis for an investigative detention, *United States v. Mendenhall* (1980) and *Reid v. Georgia* (1980). The principles of these two cases would establish the parameters of police use of these profiles.

In *Mendenhall,* the defendant was observed by two DEA agents in the Detroit Metropolitan Airport and was determined to fit the "drug courier profile." Identifying the elements of the profile which were determined to "fit" here, the Court pointed out that:

> The agent testified that the respondent's behavior fit the so-called "drug courier profile"—an informally compiled abstract of characteristics thought typical of persons carrying illicit drugs. In this case, the agents thought it relevant that (1) the respondent was arriving on a flight from Los Angeles, a city believed by the agents to be the place of origin for much of the heroin brought to Detroit; (2) the respondent was the last person to leave the plane, "appeared to be very nervous," and "completely scanned the whole area where [the agents] were

standing"; (3) after leaving the plane, the respondent proceeded past the baggage area without claiming any luggage; and (4) the respondent changed airlines for her flight out of Detroit. (*Mendenhall,* 1980, ftn.1)

The agents approached Ms. Mendenhall, asked to see her ticket and identification, noting certain inconsistencies about which they inquired. One agent identified himself as a narcotics agent whereupon she became visibly nervous. Her papers were returned to her and the agents asked her to accompany them to the DEA office. She did so, where she consented to a search that revealed two packages of heroin in her clothing.

The Court considered the propriety, under the Fourth Amendment, of the initial encounter prior to her agreement to go to the DEA office and to submit to a search. Justice Stewart, joined by Justice Rehnquist wrote the majority opinion, holding that there was no seizure of Ms. Mendenhall, and thus her consent to accompany them and to be searched was free and voluntary. In concluding that Ms. Mendenhall gave her consent freely and voluntarily, the Court recognized

> It is additionally suggested that the respondent, a female and a Negro, may have felt unusually threatened by the officers, who were white males. While these factors were not irrelevant, see *Schneckloth v. Bustamonte, supra,* neither were they decisive. (*Mendenhall,* 1980, p. 558)

Interestingly, the significance of Ms. Mendenhall's race was not discussed in connection with the profiling factors that initially drew the attention of the agents to her.

Declining to acknowledge the psychological dynamics of police authority, Justice Stewart reasoned: "[N]othing in the record suggests that the respondent had any objective reason to believe that she was not free to end the conversation in the concourse and proceed on her way, and for that reason, we conclude that the agents' initial approach to her was not a seizure" (*Mendenhall,* 1980, p. 555).

The concurring opinion upheld the propriety of the search, but on a wholly different basis. Without analysis, the concurrence assumed that Ms. Mendenhall was seized, but held such a seizure to be proper under the Fourth Amendment as supported by reasonable suspicion, based upon the use of the "drug courier profile." Acknowledging that "[a]mong the circumstances that can give rise to reasonable suspicion are the agent's knowledge of the methods used in recent criminal activity and the **characteristics of persons engaged in such illegal practices**" [emphasis added] (*Mendenhall,* 1980, p. 563). With this conclusion, the propriety of police reliance on broad descriptive categorizations of personal characteristics and conduct was thus established, and the cornerstone of profiling was laid.

Reflecting the Supreme Court's evident discomfort and uncertainty with the use of profiles to establish reasonable suspicion, the decision in *Reid v. Georgia* (1980) followed on the heels of *Mendenhall.* Again, the case involved the observation, by a DEA agent, of an individual disembarking from an arriving plane and walking through the terminal. The agent observed him having a brief word with another man who was carrying a similar shoulder bag to the one carried by Mr. Reid. Although the two did not walk together, Reid was observed to occasionally look in the direction of the other man. After the two men left the terminal together, the agent approached them, requesting to examine their ticket stubs and identification, which they produced. The agent testified that they appeared nervous to him. When he asked if they would return with him to the terminal and consent to a search, they agreed. While returning, Reid bolted and dropped his bag, which was later determined to contain cocaine. Without considering the existence of a "seizure" to implicate the Fourth Amendment, the *per curiam* opinion held that the profile factors identified were inadequate to establish reasonable suspicion.

> We conclude that the agent could not, as a matter of law, have reasonably suspected the petitioner of criminal activity on the basis of these observed circumstances. Of the evidence relied on, only the fact that the petitioner preceded another person and occasionally looked backward at him as they proceeded through the concourse relates to their particular conduct. The other circumstances describe a very large category of presumably innocent travelers, who would be subject to virtually random seizures were the Court to conclude that as little foundation as there was in this case could justify a seizure. Nor can we agree, on this record, that the manner in which the petitioner and his companion walked through the airport reasonably could have led the agent to suspect them of wrongdoing. Although there could, of course, be circumstances in which wholly lawful conduct might justify the suspicion that criminal activity was afoot, see *Terry v. Ohio,* supra at 27-28, this is not such a case. The agent's belief that the petitioner and his companion were attempting to conceal the fact that they were traveling together, a belief that was more an "inchoate and unparticularized suspicion or 'hunch'," 392 U.S. at 27, than a fair inference in the light of his experience, is simply too slender a reed to support the seizure in this case. (*Reid,* 1980, p. 441)

The Court's language suggests that reasonable suspicion requires particular conduct by the person to be detained which would "justify the suspicion that criminal activity was afoot" (*Terry v. Ohio,* pp. 27–28), rather than "circumstances [describing] a very large category of presumably innocent travelers who would be subject to virtually random seizures" (Reid, 1980, p. 441).

Returning again to the issue of the DEA "drug courier profile" as constituting reasonable suspicion on which to base an investigative detention, in *United States v. Sokolow* (1989), the Supreme Court examined the particular factors considered by the agents at the time they seized Mr. Sokolow. Those factors included purchase of airline tickets in cash, taken from a larger roll of cash, travel under a name that the agents were unable to verify, lengthy travel for a short stay in a "drug-source" city, unchecked luggage, nervousness, and attire. Finding reasonable suspicion to have been established, the Court held: "Any one of these factors is not, by itself, proof of any illegal conduct, and is quite consistent with innocent travel. But we think, taken together, they amount to reasonable suspicion" (*Sokolow,* 1989, p. 9). The attire noted by the agents was a black jumpsuit and gold jewelry. Although members of different ethnic groups might typically select certain types of attire, the Court did not indicate any linkage between this attire and ethnicity, nor did they indicate how the agents had determined such attire to be indicative of involvement in drug trafficking. The Court belied any reliance on the fact that the various characteristics were included within the DEA drug courier profile—rather they held that the factors, independently of a "profile," were sufficient as a basis for reasonable suspicion. The majority opinion discounted any significance attached to the inclusion of the observed factors in a profile, stating:

> We do not agree with respondent that our analysis is somehow changed by the agents' belief that his behavior was consistent with one of the DEA's "drug courier profiles" (Brief for Respondent 14-21). A court sitting to determine the existence of reasonable suspicion must require the agent to articulate the factors leading to that conclusion, but the fact that these factors

may be set forth in a "profile" does not somehow detract from their evidentiary significance as seen by a trained agent. (*Sokolow,* 1989, p. 10)

This effort to divorce the analysis of the factors from the inclusion of those factors in a "profile" was possibly a response to the dissent's frontal assault on the adequacy of the DEA's profiles, based upon their internal inconsistencies and "chameleon-like" quality. The dissent could not have been more focused on this issue, stating:

> In asserting that it is not "somehow" relevant that the agents who stopped Sokolow did so in reliance on a prefabricated profile of criminal characteristics, ante at 10, the majority thus ducks serious issues relating to a questionable law enforcement practice, to address the validity of which we granted certiorari in this case. (*Sokolow,* 1980, p. 14)

These "drug courier profile" cases indicate the Supreme Court's perception that the profile elements are nothing more than a collection of factors which, in any given case, might well constitute reasonable suspicion to justify an investigative detention[1], and yet in other cases they may not. As in *Reid,* the inclusion of a particular element in a "profile" does not automatically lead to a finding of reasonable suspicion. The fact that a police officer may rely upon certain factors presented in training as part of a "profile" does not obviate the need to convince a court that, in a particular case, the profile elements relied upon are sufficient to establish the quantum of facts necessary for reasonable suspicion of the particular suspect subjected to the investigative detention. It appears from the Court's somewhat contradictory decisions, if that quantum is met as in *Sokolow,* any criticism of the profile as a whole becomes irrelevant. If the quantum of facts is not met, as in *Reid,* the fact that some profile factors were observed will not automatically result in a finding of reasonable suspicion.

Hence, "profiling" has utility as a training and intelligence device which, when used appropriately, does not in any way compromise the Fourth Amendment rights of the individuals who are subjected to an investigative detention, but the Court has been non-specific about the number or types of profile factors needed to amount to *reasonable* suspicion. Although, with regard to the inclusion of race or ethnicity as a factor in a "profile," the law has long been clear, from the time of *Brignoni-Ponce,* that no investigative detention may be predicated solely thereupon. The reasoning of *Reid* would quite properly lead to the conclusion that race as the sole basis of detention would improperly include within its sweep a large group of innocent travelers who had presented no suggestion of personal involvement in criminal activity.

The cases concerning the "drug courier profiles" are conceptually consistent with the requirement that, in order to justify an investigative detention, the officer must have "a *particularized and objective* basis for suspecting the *particular person* stopped of criminal activity—a requirement that the circumstances presented to the officer raise a suspicion that *the particular individual* being stopped is engaged in wrongdoing" (*United*

---

[1] An investigative detention, also known as an investigatory stop, field stop, or *Terry* stop, is a detention made by an officer in the field "for the purpose of gathering further information upon which to base a decision as to whether or not to arrest the suspect" (Miller et al. 1986, p. 212). The additional information is typically gathered through questioning the suspect and observing his or her demeanor, responses, and reactions during such questioning.

States v. Cortez, 1981, p. 418). In applying these principles, the courts have been willing to reject a finding of reasonable suspicion when race is either the sole basis of the detention or is included with other factors which, all together, encompass a large number of innocent individuals. (*Brignoni-Ponce, Delaware v. Prouse,* and *Reid;* see also *State v. Soto*)

RACE AS AN ELEMENT OF THE REASONABLE SUSPICION NECESSARY TO INITIATE AN INVESTIGATIVE DETENTION

While the courts have rejected the use of race as the sole basis for an investigative detention, the debate on "racial profiling" has led to a call for total prohibition of the consideration of race in any manner by police as a basis of an investigative detention. The consent decree in the New Jersey federal litigation arising from racial profiling in turnpike vehicle stops provides:

> State troopers may not rely to any degree on the race or national or ethnic origin of motorists in selecting vehicles for traffic stops and in deciding upon the scope and substance of post-stop actions, **except where state troopers are on the look-out for a specific suspect who has been identified in part by his or her race or national or ethnic origin**. (*United States v. State of New Jersey and Division of State Police of the New Jersey Department of Law and Public Safety,* 1999) [emphasis added]

While understandable in the context of widespread perception of discriminatory policing, at first glance, this call ignores the legitimate uses of race as an identifying trait of individuals. Rather than a blanket prohibition, both the police and the minority community would be well served to distinguish between the legitimate and illegitimate uses of this personal descriptor within investigative profiles.

Certainly, as provided for in the "except[ion]" portion of the consent decree, police should properly consider race as *one* appropriate factor upon which to base an investigative detention when a specific crime is reported with race included as one of the identifying characteristics of the perpetrator. Not only would it be irrational to ignore the reported race of a perpetrator but such a rule would result in the detention of persons who did not possess this most basic identifying characteristic. If a robbery is reported as having been carried out by a White male, police should properly consider the reported race to eliminate non-Whites from suspicion. The race descriptor serves a proper function of adding an element of particularization to the description of a suspect. Adhering to the requirement of particularized reasonable suspicion, it would be unreasonable to detain non-Whites for this crime, just as it would be unreasonable to detain all Whites. Reasonable suspicion requires specific additional descriptive elements to avoid the inclusion of large groups of innocent persons within the description. In *Washington v. Lambert* (1996) the U.S. Court of Appeals for the Ninth Circuit criticized the generality and vagueness of a description of supermarket robbers as two African American males, one fairly tall and one fairly short, as being applicable to a "significant percentage" (p. 1191) of African American males.

Another use of race as an appropriate element of reasonable suspicion might be in those situations in which race is directly and demonstrably related to involvement in criminal activity, such as membership in ethnic gangs. It would be irrational to prohibit police from considering race when investigating an ethnic gang in which race is a requirement of membership.[2] Likewise, the courts have accepted the propriety of considering ethnicity as **one factor** in reasonable suspicion when investigating unlawful entry of "undocumented persons" at a fixed checkpoint at the border (*United States v. Martinez-Fuerte*, 1976). *Martinez-Fuerte* established that the referral to a secondary inspection area near the Mexican border, largely based on "apparent Mexican ancestry," was not a constitutional violation by saying that "different considerations would arise if, for example, reliance were put on apparent Mexican ancestry at a checkpoint operated near the Canadian border" (p. 564, ftnt 17).

To the extent that the consideration of race as an element of reasonable suspicion adds particularization, the courts have accepted its consideration, but never as the sole element upon which suspicion is based. In this author's opinion, by this reasoning, race, together with other descriptive elements, could properly be included within a profile, so long as other descriptive factors served to properly narrow the pool of suspects. To mandate police to ignore race from any consideration defies both precedent and logic.

As noted previously, whether or not race is expressly included within the matrix of a profile, the courts will determine the validity of a detention by reviewing the sufficiency of the information known to the police officer against the standard of reasonable suspicion. That review takes into account the fact that police will make inferences and deductions based upon the facts of which they are aware. As stated in *United States v. Cortez* (1981):

> The idea that an assessment of the whole picture must yield a particularized suspicion contains two elements, each of which must be present before a stop is permissible. First, the assessment must be based upon all of the circumstances. The analysis proceeds with various objective observations, information from police reports, if such are available, and consideration of the modes or patterns of operation of certain kinds of lawbreakers. From these data, a trained officer draws inferences and makes deductions—inferences and deductions that might well elude an untrained person.
>
> The process does not deal with hard certainties, but with probabilities. Long before the law of probabilities was articulated as such, practical people formulated certain common sense conclusions about human behavior; jurors as factfinders are permitted to do the same—and so are law enforcement officers. Finally, the evidence thus collected must be seen and weighed not in terms of library analysis by scholars, but as understood by those versed in the field of law enforcement. (*Cortez*, 1981, p. 418)

To the extent that the courts defer to the police to draw inferences and make deductions from information and from modes and patterns of operation of certain kinds of lawbreakers, police agencies would be well served to scrutinize the nature of these deductions and inferences based upon race when race is included as an element of reasonable suspicion, whether or not as a part of a profile. When the inferences and deductions that underlie the use of race in a profile result in the inclusion of substantial numbers of innocent members of a racial/ethnic group, the courts have been **un**willing to recognize "reasonable suspicion" as having been established. For example, in *United States v. Jimenez-Medina* (1999), the U.S. Court of Appeals for the Ninth Circuit reasoned:

---

[2] Ethnicity alone cannot be the basis for suspecting a person of gang membership (see *City of Chicago v. Morales*, 1999, and *City of Chicago v. Youkhana*, 1995).

> This Circuit has held that reasonable suspicion must not be based on "broad profiles which cast suspicion on entire categories of people" (*Rodriguez-Sanchez*, 23 F.3d at 1492). The rationale upon which the "reasonable suspicion" doctrine is based, a doctrine that thwarts the notion of liberty and freedom from state intrusion in a mobile society, must be on an objective basis for suspecting that a particular person is engaged in criminal activity, lest we "sweep many ordinary citizens into a generality of suspicious appearance merely on hunch" (*Rodriguez*, 976 F.2d at 596) Reasonable suspicion cannot rest upon the hunch of an experienced officer, even if the hunch turns out right. The requirement of objective fact to support an inference of wrongdoing eliminates the need to deal with a police stop that rests on constitutional intuition. (*U.S. v. Jimenez-Medina*, 1999, p. 756)

Not only is the use of overly inclusive profile factors constitutionally suspect, but, as the same court has pointed out in *United States v. Montero Camargo* (2000), the practice is not effective policing:

> Whereas here, the majority (or any substantial number) of people share a specific characteristic, that characteristic is of little or no probative value in such a particularized and context-specific analysis. (*U.S. v. Montero Camargo*, 2000, p. 1131)

Such holdings have led to the current, widespread perception that "profiling" is nothing more than a euphemism for racist policing and have resulted in a climate of condemnation of this investigative tool and a focus only on its abuse, rather than on what should be its appropriate use.

DISPARATE ENFORCEMENT OF THE LAW—THE ABUSE OF PROFILING

The current controversy, which has been labeled "racial profiling," is predicated upon statistical anomalies in the incidence of police seizures of highway travelers of different ethnicities (*State v. Soto*, 1996). Both anecdotal and statistical evidence have been marshaled to illustrate that minorities are targeted by certain police agencies for so-called pretext traffic stops in which a vehicle stop, justified by some minor traffic infraction, is followed by an extended detention and search of the vehicle and passengers. Notwithstanding dispute regarding the validity of studies establishing such anomalies, they have been accepted by courts in vigorously contested litigation and thus should be taken as sufficient to establish serious issues regarding both police credibility and community perception of unequal justice.

The concept of "profiling" arises from the assertion that race is included, explicitly and implicitly, as a factor in "drug courier profiles" developed by the DEA and utilized by state and local police as a basis for the discretionary selection of the particular vehicles which are subjected to pretextual traffic stops. The allegation at the heart of the "racial profiling" controversy is "that the police exercise this discretionary power primarily against African-Americans and Latinos" (Harris, 1999, p. 3).

The pretext traffic stop was recognized as a constitutionally acceptable policing tactic after the Supreme Court approved the practice in *Whren v. United States* (1996). In that case, a police officer, acting on probable cause that a vehicle was in violation of the traffic code, stopped the vehicle ostensibly for the traffic violation, with the true purpose being to investigate drug-dealing activity. When the officer approached the vehicle to give a warning regarding excessive speed and other violations, he observed contraband in plain view. The Supreme Court refused to invalidate the stop of the vehicle, or the seizure of contraband which followed from the stop, holding:

> Here, the District Court found that the officers had probable cause to believe that petitioners had violated the traffic code. That rendered the stop reasonable under the Fourth Amendment, the evidence thereby discovered admissible. (*Whren*, 1996, p. 819)

The Court recognized the concern that, because virtually everyone may well be in violation of some minute provision of the vehicle codes, the decision to stop some motorists and not others might well be predicated not upon the traffic violation itself, but rather on a selection process which is impermissibly based upon race. Acknowledging the impermissibility of such disparate enforcement, the Court directed that relief for such a Constitutional violation should be found in the Equal Protection Clause, rather than in the Fourth Amendment.

The *Whren* decision has raised serious concerns among civil libertarians, in part, because the federal Supreme Court's decision contradicted several lower court decisions dating back to 1968 (*United States v. Millio,* 1984; *State v. Davis,* 1983; *People v. Holloway* (dissenting opinion), 1982; and *Amador-Gonzalez v. United States,* 1968). In those cases, the lower courts were concerned that by allowing pretextual stops, police officers would be in a position to look for or manufacture "grounds for an arrest for a minor offense in order to search for evidence of another suspected crime for which there was no probable cause. . . " (*State v. Davis,* p. 726).

Hence, according to the reasoning of such lower courts, the illegal motive behind the stop rendered an otherwise valid arrest invalid (Miller, et al, 1986). Judge Levin, dissenting in *People v. Holloway* explained:

> The constitution permits the police to search in order to facilitate an otherwise lawful arrest. It does not permit them to arrest in order to facilitate an otherwise unlawful search. If this practice were permitted, any minor offense committed by a significant proportion of the population could be used by the police as a basis for arresting and searching whomever they pleased. (p. 413 as cited in Miller et al., 1986, p. 186).

At the heart of the racial profiling controversy is both the potential lack of probable cause to believe that occupants of a particular automobile are engaged in crimes other than motor vehicle violations and whether the racial identity of the occupants is what is motivating officers to exercise their discretion to stop one vehicle as opposed to another, when both are engaged in the same or similar traffic-related crimes.

By making the officer's underlying motive(s) for the stop irrelevant, the *Whren* decision clarifies the legality of the use of pretext to stop vehicles that are, in fact, in violation of traffic laws. However, it provides little guidance on how to dissuade police officers from exercising their discretionary authority in ways that do not violate the rights of some motorists, while observing the rights of others. The *Whren* court notes:

> We think these cases foreclose any argument that the constitutional reasonableness of traffic stops depends on the actual motivations of the individual officers involved. We of course agree with petitioners that the Constitution prohibits selective enforcement of the law based on considerations such as race. But the constitutional basis for objecting to intentionally discriminatory application of laws is the Equal Protection Clause, not the Fourth Amendment.

Subjective intentions play no role in ordinary, probable cause Fourth Amendment analysis. (*Whren,* 1996, p. 813)

A multitude of state courts have followed the *Whren* principle to allow the so-called pretext stop, notwithstanding the recognition that it affords an opportunity for discriminatory enforcement, an opportunity which has been demonstrated by studies of police utilization of this technique. For example, in *People v. Robinson* (2001), the highest court of New York state adopted the reasoning of *Whren,* notwithstanding its express acknowledgment that

> [t]he real concern of those opposing pretextual stops is that police officers will use their authority to stop persons on a selective and arbitrary basis. . . . We are not unmindful of studies . . . which show that certain racial and ethnic groups are disproportionately stopped by police officers, and that those stops do not end in the discovery of a higher proportion of contraband than in the cars of other groups. The fact that such disparities exist is cause for both vigilance and concern about the protections given by the New York State Constitution. Discriminatory enforcement has no place in our law. (*People v. Robinson,* 2001, p. 153)

While the recognition that selective enforcement is constitutionally offensive has significance, limiting individual redress of such unconstitutional behavior to an action based on the Equal Protection Clause makes prevailing against such a violation a remote possibility. The difficulties of successfully challenging impermissible selective enforcement of the law are considerable (Maclin, 1998, pp. 354–62; *United States v. Armstrong,* 1996).

On the other hand, the utility of the *Whren* decision to police agencies is evident in highway enforcement operations. Once a traffic violation is observed, the officer has discretion whether or not to stop the violator and make contact with the vehicle. Significantly here, the "profile" is not the basis of the Fourth Amendment seizure of the vehicle; rather, the seizure is constitutionally acceptable because it is predicated upon probable cause that a traffic violation has occurred. The relevant issue then becomes the Fourth Amendment justification for the *search,* since probable cause arising from the traffic violation has already functioned under *Whren* to justify the stop. Under previously decided case law, once stopped, the officer is entitled to direct the occupants, both driver and passengers, out of the car (*Pennsylvania v. Mimms,* 1977; *Maryland v. Wilson,* 1997). However, neither *Whren,* nor *Mimms,* nor *Wilson* authorizes an automatic search of the vehicle.

In order to remain within the legal limits of the Fourth Amendment, as the encounter evolves, the officer must obtain some further factual basis before initiating a search, whether by observing materials in plain view, obtaining consent, etc. The evolving nature of the encounter, and concomitant development of an adequate Fourth Amendment basis for increasing police intrusion is an unremarkable, and long-established, feature of Fourth Amendment jurisprudence. However, the development of this jurisprudence has not been without some complications.

For example, in 1998, in *Knowles v. Iowa,* the Supreme Court invalidated an Iowa statute that allowed a search incident to arrest to be conducted in the course of a traffic stop for a violation which was handled by the issuance of a citation (motor vehicle summons/"ticket") rather than by an arrest. Finding no justification for a "full field-type search" absent an arrest, the Court distinguished a "citation" situation from a custodial "arrest" and declined to extend authority to search to a case in which the officer might have arrested the violator but elected not to do so. While this decision does not directly affect the authority of traffic enforcement under *Whren* to make a vehicle stop based on a traffic violation, it suggests that the Court may be willing to view detentions for traffic violations in a different light than other seizures. *Knowles* points out that the traditional justifications for a search "incident to arrest," namely officer safety and preservation of evidence, are not present in the traffic violation situation to the same extent as they might be in a custodial arrest. Although the reasoning of *Knowles* seems to preclude a search "incident to arrest" conducted upon the issuance of a citation for a traffic violation, no Fourth Amendment principles prohibit the officer from seeking voluntary consent to search, from making plain view observations, or from conducting a *Terry* pat-down if there is reasonable suspicion that the occupant(s) may be armed. Such investigative efforts remain appropriate once the initial stop has been justified.

Notwithstanding the Fourth Amendment propriety of the pretextual traffic stop and, potentially, the ensuing search, aspersions are cast on the police for selectively targeting minorities for enforcement of the traffic laws as a pretext and prelude to intrusive seizures and searches. As noted previously, litigation against police agencies in New Jersey (*United States v. State of New Jersey, et al.*), Maryland (*Wilkins v. Maryland State Police*), Illinois (*Chavez v. Illinois State Police,* 2001), and elsewhere has utilized statistical studies of racial disparities in traffic enforcement, with varying degrees of success. The Traffic Stops Statistics Study Act of 1999 was introduced in Congress calling for a nationwide study by the Attorney General of stops for traffic violations and directing the Attorney General to perform an initial analysis of existing data, including complaints alleging profiling and other information concerning traffic stops motivated by race and other bias. The statistical studies and analyses are all directed toward an examination of selective enforcement of the traffic laws, an equal protection question under the Constitution. Notwithstanding that focus, these studies, and eventually, their results and analyses, carry the connotation of examining "racial profiling."

In Maryland for example, during 1995, statistics from the State Police indicate that four times as many cars being driven by Black motorists were stopped as were cars being driven by White motorists (409 versus 97) on suspicion of drug possession, and drugs were found in only 33 percent of the Black-occupied cars (Russell, 1998, p. 42). In New York, in 1998 a special unit stopped and frisked 45,000 mostly Black and Latino people, seizing 2,072 guns (De La Cruz, 1999). Unlike the FAA profiles of hijackers which boasted a success rate of 90 percent, these New York stops indicate an accuracy rate of less than 5 percent. Such inaccuracies give rise to grave concerns that the police are abusing rather than using "profiling" as an investigative tool by focusing too much on race to the exclusion of other factors. Or, for other reasons, the profiles upon which these law enforcement agents are relying are faulty since they do not appear to sufficiently differentiate the factually guilty from the factually innocent. Yet another explanation for these statistical anomalies might be that, like in *Reid,* with or without reliance on a profile, the police may be taking action before they have acquired the requisite amount of factual evidence amounting to reasonable suspicion. Absent careful, analytic distinction between the concepts of selective enforcement and profiling, police face the potential loss of the constitutionally tested and approved tool of profiling, by virtue of its, perhaps, misguided association with discriminatory police practices.

CONCLUSION

The concept of "racial profiling" by police agencies has been much maligned in the volatile debate concerning selective and discriminatory enforcement of the law. However, the technique of profiling has gained acceptance by various police agencies and by the courts. It is recognized as an investigative tool, but not as a substitute for the time-tested Fourth Amendment requirements of reasonable suspicion and probable cause. For over two decades, police agencies have successfully used profiling so long as the use of race is not the sole or primary basis for the detention of an individual.

Profiling has come under a critical spotlight by virtue of its association, in the public mind, with claims of discriminatory policing. That is, statistics and anecdotal accounts indicate that in some locations, investigatory stops and/or searches are disproportionately being conducted in situations where the subjects are members of minority groups, and the percentages of unfounded stops and/or searches in these locations run high. While, as noted above, there may be multiple explanations (including ones not related to racial animus) for this apparent racially disparate impact of police search and seizure procedures, racism and intentional discrimination may quickly be blamed as the culprits. This confusion may well lead to a misguided attempt, by courts and politicians, to end discriminatory policing by banning or restricting the use of profiling. Such an effort would not only fail to resolve the discrimination but would also lead to the loss of a valuable investigative tool. Only by scrupulous avoidance of any abuses of profiling can the police preserve this tool and the acceptance of its value by the courts.

REFERENCES

Amador-Gonzalez v. United States, 391 F.2d 308 (5th Cir. 1968).

Becton, C. L. (1987). The drug courier profile: "All seems infected that the infected spy, as all looks yellow to the jaundic'd eye." *North Carolina Law Review,* 65, 417.

Chavez v. Illinois State Police, 27 F. Supp. 2d 1053 (N.D. Ill. 1998), *aff'd* 251 F.3d 612 (7th Cir. 2001).

City of Chicago v. Morales, 527 U.S. 41 (1999).

City of Chicago v. Youkhana, 277 Ill. App. 3d 101 (1995).

De La Cruz, D. (February 6, 1999). Elite street crime unit under scrutiny following police shooting. Associated Press state and local wire.

Delaware v. Prouse, 440 U.S. 648 (1979).

Greene, P. S., and Wice, B. W. (1981). The DEA drug courier profile: History and analysis. *South Texas Law Journal,* 22, p. 261.

Hall, S. E. (1993). A balancing approach to the constitutionality of drug courier profiles. *University of Illinois Law Review,* 1007.

Harris, D. (June 1999). *Driving while black, racial profiling on our nation's highways. An American Civil Liberties Union special report.* New York: American Civil Liberties Union, Department of Public Education.

Ingram, S. (Summer, 1998). Note: If the profile fits: Admitting criminal psychological profiles into evidence in criminal trials. *Washington University Journal of Urban & Contemporary Law,* 54, 239.

Knowles v. Iowa, 525 U.S. 113 (1998).

Maclin, T. (1998). Race and the Fourth Amendment. *Vanderbilt Law Review,* 51, 333.

Maryland v. Wilson, 519 U.S. 408 (1997).

Miller, F., Dawson R., Dix G., & Parvas, R. (1986). *The police function*, 4th ed. Mineola, NY: Foundation Press, Inc.

Office of the New York State Attorney General Eliot Spitzer. (December 1, 1999). *The New York City Police Department's "stop & frisk" practices: A report to the people of the State of New York from the Office of the Attorney General.* New York: Office of the Attorney General.

Pennsylvania v. Mimms, 434 U.S. 106 (1977).

People v. Holloway, 416 Mich. 288 (1982); cert. denied 461 U.S. 917 (1983).

People v. Robinson, 741 NYS 2d 147 (2001).

Reid v. Georgia, 448 U.S. 438 (1980).

Russell, K. (1998). *The color of crime.* New York: New York University Press.

Smith, D. (Fall, 1998). Comment: Passenger profiling: A greater terror than terrorism itself? *John Marshall Law Review,* 32, 167.

State v. Davis, 35 WN. App. 724 (1983).

State v. Soto, 324 N.J. Super. 66, 734 A.2d 350 (1996).

Terry v. Ohio, 392 U.S. 1 (1968).

Thompson, A. C. (October, 1999). Stopping the usual suspects: Race and the Fourth Amendment. *New York University Law Review,* 74, 956.

United States v. Armstrong, 517 U.S. 456 (1996).

United States v. Brignoni-Ponce, 422 U.S. 873 (1975).

United States v. Cortez, 449 U.S. 411 (1981).

United States v. Jimenez-Medina, 173 F.3d 752 (9th Cir. 1999).

United States v. Lopez, 328 F.Supp. 1077 (E.D.N.Y., 1971).

United States v. Martinez-Fuerte, 428 U.S. 543 (1976).

United States v. Mendenhall, 446 U.S. 544 (1980).

United States v. Millio, 588 F.Supp. 45 (W.D.N.Y. 1984).

United States v. Montero Camargo, 208 F.3d 1122 (9th Cir. 2000).

United States v. Sokolow, 490 U.S. 1 (1989).

United States v. State of New Jersey and Division of State Police of the New Jersey Department of Law and Public Safety, No. 99-5970 (MLC) (D. New Jersey, 1999).

U.S. Department of Justice, Drug Enforcement Administration. *Operations Pipeline and Convoy* (retrieved February 1, 2002). *www.usdoj.gov/dea/programs/pipecon.htm*

U.S. General Accounting Office. (March, 2000). Report to the Honorable Richard J. Durbin, United States Senate United States Customs Service: Better targeting of airline passengers for personal searches could produce better results. Washington, DC.

Washington v. Lambert, 98 F.3d 1181 (9th Cir. 1996).

Whitfield v. Board of County Commissioners, 837 F.Supp. 338 (D. Colo. 1993).

Whren v. United States, 517 U.S. 806 (1996).

Wilgoren, J. (1999, April 9). Police profiling debate hinges on issue of experience vs. bias. *New York Times,* B1.

Wilkins v. Maryland State Police, Civil Case No. CCB-93-468 (D. Md. 1995).

Wisotsky, S. Professor of Law, Nova University Law Center, *Prepared statement before the Select Committee on Narcotics Abuse and Control, House of Representatives, concerning: A new beginning in U.S. drug policy,* September 29, 1988.

5

Police Ethics and Minority Communities

John Kleinig

T alk of *police ethics* is none too clear. At least two understandings suggest themselves. The phrase can be taken to signal a distinctive set of ethical values or principles that govern police work—moral prerogatives that police can call upon in justifying their conduct (see Kleinig, 1996, p. 279 for a discussion of the distinction between ethics and morality). Or the phrase can be taken to characterize a certain kind of social fact, namely, that police tend to be a law unto themselves—they do and get away with things that are forbidden to other members of the community. To the disenchanted, *police ethics* may appear to be something of an oxymoron, a fusing of seemingly incompatible ideas.

Despite these initial appearances, talk of *police ethics* is intended neither as an oxymoronic joke—like "jumbo shrimp"—nor as a claim that there is a set of ethical principles to which police alone may appeal. Like its neighbors, nursing ethics and research ethics, police ethics is differentiated by context rather than by substance. That is, by virtue of the work that they do, and the responsibilities they acquire as part of that work, police—like nurses and researchers—must face ethical decisions that differ from those likely to be encountered in the course of an ordinary life. Most of us, for example, will never need to determine whether or not to use a firearm against another, or how to obtain information concerning a criminal suspect's activities, or whether to initiate or continue a high speed pursuit. Police ethics is distinguished by its concern with decision making in these contexts—often generated by occupational prerogatives—rather than with the enunciation of some distinctive ethical stance (see Luban, 1988, pp. 129–133, for a discussion on lawyers' ethics, which can be restated for police ethics, Kleinig, 1996, pp. 49–50).

In this chapter, I expand on this understanding, first, by examining some of the contextual underpinnings of policing and the implications that these have for a police ethic.

Then I develop what I term an ethic of police professionalism.
larly concerned to identify some of the ways in which such an
concerns in police-citizen encounters.

FOUNDATIONAL ISSUES

Within liberal democratic societies, the ethical foundations of]
particular conception of the policed or governed. I say "policed or governed" because police have traditionally been agents of government. More importantly, though, government
has been traditionally conceptualized as an agent of the governed—albeit indirectly through
some form of representation.

The underlying assumptions are well expressed in the U.S. Declaration of Independence (1776). The Declaration asserts that there are certain "self-evident" truths—including
an equality of human worth and the attribution to individuals of various "unalienable Rights"
(most centrally rights to "Life, Liberty and the pursuit of Happiness"). Although the Declaration refers to these fundamental possessions as endowments of a Creator, writers in the tradition have also sought to provide them with a more secular source—the rational nature of
human beings (Locke, 1690). By virtue of the capacity that humans have for deliberating on
their behavior and the power they have to make decisions on the basis of deliberative as-
sessments of alternatives available to them, they are entitled to be treated as authors of what
they do and what happens to them. They are, in other words, to be acknowledged as posses-
sors of rights to "Life, Liberty and the pursuit of Happiness." Rights thus construed are
morally privileged claims, deservedly protected or secured by means of force.

If such rights are to be more than bare assertions, however, social conditions need to
exist in which they can be productively exercised. The Declaration therefore recognizes that
"to secure these rights, Governments are instituted among Men, deriving their just powers
from the consent of the governed." Government, with its constitutive institutions, exists to
ensure that natural or moral rights have practical import. It is the peculiar and strategic
strength of this "contractarian" view that it seeks to affirm governmental authority without
derogating from individual autonomy. The government that exercises its authority legisla-
tively, judicially, and executively (Locke, 1690, ch. 9), has been authorized to do so *by those
over whom it exercises such authority.*

The foregoing sketch outlines the liberal democratic tradition (or, perhaps, myth) by
which we live. It has broad public support, though the details—and sometimes even the
framework—are vigorously debated. That, however, is not a topic for the present occasion.
More to the point is the implied chain of authority—from individual to society to government to police—and the significance that this has for policing and police ethics.

As early writers in the social contract tradition saw it, agencies of government, including the police, were answerable to citizens for the ways in which they exercised the authoritative power that was entrusted to them. In these early formulations, the authority
vested in governmental agencies extended no further than the protection of fundamental
rights. The provision of social services was not included in the governmental mandate. Although there are still (libertarian) defenders of that original position, most supporters of the
tradition believe that the governmental role has evolved from its essentially protectionist
function to one that is more welfare oriented (cf. Nozick, 1974, with Rawls, 1971). The

rights to life, liberty, and the pursuit of happiness have been increasingly interpreted to include not merely security against the predations of others, but also some kind of assurance that the wherewithal of life, liberty, and pursuit of happiness will be available to all (Ritchie, 1894). The United Nations Universal Declaration of Human Rights (1948), with its 30 articles, including rights to education, health care, and holidays with pay (Arts. 26, 25, 24), exemplifies the shift that has occurred, though few if any governments could be said to have implemented all its provisions.

The shift in governmental concern has been paralleled by a shift in the role of police. From an early understanding of police as mere protectors (executors) of human rights—that is, as law enforcers and crime fighters—we now accord them a broader responsibility for securing and maintaining social peace. Police have educational, social service, and order-maintenance responsibilities along with those involved in deterring crime and the detection of criminals.

This brief overview of foundations already allows us to note some of the broader ethical questions that confront policing—policing as a social institution and policing as an occupational choice. First, there are pressing questions surrounding the ethical basis of police authority. Although the social contract tradition locates police authority in the consent of the governed, it is clear from the actual history of governmental institutions—in the United States, at least—that the "governed" have often had remarkably little input into the shaping and control of those institutions. Many early defenders of the social contract tradition and its American expression (the Founding Fathers, for example) saw no problem in asserting human equality and rights at the same time as they perpetuated the practice of slavery and the chattel status of women. We may now wonder how that could be so—though there were in fact many 19th-century defenders of both practices who believed that no incompatibility was involved. For many, these demeaning practices had biblical and other philosophical supports, though a modern student of either the Bible or philosophy might see such supports as tendentious, if not hollow (see Blanchard, 1846, for an instructive 19th-century debate). What we might generously attribute to widespread moral blindness may have been formally expunged from the books. Nevertheless, the residues of these practices remain in social life—in the educational and economic opportunities of the descendants of slaves, in the persisting divisions of domestic labor and employment opportunities, and in spoken and unspoken public attitudes.

Policing in the United States began and evolved in an era of formal and manifest racial (and other) discrimination. The first U.S. police departments were established in the 1840s. Not only were police expected to enforce racially discriminatory laws—whether of the fugitive slave kind of the 19th century or the segregationist kind of the 20th—but they were permitted and often expected to use their discretion in discriminatory ways. Police may not have been more deeply racist than other members of society, yet because they possessed power that others lacked, their work was likely to bring them into adversarial contact with Black America (McWhorter, 2001). It was many years before Blacks were given opportunities for peace officer status, and even now Blacks are generally underrepresented and often subject to discriminatory treatment within police departments (Chivers, 2001; Dulaney, 1996; Lardner & Reppetto, 2000, ch.12). Though the most egregious cases of discrimination tend to relate to the descendants of slaves, some of these observations are also true of women and other minorities in policing (e.g., Hispanics, Jews).

This history, including its contemporary remainders, might lead us to wonder whether certain members of our society can properly be construed as parties to the social contract—that is, whether the familiar forms of governmental authority can be seen as representing their interests along with those who have traditionally possessed more social power and who have given U.S. legislative, judicial, and law enforcement institutions most of the shape and content they have. Although this is a question that we all might reasonably ask, given the ways in which politicians have regularly corrupted the political process (Burrows, 1984), it is a question that is posed most acutely for those who have usually been made to bear most heavily the burdens of legislation, judicial decision making, and law enforcement (Lawson, 1990).

Although the question just raised goes to the very heart of political authority, it might be addressed with equal appropriateness to the particularities of legislative decision making and the administration of law. To use a contemporary example, federally mandated penalties for the possession of crack cocaine are substantially higher than those for the possession of cocaine powder, and this penal differentiation significantly disadvantages Black drug users (who, even if they do not use crack cocaine more frequently than White users, are more likely to be arrested for it). What is it that makes crack cocaine *so much more* troublesome (given that we support its criminalization in the first place) that one segment of the community tends to be much more heavily penalized than another? And, given that rates of drug use are comparable for minorities and Whites (Butler, 2000), why is it that the enforcement of drug laws impacts so much more heavily on minority society? Is there intentionally selective enforcement, whether reflective of overtly racist attitudes or the more subtle racial prejudice of profiling? Is it that economic and social factors make minorities more vulnerable to the sweep of law enforcement?

I pose these questions, not to answer them, but to indicate how ethical issues are to be found in the deepest recesses of policing—raised by its very role as an expression of "the rule of law." Not only are there issues of ethical significance here, but ethical issues of concern to those whose citizenship is also associated with minority status.

This said, however, it is important to recognize the moral basis of policing. Policing is not only a secure and challenging occupation, with various opportunities for personal advancement and fulfillment, but also—and more particularly—it serves a vital and morally significant social function. As I will later suggest, an appreciation of this social function—what I have termed "social peacekeeping" (Kleinig, 1996)—and the standards and values associated with serving this function appropriately, is central to an ethic of police professionalism (Kleinig, 1999). By social peacekeeping, I mean the securing and maintenance of a social environment in which individuals are able to flourish (see Kleinig, 1996, ch. 2, for a more developed discussion of this concept). Its model is the "king's peace," not the more substantive social doctrine associated with "peacemaking" ideology (Fuller, 1997). The peacekeeping account of police work puts crime fighting into a larger and less adversarial framework and does not confuse one of policing's means (the use of coercive force) with part of its *raison d'être*.

OCCUPATIONAL ISSUES

The formalization of modern policing—in London in 1829 and in New York some 15 years later—brought with it the need to develop task-specific ethical as well as administrative rules so that the powers accorded to police in what was originally their crime preventive and crime investigative work would be subject to societally acceptable constraints. Rowan and Mayne's *General Instructions* (1829) comprised a mixture of moralized admonitions along with administrative rules designed to protect the people of London from predation and disaster as well as to assure them of their safety. Later, some of these admonitions were extracted as a series of "Maxims for the General Guidance of Police Officers" and were widely distributed in England and its colonies. This was the first code of ethics for police (see Kleinig and Zhang, 1993, for a reproduction of these Maxims used for the New South Wales (Australia) Police in 1870, as well as the other codes referred to in this chapter).

In the United States, departmental manuals, mostly after the general fashion of Rowan and Mayne (1829), prevailed until August Vollmer's protégé, O.W. Wilson, was appointed in 1928 to head the Wichita (Kansas) Police Department. In quick order, Wilson drew up what he referred to as "Our 'Square Deal' Code" along with a detailed manual. The code was designed to assure the residents of Wichita that they could now expect a square deal from their previously troubled police department. Wilson's code was significant because much of its phrasing prefigured the International Association of Chiefs of Police (IACP) Law Enforcement Code of Ethics (see Kleinig & Zhang, 1993), the most widely used of all law enforcement codes. Wilson subsequently became a member of the Committee that in 1955 drew up the Californian Peace Officers' Research Association code of ethics, the immediate predecessor of the IACP Code. Between the localized Wichita code and its national successor, the FBI under J. Edgar Hoover produced its own Pledge in 1937, and this functioned as a national code until the IACP adopted its code in 1957 (see Kleinig & Zhang, 1993, p. 34).

Codes of ethics have always had a somewhat ambiguous social role and problematic moral status, but the emergence of O.W. Wilson's 1928 code was associated with another movement that has considerable significance for framing the ethical content of policing. As students of police are well aware, August Vollmer is generally regarded as the father of professionalized policing. His opus magnum, *The Police in Modern Society,* was published in 1936, and soon after, in 1938–1939, the IACP's Committee on the Professions reported inter alia that it was essential, were policing to be professionalized, for departments to develop a code of ethics that would mediate relations between police and the public they served (Kleinig, 1996, p. 34).

Police professionalization and the development of a police ethic have thus tended to go hand in hand. Although I take the view that the professional*ization* of police—if thought of as aspiring to a particular social status and the narrowing/specialization of police work—is not generally a good thing, I believe that professional*ism* in policing is crucial, and that police ethics should be seen primarily as an ethic of professionalism (Kleinig, 1996, ch. 3). I ground this skepticism toward professionalization in what I see as the general-skills character of much basic police work (e.g., crowd and traffic control, brokering responses to crisis situations), as well as the belief that professionalization tends to be associated with paternalism, the distancing of service, and the perpetuation of social discrimination (cf. Kultgen, 1988).

What I mean by *professionalism* is a commitment to the role of police officer (social peacekeeping) that reflects a competent determination to fulfill the elements of that role to the greatest possible degree. The role of police officer should be a source of pride to those who perform it, not especially because of the social standing they acquire thereby (though they may also be socially well regarded), not especially because of the organization to which they belong (though it might also include that), not especially because of the people with whom they work (though this too they can also hope for), but because they are engaged in an important—indeed crucial—social task, and it is important to them that they do it as well as they can. Professionalism so understood is not the exclusive province of the traditionally "learned professions," but can be associated with any occupation—from janitor to aircraft controller. Each may aspire to excellence in his or her role.

Although police organizations frequently confuse professionalism with professionalization (Kultgen, 1988; Kleinig, 1996), adoptees of the 1991 revision of the IACP's Law Enforcement Code of Ethics appropriately recognize that "[they] alone [are] responsible for [their] own standard of professional performance and will take every reasonable opportunity to enhance and improve [their] level of knowledge and competence" (Kleinig & Zhang, 1993, p. 93). Such professionalism involves not only a commitment to the continuing enhancement of technical understanding and skill, but also a growth in ethical awareness and conduct as police services are delivered to the wider community.

There are several areas in which an ethic of professionalism will make itself distinctively evident.

Accountability

The authority that police possess is first and foremost a recognition *by others* that police have certain prerogatives or powers. Authority is a form of social recognition rather than an inherent quality of being (see Hart, 1960, for the classic discussion of the social recognition that distinguishes the *authority* of police from the *coercive power* of the gunman). Ideally it involves a recognition that those who are given such powers are competent to exercise them—that is, that those who are given or accorded authority should be (expert) authorities in that for which they are given authority. The others on whose behalf such powers are exercised comprise—as we earlier observed—the larger society of which they are a part. It is by virtue of this connection between police authority and societal recognition that police are socially accountable or answerable for what they do. And rightly so, for, given the presumptions of liberal democracy, those over whom authority is exercised should be able to review and even influence its deployment.

This account of police authority already points to a significant problem with respect to policing in racially divided communities. It is not uncommon for the "social recognition" that police have to be most heavily concentrated among members of the dominant social group—in the United States, to a White middle class (Gallup, 2000). Those who populate what might be seen as a social underclass—predominantly Black and Hispanic—are often more inclined to view police as an "occupying army." They are gunmen "writ large" rather than authoritative social peacekeepers. That they come to be viewed in this way is largely a result of their lack of accountability to this segment of the population.

In the first instance, accountability involves transparency of behavior, in which what is done under the color of police authority can be understood and scrutinized by those over whom it is exercised. This is often subverted by the so-called blue wall of silence, which disenables those outside the organization from getting access to accurate information (Kleinig, 2001). Even so, there are various familiar mechanisms intended to ensure such accountability. Within police departments themselves efforts are made to promulgate administrative rules or regulations that prescribe or limit police responses and to establish clear chains of responsibility, reporting mechanisms, effective investigative bodies, and effective training programs. As they have actually been implemented or administered, however, these internal mechanisms have rarely been sufficient to secure an appropriate accountability. Legislative and judicial bodies, civilian review boards, media organizations, and citizens in individual and collective activity, have therefore attempted to provide additional external monitoring of what the police do and have thereby sought to hold them accountable for their behavior.

These are all important mechanisms of accountability, though they do not always provide the same or even compatible oversight, and—as we might have surmised from earlier remarks—some of them may even be skewed to certain populations or perspectives that are not "representative" of the society that is being served. Media and citizens groups might well reflect particular biases; courts are not always paradigms of impartiality; legislative bodies may be swayed by the power of prejudiced interest groups, and so on. Those who followed the Rodney King case in Los Angeles (Skolnick & Fyfe, 1993) or the New York trial of Francis Livoti in the death of Anthony Baez (Purdy, 1996; Weiser, 1998) will be acutely aware of the extent to which—even in a social environment significantly removed from the egregious prejudices of the pre–civil rights era—the mechanisms of social accountability can still be manipulated to favor narrow social interests. If for no other reason than this the plurality of accountability mechanisms is to be welcomed, for with such plurality there tends also to be diversity and thus a potential for correcting misperceptions and misjudgments.

These various mechanisms, however, do not cut to the heart of what accountability is about, at least as it is conceived and fostered within an ethic of professionalism. *Professional* accountability is preeminently personal, though not private. It is a commitment that professionals have to the standards that are implicit in the public service they provide. Whereas most accountability mechanisms are—and are often seen as—social impositions, the professional's accountability is motivated by an internal disposition, and though that may not always involve an acceptance of or a commitment to every social mechanism of accountability, it will be directly associated with the occupation's *raison d'être* (or purpose). One of the common complaints about external accountability mechanisms is that they fail to secure or "measure" what they are designed to secure or measure (this is a common problem for all forms of assessment, especially where what is assessed is characterized qualitatively rather than quantitatively). But professional accountability, understood as an internal commitment to the liberal democratic values and standards that give the occupation its social *raison d'être,* is tied directly to the achievement of those ends that external measures can assess only indirectly and imperfectly.

In other words, although professional accountability has regard—as all accountability must—to societally accepted standards (in this case the recognized or at least validated norms of professional behavior), measuring up to such standards is a function of the practitioner's commitment rather than of mere conformity to organizational or societal demands. One *holds oneself* to such standards. The truly professional will take pride in what they do, and therefore in doing it well. They will see themselves as conservers of the liberal democratic values that give their occupation its social legitimacy.

I am not of course suggesting that organizational and societal accountability measures should be abandoned. Far from it. As I have outlined it, professional accountability represents an ideal rather than an achievement. It is, furthermore, an evolving rather than a fixed ideal. Although we can agree about the need to exemplify the standards that are implicit in police work, it is much more difficult to get stable agreement about what those standards are. Scholars of policing and police themselves are involved in an ongoing debate about the scope and role of police, and even if, as I have suggested, police might be best viewed as social peacekeepers, there is still a great deal of room for making the boundaries of that understanding more precise. Nor is clarity about the standards sufficient. Not all who enter an occupation are motivated by its intrinsic values and goals. Role occupants are, after all, human beings beset with the frailties and mixed motives that characterize most human beings. And, just as government is required to ensure that human association is kept in some sort of check—itself a societal accountability mechanism—so too will the various social institutions that provide or execute public services need to secure the integrity of those services by means of some form of external oversight.

Yet it needs to be kept in mind that these external mechanisms are not so much substitutes for professional accountability as its guardians. Too much heavy-handedness can destroy rather than advance an ethic of professionalism, just as too great an emphasis on college examinations can destroy the educative process. Every effort should be made to develop in police a conception of what they do that fosters pride in service, an intense satisfaction in fostering social peace—a social environment in which all stakeholders are given opportunities to flourish. When the work of police officers is dominated by a sense that others are always looking over their shoulder, it becomes rigidly rule bound and morale breaking.

In a society that manifests strong racial and other divisions, professional accountability of the kind I have been articulating is easy to corrupt and difficult to inculcate. For what "fostering social peace" means is likely to be affected by the social milieu in which one has been raised, and that is one in which race, gender, class, religious, and other divisions are prominent. In such a social environment, the very dispositions one develops are likely to distort the realization of a societally comprehensive professional accountability. Existing socioeconomic and geographic divisions become a status quo to be preserved, and White Protestant middle-class behavior becomes the social norm to be enforced. Only with greater recruitment of and input from minority populations is this notion of social peace likely to become more encompassing.

Particularly destructive of the goal of social peace is an "us-them" dichotomy that corrupts police organizations, one in which service to the wider society is trumped by an ethic of the garrison—the need to secure the organization and its members against any outside criticism or review (Kleinig, 2001). This inversion of values was tellingly illustrated a few years ago by a case in which police left a pregnant minority (Asian) woman to die on the floor of a restaurant while they rushed off to the aid of other officers who were under fire. Asked to explain, they reported: "My main job is to protect my partner and make sure I go home every night" (Junod, 2000, p. 116). Not only was there an undervaluing of the life of a *minority* member of the society, but there was a further undervaluing of *members of the society* vis-à-vis colleagues. No doubt police solidarity has an importance and engenders satisfactions of its own, but as professionalism this particular expression fell significantly short.

How such divisions and dichotomies are to be overcome is a difficult logistical problem. Apart from the broader recruitment policies mentioned, there is a need to look at the whole process of training and education. There is every reason to think that from the day on which they enter the police academy officers are encouraged to bond in ways that easily distort themselves into adversarial and self-protective *modi operandi*.

The Exercise of Discretion

One of the hallmarks of traditional professionals is their discretionary autonomy. The extended study they have undertaken and then applied is intended to give them a sufficiently rich familiarity with and understanding of their field to fit them for making informed judgments about how their services are best provided. Although doctors, lawyers, architects, and engineers may consult with each other, they are not normally required to defer to those others in the recommendation of services.

In respect of discretionary authority, police are both similar to and different from traditional professionals. They are similar in that their work necessarily involves the exercise of considerable discretion. It is, moreover, a discretion that may involve decisions of life and death. They differ, however, in that they are usually less prepared for the discretion they will have to exercise—educational entry requirements are lower and their training is much shorter. Partly in consequence of this, they are, unlike traditional professionals, answerable to superiors for the decisions they make. It is frequently remarked that in policing, unlike the traditional professions, those with the least knowledge and experience are given the greatest (or at least most profound) discretion. They are directly authorized to exercise power that may mean the difference between life and death.

There may be some confusion here. Although a great deal of first-line police work is unsupervised, and therefore officers have many opportunities to exercise their judgment about how to respond to situations calling for their decision, the mere *capacity* to exercise judgment is not the same as having discretion. This is the mistake in Kenneth Culp Davis's much-quoted account of discretion: "A public officer has discretion whenever the effective limits on his power leave him free to make a choice among possible courses of action or inaction" (Davis, 1969, p. 4). Discretion, rather, is a prerogative (a role entitlement), not a mere capacity. Although an officer (often) has discretion whether or not to arrest a person who has violated a law, he has no legitimate discretion to beat up someone who has shown him disrespect—even if he can get away with it (Sontag & Barry, 1997). Discretion is a normative resource, a form of authority—it is a type of social recognition constrained by laws, regulations, and other standards. It does not encompass whatever an officer may be able to choose with impunity (Kleinig, 1996a).

Nevertheless, as I will make clearer below, discretionary decision making is easily corrupted by deep-seated prejudice. Whether done informally or formally, profiling that incorporates racial characteristics leads to the discriminatory exercises of discretion. Suspicion is more likely to be aroused, probable cause more likely to be determined, and the use of force more likely to be implemented if one is Black and/or poor than if one is White and/or middle class.

The discretionary authority of first-line officers is limited by what the law, departmental regulations, and supervisors permit. These may be formidable constraints: case law and patrol guides are often lengthy and detailed. Even so, extensive discretion may be allowed to an officer. Though it has its routines, policing is not routinized. Police often go out not knowing what to expect and may subsequently need to make decisions under severe time constraints and conditions of considerable complexity and uncertainty.

Various kinds of discretionary decisions may be involved: there may be issues of scope, interpretation, priority, and tactics. In *scope* decisions, officers will need to make determinations about whether what is asked of them properly concerns them. For example, unless some criminality is likely to be involved, officers are generally not expected to resolve private disputes. However, whether a dispute is of private or public significance may not always be clear. Domestic disputes have always been challenging, and many departments have sought to deal with their uncertain status by severely limiting the amount of discretion available to officers. James Fyfe (1996) has a telling discussion of the way in which police discretionary decision making in relation to domestic disputes has been influenced not only by the murky boundaries of private and public, but also—and in particular—by discriminatory racial and homophobic perceptions.

In *interpretative* decisions, it may be clear that the behavior is of a kind that falls within the scope of police intervention, but it may remain unclear how the facts are to be interpreted—whether, for example, they can be construed as providing "probable cause" that person *A* was responsible for some prohibited behavior. Here, too, there is significant space for discriminatory interpretation. It is instructive to consider how many of those initially arrested are subsequently released, and further, how many of those belong to racial minorities.

Prioritizing decisions are needed when demands on police resources exceed the resources available. Should police spend their energies on ticketing jaywalkers or turnstile jumpers when people are being mugged or cars stolen? These may not always be simple decisions. If, as some have argued, there is a significant correlation between being a turnstile jumper and being involved in more serious offenses, there might be some reason for devoting some limited resources to what might otherwise be seen as low priority offenses. Certain interpretations of the so-called Broken Windows approach argue as much. They are, however, problematic in much the same way that profiling is. Those affected by so-called zero-tolerance or quality-of-life policies belong disproportionately to "visible" minorities, and in a disproportionate number of cases those arrested for quality-of-life offenses are not also wanted for more serious offenses.

Finally, in *tactical* decisions police must decide what means to use when intervening— whether to use pepper spray or a baton, whether to reprimand or summons, and so on. Once again, as the Amadou Diallo case in New York showed, one is much more likely to be perceived as a threat if one is Black than if one is White. Tom Junod reports revealingly on Commissioner Timoney's fix on the case: "[Timoney] will deliver a reasoned and impassioned defense of the cops who shot forty-one bullets at Amadou Diallo only to turn around and say, in the end, that 'there's one thing you can't get around in that case, and that's the fact that if Amadou Diallo was an immigrant from Belfast, Ireland, he'd be alive today. That's just a fact, because if you look closely at police shootings, you'll see that race is the dominant factor'" (Junod, 2000, p. 156).

Although the use of discretion is necessitated by the complexity of situations and the limited resources that police have available to them, wide discretion generates significant ethical problems for a liberal democratic polity (Kleinig, 1998; Reiman, 1996, 1998). At bottom, discretionary authority returns to individuals a power that liberal democratic regimes have sought to restrict. Kings and tyrants who wield or arrogate to themselves the power to decide for others, remove from the governed any security that they will not be subject to arbitrary and discriminatory fiat. The "rule of law, not of men" that is central to liberal democratic government is meant to restore to the governed not only some control, but also predictability and fairness. Thus, at the same time as discretion provides opportunities for nuanced, wise, and fair decision making, it also reintroduces the monarchical potential for arbitrariness and discrimination.

Even though the discretionary authority of police is not of the same order of magnitude as that of kings and tyrants, it may nevertheless display the same defects. Police officers who arrest as a result of personal pique or who are more inclined to arrest or maltreat blacks, gays, and other minorities, succumb to the very same deficiencies that provoked the rebellion against monarchies in favor of parliamentary or republican rule. It is partly for this reason that police discretion is often severely constrained, even though social situations are complex and might—in particular cases—call for a more nuanced response than the rules allow. But it is for this very same reason important that police be educated in the kinds of factors that make for wise discretion. An ethic of professionalism will be concerned to provide this (Kleinig, 1999).

Officer Culture

Much has been written on police culture, particularly on police solidarity (Skolnick, 1994). The latter has a distinctive character and varied sources. Among those sources are a sense of vulnerability and threat, a need that police feel for protection, and a belief that that protection can come only from other officers; a recognition that decisions must be made not only under severe time constraints but also under conditions of uncertainty, and a desire therefore not to be second-guessed; a model of policing that emphasizes the "thin blue line" and crime fighting, that fosters suspiciousness and encourages a division of the world into "us" (officers) and "them" (everyone else); the pragmatic imperatives of the job, driven by pressures within and outside the organization; and constant oversight by bosses, the media, and the public.

One result of these factors is a culture that is—for the most part—close, closed, and intensely self-protective. It finds its most notorious expression in what is often referred to as the blue wall of silence, a refusal of officers to pass on any information that would be damaging to another officer. In fact it often goes further than this, to a refusal of equally ranked officers even to criticize one another. By virtue of the blue wall, the use of excessive force, discriminatory conduct, and unconstitutional tactics may go unchecked, and corruption has frequently flourished. Given that the victims of police misconduct are more likely to be members of minority groups, the blue wall reinforces the alienation that often exists between them and the police (Kleinig, 2001).

The blue wall—under its general appellation, the "code of silence"—is not unique to policing. It is a staple of friendship and familial relations, it is found in business organizations and government bureaucracies; even the professions maintain it. Indeed, any association that feels itself to be under outside threat will foster such a code, and any associational member who values the association will be inclined to adopt it. At its heart, the code of silence expresses the loyalty of those who value a particular associative bond and wish to secure it and the parties to it from external threat (Kleinig, 2001). Thus understood, the code of silence has an important associative function.

But the code—and certainly its "blue wall" variant—is frequently made to do much heavier duty. Not only is it used to preserve valued relationships against *illegitimate* threat, but it is also used to shield corruptive or deviant associations from *corrective* intervention. In the case of policing, this is particularly troublesome, since the authority vested in police is grounded in a presumption of public service. Even if police officers themselves see their associational bonds as possessing intrinsic value for them, the fact that they are *police* bonds subjects them to a further level of scrutiny—public accountability. It is partly for this reason that appeals to loyalty are ethically insufficient to secure the blue wall against breaches. Breaches are deterred as much by fear of retaliation as by any appeal to associational virtue. Officers cognizant of their public duty are kept from speaking by the threat of ostracism or physical endangerment should they believe on occasion that their societal responsibilities override their associational obligations.

An ethic of professionalism cannot thrive in an environment in which the code of silence has been severed from the larger *telos* (or ultimate purpose) of policing—the securing of social peace. Such an ethic is not inimical to a code of silence as such, because associations need more strength than self-interest can supply. Loyalty is a virtue, and betrayal is an assertion of self-interest. But an ethic of professionalism remains focused on the social purpose of policing and seeks to serve its social ends as well as it is able. Although part of that service will undoubtedly include a fostering of the strengths that associational life will contribute to policing's task, associational values must nevertheless remain answerable to professional values.

Police culture, within an ethic of professionalism, must be first and foremost a culture of service—of service to the broad constituencies that make up a jurisdiction. That may be difficult to realize, particularly if police are drawn primarily from a limited number of social constituencies and there is a history of tension between those constituencies and others that fall within a department's jurisdiction. In such cases, the expression of societal interests may be colored by various forms of prejudice. A Black person who travels in a largely White neighborhood or drives a late-model car may be presumed to be "up to no good" and thus questioned as to his doings. Service so rendered is to one "community" at the expense of another.

There is some reason to think that these problems will be ameliorated—although not eliminated—as the proportions of minorities and women in policing reach a critical mass and the cultural traditions of policing are fed by other than its traditional streams. It is significant that in the Rodney King and Anthony Baez cases the two police officers who testified against their colleagues were women. One might also expect that an increasing number of Black and Hispanic officers will also contribute to a broadening of awareness and greater caution in regard to policing by cultural stereotype. But the process is likely to be slow. As the maxim "blue over black" indicates, it is anticipated that minorities who enter policing will embrace an existing police culture rather than transform it.

Management Culture

An ethic of professionalism will flourish when those who provide a service have the incentive as well as the opportunity to do the best that they can to realize the occupation's intrinsic standards—those standards embodied in its codes of ethics. When service provision provides adequate intrinsic as well as extrinsic rewards, when trust is fostered, and contributions are appropriately acknowledged, then conditions will exist in which an ethic of professionalism can flourish. Organizations that are strongly hierarchical frequently do not foster attitudes and habits conducive to professionalism. Comparative discussions of managerial and street culture in policing have often pointed to the fact that the managerial culture of many departments is not conducive to the development of such an ethic (Reuss-Ianni & Reuss-Ianni, 1983). Aphoristic wisdom such as "no good deed goes unpunished," "they can always get you," and "don't trust bosses" speaks of an environment in which trust is missing, cynicism is fed, and minimalism is encouraged. Hierarchical organizations are frequently sycophantic and punitive, and, when blame is due, tend to engage in scapegoating.

Particularly rife in many police organizations are informal strategies for advancement, the cultivation of supervisory "hooks" and "rabbis" who will create and repay loyalty by providing promotional and other opportunities. The networks thus formed replicate within the organization what exists in the larger society—diminished opportunities for members of unfavored minority groups. Not only are minority group members disproportionately underrepresented within police organizations, but they are even further underrepresented in the higher ranks of policing. When they do succeed, there is often a suspicion that they made it only as the result of despised "affirmative action." Interestingly, those who succeed because they have been "reached out to" by some "hook" or "rabbi" rarely become objects of contemptuous suspicion. Networking usually shares little of the opprobrium of affirmative action.

The military-style management culture that characterized traditional police departments has sometimes given way to a flatter organization in which the driving models have not been the militaristic but corporate. But this has brought its own challenges to an ethic of professionalism. Much business culture is bottom-line oriented, focused more on what is quantitatively measurable than on what is qualitatively required. Procedural "doing it right" has replaced substantive "doing right." Police departments are thus encouraged to set for themselves annual performance objectives, measurable in response times, arrests, reported crimes, budgetary "responsibility" and so forth, and, as with health maintenance organizations (HMOs) in medicine, efficiency has come to be purchased at the cost of the goals of the activity.

In many departments, union influence has been a further impediment to an ethic of professionalism. Unions do not have the role of a professional association—maintaining standards, sharing advances, fostering research, and so on. Their concerns are essentially industrial—the maintenance of economic and other fringe benefits, advocacy services for members in adversarial relations, contract negotiations, and so on. This has frequently brought them into conflict not only with management but also with the ideals implicit in an ethic of professionalism. Unprofessional officers have been defended, efforts to give greater weight to merit have been opposed in the name of seniority, and unreasonable conditions have been imposed on attempts to foster professionally oriented training (overtime rates, etc.). To the extent that officers who engage in discriminatory conduct have been defended and enabled to get away with it, alienation from minority communities has been exacerbated, and the uneasy position of minority officers within the organization has been perpetuated because they will have seen officers avoid the consequences of complaints that they have engaged in race-based conduct.

The point of these observations is not to challenge the legitimacy of police unions any more than my comments on management style have been an attempt to deny the legitimacy of management. Unions are able to provide important safeguards in employment environments that are heavily weighted in favor of management, and which management is often inclined to exploit. But, as with all institutional structures, unions may come to have a life of their own apart from the larger goals of policing, and the wood is lost sight of amidst the trees. If managements can be vigorously criticized for becoming punitive or performance-oriented fiefdoms, so can unions for frequently impeding sincere efforts at reform. Union activity no less than management style can perpetuate and even magnify the prejudices found elsewhere in society.

Ethical Ownership

I have been arguing that police should be encouraged to develop an ethic of professionalism—that is, an ethic grounded in the socially sanctioned purposes of policing. Apart from its appropriateness to the quality of service provided and the way it is provided, this approach has some additional things to be said for it. *First,* by stressing that a police ethic is an ethic of professionalism, we avoid the unfortunate assumption that police lack moral sensibility and need, somehow, to be initiated into the moral community. Moral development—the acquisition of a mode of social action that is sensitive and responsive to the humanity of others—

is part of our common social inheritance and, given appropriate selection procedures, we can expect that those who come into police work will, for the most part, bring with them an already developed and, in some respects, a fairly sophisticated moral understanding. We will expect them to be imbued with a reasonably clear sense of right and wrong, of justice, and some notion of, and commitment to, public service, and these will provide ready-made foundations for the further ethical nurturing that they will receive. To speak of police ethics as an ethic of professionalism indicates that what they are expected to incorporate into their understanding is, to a considerable extent, an *application* of that common moral sensibility to the specific contours of police work.

Of course, I don't want to deny that a more fundamental conscientization might also need to take place. Police are drawn from the larger society, and if segments of that larger society are characterized by racist, sexist, heterosexist, or other attitudes that are inimical to the broadly tolerationist stance of a liberal democratic society, then an ethic of professionalism may need to incorporate some explicit reference to such issues. Although the social character of many occupations may limit opportunities for the workplace expression of broader social prejudices, policing is likely to aggravate such tendencies unless real effort is made to counteract them. Higher educational requirements may constitute one agent of amelioration, but frequently a more explicit engagement with social illiberality will be needed. Officers need to grasp a deeper understanding of the moral sources of their authority.

Second, understanding police ethics as an ethic of professionalism conceives of it in a way that should comport well with the outlook of those who have chosen to make policing their career. Professionalism bespeaks a certain pride in doing what one does, a sense not only of its worthiness, but also of the worthiness of doing it well. Professionalism in policing is expressive of a commitment to the specific form of public service to which police work is devoted. An ethic of professionalism does not represent itself as something external and alien to the otherwise viable and ongoing activity of policing, but as an integral part of good policing practice. A person who wishes to do well as a *police officer* will already have reason to adopt an ethic of professionalism. Unless a person has entered into policing from the crassest of motives or has had his or her work values eroded by cynicism, an ethic of professionalism is likely to find ready ownership among those who have chosen such work. No doubt some do enter policing for reasons that augur badly for the quality of service they will subsequently provide, but most will be initially motivated by factors that will be compatible with the development of a professional ethic (Maghan, 1988).

And *third,* conceiving of police *ethics* as an ethic of professionalism provides a cultural base for effective self-policing. All police organizations must wrestle with the problem of a culture that protects its own. For the most part, they promulgate rules that require officers to *report* misconduct, corruption, and so on, without regard to the horizontal bonds of operational officers, the seriousness of infractions, or the most productive strategies for dealing with them. I do not of course wish to challenge the obligatoriness, on some occasions at least, of reporting the infractions of others. Indeed, it may be wise as well as politic to have rules requiring such reporting. But one of the important contributions that the acceptance of an ethic of professionalism can make is to imbue its adherents with a commitment to the work they are doing that will not tolerate its subversion or denigration—whether from misconduct, corruption, or just plain incompetence—and will express its judgment directly to those involved, even if not to a superior or outside monitor. A culture in which the willful shortfalls of others are tolerated or condoned is one in which the commitment to professionalism has been abandoned. If the only recourse available for dealing with infractions is reporting them to superiors, a culture of professionalism has not taken root (see Martin, 1992).

An ethic of professionalism must convey to those who have chosen a policing career that what they have taken on is not just a job, but a commitment, and not just commitment to an organization, but more particularly to a morally important social task—to a set of standards and values that does not set them apart from the community, but in service to it, a set of values with which they can identify not only as the citizens they are but also as the officers they are. However, although an ethic of professionalism is grounded in the reality of their status as citizens and as officers, it also functions as an ideal—fostering in them a conception of citizenship and police work that rises above the racist, sexist, sectarian, and homophobic prejudices that often scar real societies and police departments.

An ethic of professionalism is a reminder of the high calling to which police have committed themselves (see Kleinig, 1999).

PROFESSIONAL ETHICS IN A DIVERSE CULTURE

For the most part I have spoken of the *society* that police serve rather than the *community.* I have done this deliberately, for "community" conveys a greater sense of unity and shared purpose than "society." American society has always comprised an uneasy articulation of communities, and population growth and increased urbanization have exacerbated some of those social tensions even as civil rights legislation has succeeded in removing some of the older formal divisions. Police have frequently found themselves caught in the interstices of communal diversity. In a society deeply divided over abortion, they have found themselves policing demonstrations at abortion clinics. They are sometimes called to intervene in domestic disputes in which, as part of her lot, the mistreated party is culturally conditioned to accept the abuse that has prompted the call. And, even if no longer acting as the explicit agents of a separationist culture against the clamor for civil rights, they now find themselves the object of protest as incident after incident suggests that ancient prejudices have not yet been overcome.

The cultural tensions that affect police may be of several different kinds. First of all, the officers themselves may have little personal sympathy for the behavior that they are being asked to secure. A devout Catholic officer who is expected to ensure that women have ready access to an abortion clinic may feel torn between personal beliefs and occupational demands. Officers may be expected to ensure the orderly conduct of an authorized neo-Nazi or anti-White or anti-police demonstration even if they feel they are assisting causes that are fundamentally inimical to their personal values or interests.

Second, independently of their own views, officers might be called to act in matters that express deep societal divisions. In such cases, their involvement might be taken to identify them with a particular position. In many circles, the policing of anti-Vietnam demonstrations in the 1960s and 1970s did not enhance the public image of police. In the 1980s, British police who were deployed to secure Mrs. Thatcher's efforts to break the coal mining unions found themselves tarnished by the experience. In some cases, police involvement has served not only to identify them with one side in a particularly divisive issue, but has also enabled them to play out prejudices with which they were themselves infected.

Birminghamm, Alabama police in the early 1960s were not just the neutral or passive agents of "Bull" Connor but willing conservators of racist policies (McWhorter, 2001).

Finally, police are sometimes confronted with and called to respond to the nontraditional practices of marginal(ized?) or newly immigrant groups. In some cases, laws may already be in place to provide a (sometimes controversial) resolution of the issue, but in other cases there may exist no societal determination, even though the practices are significantly nonconventional. Cockfighting, ritual animal slaughtering, polygamy, snake handling cults, child-bride arrangements, and more recently clitoridectomy and infibulation have posed cultural challenges to the police (and the broader society). How diverse may diversity be? The question is ultimately for the broader society to deal with; yet it is often the police who must initiate the first social responses to new practices.

Although a single situation might be expressive of more than one of these tensions, each raises its own challenges for a professional ethic. The first kind of case reminds us that when officers assume a certain role, they also accept the constraints implicit in that role, and—to a significant extent—defer to the demands of that role when it comes into conflict with their own personal convictions. Insubordination constitutes a serious failure in police work. In such cases, they do not sacrifice their convictions as much as recognize that one conviction (deference to orders of senior officers or the law) normally overrides another. In other words, they acknowledge the moral importance of the role of police and of their need to ensure that what is lawful or lawfully demanded is socially secured. A person who takes on the role has to be prepared to give priority to the moral conviction involved in that decision over others that they have. It is not of course a rigid prioritization. Situations may sometimes arise in which an officer believes that his or her moral convictions accord precedence to a "private" commitment over the values embodied in securing the law. Where this is so, an officer may decide that it is better to resign than to continue in the role, for the role is no longer morally viable. Occasionally, an officer may believe that opposition (open or subversive disobedience) to what is required is better than resignation. Consider the situation of 19th century officers required to enforce runaway slave laws or 20th century German officers required to enforce some of the more discriminatory Nazi laws. Although a professional ethic gives considerable weight to the values secured by the role, just because it is an ethic it recognizes that there may sometimes be situations in which the role itself needs reconstruction. There is no absolutism about an ethic of professionalism (Applbaum, 1998).

In the second kind of case, a professional ethic requires that police attempt to respond to social divisions in such a way that leaves it clear that their role is one of seeking to secure or ensure social peace rather than one of taking sides on some deeply divisive issue. They will demonstrate this primarily in the way in which they go about their peacekeeping role. P. A. J. Waddington observes that when police turned out in full riot gear to control demonstrations against the shipping of veal calves from England—in effect to ensure that trucks bearing veal calves could gain access to the wharf to discharge their cargo—they made it appear that they were in favor of what was being done, and thus identified themselves with a position that they could later come to regret (Waddington, 1995; cf. Waddington, 1991). More locally, the speed with which police charged a Harlem rally after it continued beyond its allotted time left the strong impression that they were doing more than ensuring compliance with regulation. They were acting as the agents of a certain kind of social disapproval (Barry, 1998). Although the role of police is an essentially conservative one, it must sometimes be exercised in a way that allows for a changing status quo. They must not show themselves to be opposed to change as such, only to change that is not secured through democratically acceptable means. Police would have come out of the civil rights struggles much better had they not appeared to be (and indeed been) the agents of resistance to change rather than guarantors of social order. Many demonstrations would have gone much better had there been prior negotiations between police and the organizers of demonstrations so that an understanding could be reached about how the goals of each could be most effectively served. Demonstrations and civil disobedience are democratically acceptable practices, and police need to develop strategies for responding to them that do not have the effect of undermining their own legitimacy.

In some respects, the third kind of case is the most difficult, though it is probably the one that police are least likely to confront. It requires that police extrapolate from the social status quo and be able to say, in effect: "That kind of behavior may well be acceptable in the place from which you've come. But in the place to which you've come, it does not (yet) have legitimacy. And therefore we cannot condone it. In coming here, you have also had to accept a range of constraints to which you might not have been subject in your homeland. And this too is one of those constraints. Unless or until those to whom we have given legislative responsibility rule otherwise, we cannot condone what you are doing. Although we recognize that it is culturally important to you, you have chosen to live that culture in this place and therefore you must—for the time being, at least—conform to our norms." In cases such as these, police must use their discretion to reflect what is likely, for the most part, to be a broad cultural understanding, one that can distinguish between what is merely culturally alien and what is culturally unacceptable. In a liberal democratic community, that will first and foremost involve a consideration of the effect that the practice has on others, whether it merely grates or instead infringes on their securable interests.

There is, however, a variant on the third case that is more commonly encountered and for which police have often shown limited cultural tolerance. Of the groups that comprise the wider American society, some are frequently characterized by social behavior that violates no rights but simply offends the sensibilities of some police officers. The social habits of the homeless, gay culture, and even African Americans may be alien to the social milieu from which most officers are drawn (Williams, 2000). In such cases, responses may be complicated by that social and cultural distance. What is called for here is not simply wise discretion but a greater capacity for toleration of difference, for recognizing that there are alternative ways of leading a life and that it is not for the police to pass judgment on ways of living with which they cannot themselves identify.

If police officers are to develop an ethic of professionalism that is adequate for the cultural diversity of a modern liberal democracy, it is essential that they familiarize themselves with the broad spectrum of understandings that a liberal democracy can accommodate as well as the actual diversity that it currently accommodates. In negotiating the tension between these, they will need to develop strategies that conserve, but do not inhibit ordered change. In many police academies, it is now common to include curricular materials designed to familiarize officers with the cultural traditions of the groups they are likely to encounter. This is one step in the right direction. But it is unlikely to bridge the cultural divide unless police officers also gain some personal familiarity with the groups in question. One way in which that is likely to happen is through recruitment of officers from these groups. In addition, however, it will also be necessary to establish some ongoing connection between police departments and the groups in question through the local associations they are likely to have formed.

CONCLUSION

In focusing on the broad contours of a professional ethic, I have attempted to indicate how an ethic of professionalism is more than just ethics in general—a broad call for good character—but is also an attempt to explicate the implications of good character for a specific occupational role. In such cases, the occupational role will carry with it certain prerogatives and responsibilities that shape what is morally acceptable and what is not. A more fine-grained exploration of these occupational privileges and duties would have us look, for example, at the use of force and particular kinds of force; at the use of deception and at different kinds of deception in different contexts; at the intersection of an officer's role with his or her private life; and so on. In particular, it would require that we pay special attention to the ways in which these already complex issues are easily infected by various social prejudices—ethnic, racial, gender, sexual, sectarian, and so on. Even though a professional ethic is not identical with ethics in general, it must—ultimately—answer to broader ethical constraints, and if a society still carries with it the baggage of historical prejudice, this will inevitably seep into the lives and decision making of its professionals. Police, as bearers of a professional ethic, do not stop being citizens subject to broader ethical constraints, and, like other citizens, they are not exempt from the self-examination that is the responsibility of every individual. The prejudices of their social milieu may explain but do not excuse the flaws that frequently appear to mar their occupation's handling of diversity.[1]

REFERENCES

Applbaum, A. (1998). Professional detachment: The executioner of Paris. In *Ethics for Adversaries,* Princeton, NJ: Princeton University Press.

Barry, D. (1996, September 6). Confrontation in Harlem: The overview; rally in Harlem ends in clashes with police. *New York Times,* p. B1.

Blanchard, Rev. J. (1846). *A debate on slavery.* New York: Negro University Press.

Burrows, E. G. (1984). Corruption in government. In J. Green (Ed.), *Encyclopedia of American political history.* New York: Scribner.

Butler, P. (2000). Class-based remedies for the poor. In W. H. and J. Kleinig (Eds.), *From social justice to criminal justice: Poverty and the administration of criminal law.* New York: Oxford University Press.

Chivers, C. J. (2001, April 2). For black officers, diversity has its limits. *New York Times,* p. A1, B5.

Davis, K. C. (1969). *Discretionary justice.* Baton Rouge, LA: Louisiana State University Press.

Declaration of Independence. (1776). [On-line] Available: *http://www.nara.gov/exhall/charters/declaration.*

Dulaney, W. M. (1996). *Black police in America.* Indianapolis: Indiana University Press.

Fuller, J. (1997). *Criminal justice: A peacemaking perspective.* Boston: Allyn & Bacon.

Fyfe, J. J. (1996). Structuring police discretion. In J. Kleinig (Ed.), *Handled with discretion: Ethical issues in police decision making.* Lanham, MD: Rowman & Littlefield.

---

[1] In preparing this paper for publication, I am grateful for the assistance of Chris Fisher. Delores Jones-Brown and Karen Terry provided useful editorial advice on an earlier draft.

Gallup Organization. (2000). Perceptions of black and white Americans continue to diverge widely on issues of race relations in the U.S. [On-line] Available: *http://www.gallup.com/poll/releases/pr000228.asp.*

Hart, H. L. A. (1994). *The concept of law* (Rev. ed.). Oxford: Clarendon.

Junod, T. (2000, June). The last cop in Camelot. *Esquire,* 112–122.

Kleinig, J. (1996). *The ethics of policing.* New York: Cambridge University Press.

Kleinig, J. (1998). Selective enforcement and the rule of law. *Journal of Social Philosophy, 29,* 117–131.

Kleinig, J. (1999). Ethics in police training. *Australian Journal of Professional and Applied Ethics, 1,* 14–27.

Kleinig, J. (2001). "The blue wall of silence": An ethical analysis. *International Journal of Applied Philosophy,* 15, 1–23.

Kleinig, J., with Zhang, Y., (Eds). (1993). *Professional law enforcement codes: A documentary collection.* Westport, CT: Greenwood.

Kleinig, J. (Ed.) / (1996a). *Handled with discretion: Ethical issues in police decision making.* New York: Rowman & Littlefield.

Kultgen, J. (1988). *Ethics and professionalism.* Philadelphia: University of Pennsylvania Press.

Lardner, J., & Reppetto, T. (2000). *NYPD: A city and its police.* New York: Henry Holt & Co.

Lawson, B. (1990). Crime, minorities, and the social contract. *Criminal Justice Ethics, 9,* 16–23.

Locke, J. (1690). *Two treatises of civil government.* New York: J. M. Dent & Sons. (reprinted 1955).

Luban, D. (1988). *Lawyers and justice: An ethical study.* Princeton: Princeton University Press.

Maghan, J. (1988). *The 21st century cop: Police recruit perceptions as a function of occupational socialization.* Dissertation—City University of New York Graduate Center—John Jay College of Criminal Justice.

Martin, M. W. (1992). Whistleblowing: Professionalism, personal life, and shared responsibility for safety engineering. *Business and Professional Ethics Journal, 11,* 21–40.

McWhorter, D. (2001). *Carry me home: Birmingham, Alabama, the climactic battle of the civil rights revolution.* New York: Simon & Schuster.

Nozick, R. (1974). *Anarchy, state, and utopia.* Oxford: Basil Blackwell.

Purdy, M. (1996, October 9). Bronx judge explains acquittal of officer in choking death. *New York Times,* p. B1.

Rawls, J. (1971). *A theory of justice.* Cambridge, MA: Harvard University Press.

Reiman, J. (1996). Is police discretion justified in a free society? In J. Kleinig (Ed.), *Handled with discretion: Ethical issues in police decision making.* Lanham, MD: Rowman & Littlefield.

Reiman, J. (1998). Against police discretion: Reply to John Kleinig. *Journal of Social Philosophy, 29,* 132–142.

Reuss-Ianni, E., & Reuss-Ianni, F. A. J. (1983). Street cops and management cops: The two cultures of policing. In M. Punch (Ed.), *Control in the Police Organization.* Cambridge, MA: M.I.T. Press.

Ritchie, D. G. (1894). *Natural rights: A criticism of some political and ethical conceptions.* New York: Macmillian.

Rowan & Mayne. (1829). *General Instructions.* London: His Majesty's Stationery Office.

Skolnick, J. (1994). *Justice without trial: Law enforcement in democratic society.* New York: Macmillan.

Skolnick, J., & Fyfe, J. J. (1993). *Above the law: Police and the excessive use of force.* New York: The Free Press.

Sontag, D., & Barry, D. (November 19, 1997). Challenge to authority: A special report; disrespect as a catalyst for brutality. *New York Times.* p. A1.

United Nations. (1948). *Universal Declaration of Human Rights. www.un.org/overview/rights.html*

Vollmer, A. (1936). *The Police in Modern Society.* Berkeley: University of California Press.

References

Waddington, P. A. J. (1991). *The strong arm of the law, armed and public order policing.* Oxford: Clarendon.

Waddington, P. A. J. (February, 1995). Two wrongs can make a right, *Police Review, 103,* 12.

Weiser, B. (1998, June 27). Ex-officer guilty in choking death. *New York Times,* pp. A1, B1.

Williams, L. (2000). *It's the little things: The everyday interactions that get under the skin of Blacks and Whites.* New York: Harcourt Brace.

6

Fixing Broken Windows or Fracturing Fragile Relationships?

Eugene O'Donnell

"Repressiveness is the worst kind of police-community relations possible. No one likes to be pushed around, to be denied his rights, and few will readily forget or forgive it. Police brutality, sweep arrests, roundups of people where there is no probable cause—these embitter beyond all other acts."

> Ramsay Clark, Former U.S. Attorney General
> *Crime in America*
> 1970 (p. 161)

"In all my travels and interviews across the United States, I rarely met a Black male who had not been unjustly hassled by a White officer."

> David Shipler, Pulitzer Prize Winning Author
> *A Country of Strangers: Blacks and Whites in America*
> 1997 (p. 384)

"Very early, I learned to handle the police with caution and self-control. I remember the police cruising through Cleveland Avenue one night, stopping when they noticed me hanging out with the white kids from the neighborhood. We weren't doing anything, just talking. The policeman got out of his car, came over, looked at us, looked at me, then looked at me again. He asked me what we were doing. 'Nothing, just talking,' we said and explained that we lived in the neighborhood. I pointed and said calmly: 'That's my house over there, Officer.'

> He looked at me hard and said finally: 'You go home. The rest of you be careful.' I went home without any further discussion. It was not fair, but I didn't expect the police to be fair."
>
> Andrew Young, Former United States Ambassador
> to the United Nations
> *An Easy Burden*
> 1996 (pp. 36–37)

In 1982, James Q. Wilson and George Kelling published an article in the *Atlantic Monthly* magazine that rocked the world of policing. The article, "Broken Windows: Police and Neighborhood Safety," declared that police departments were complicit in the decline of urban America. Wilson and Kelling maintained that the police had shied away from watchman-style policing because they feared the consequences would include criticism for being overzealous or, worse, provoking civil unrest (Wilson & Kelling, 1982).

The *Atlantic Monthly* article and the follow-up book, *Fixing Broken Windows* by Kelling and Cole (1996), maintained that the police should enforce minor laws in an effort to create an atmosphere where more serious crimes would be discouraged. The article focused on the broken window within a community as the symbol of a steady trend toward deterioration of that neighborhood. If responsible people within the community failed to repair the broken window, then the community would spiral into more disorder and eventually be seriously damaged.

The *Broken Windows* essay suggested that the police enforce "quality of life" crimes by sanctioning persons for minor offenses (see Bennett, DiIulio, and Walters, 1996). Though the article received glowing reviews and was praised for its simplicity and straightforwardness, in actuality it represented a dangerous invitation to ignore the history and complexity that surround police-community relationships. Whether intended or not, this article provided a roadmap for police abuse of power, particularly within minority communities.

The premise of this chapter is that there is nothing new about the Broken Windows approach. The American police have a long history of targeting "undesirables" who are often minorities in low socioeconomic communities. The idea of using minor ordinances to crack down on disorderly street conditions had been tried and found to be legally dubious, as well as wasteful with time and resources. If the history of American policing has taught us anything it is that there is no easy solution to the "crime problem" and that the answer to long-term, entrenched problems is not available at any police headquarters. Policing is complex. Public policy that addresses long-standing social inequities is no less so.

This chapter also argues that Broken Windows not only deliberately ignored the often painful lessons learned by law enforcement, particularly in the decades of the 1960s and 1970s, but was offered as a political decoy to divert attention from more serious and more enduring societal problems such as discrimination and poverty. After American cities erupted in riots over civil rights in the 1960s, several investigative commissions were established to address the underlying causes for the unrest. Most of these commissions pronounced America in need of substantial repair. Wilson and Kelling, along with other conservatives, used the Broken Windows argument to sidestep these demands, insisting that the police could be the key players in restoring urban America.

However true it may be that the police should act affirmatively to reassert a sense of community safety and security, the police role in a democracy is necessarily a limited one. The police are not always in the best position to diagnose or care for problems, and Americans must be wary about suggestions that simple solutions can be found for deep and enduring social divisions. The lessons learned from the 1960s are just too valuable to be discarded, as some offer a vision of America where all the action is at the police station or the local lockup.

AMERICAN POLICING: A (BRIEF) HISTORY

The story of police-community relations in the United States is an examination of race relations (Walker, 1999). The racial features of law enforcement make many uneasy; thus, some textbooks about the police and community relations don't mention race at all or do so just in passing. The relationship between the police and minorities has been characterized by long-standing tensions, documentation of which appears throughout the literature of law enforcement (Richardson, 1974). The exact causes for these tensions are many, but it is certainly true that the police play a central role in perpetuating a legal system that many minorities, especially African Americans, see as unfair (Kennedy, 1997).

The criminal justice system was one of the major instruments of White supremacy after the Civil War in the South (Walker, 1999), though police abuse was far from unknown in the North (Richardson, 1974). Public opinion polls continue to show a chasm between Whites and Blacks (and other minorities) in how they perceive the police. Much of the contemporary debate about policing surrounds the brutalizing of individuals by the police, while dysfunctional police-community relationships in fact may be tied as much to "petty indignities" (e.g., verbal abuse, stopping and frisking) to which minorities are disproportionately subjected (Silberman, 1964). These are significant police intrusions into the lives of individuals that can give rise to community tensions and discord between the police and the community (Goldstein, 1977). The police cannot do an effective job without the support of the community (see, for example, Rubinstein, 1973), and this support is likely to be withheld by individuals who view the police as abusive or callous. Unfortunately, the police are sometimes eager to enforce laws and, while doing so, ignore the public's civil rights and civil liberties (Sparrow, Moore, & Kennedy, 1990).

In his book, *Crime and Punishment in American History*, Lawrence Friedman (1993, p. 104) underscores the long police history of targeting those viewed as undesirables:

> By the second half of the century, the police were in place as an army that could be mobilized in the struggle against the tramp. The police preserved the public peace; they monitored public spaces. They 'trawled' common areas of the city; and they tended to fasten their grip on drunken foreigners, on suspicious, vagrant men, homeless men, men who loitered, men who looked and dressed in a disreputable way, strangers, the unkempt, the unseemly. Thousands of arrests fell into the garbage pail categories that made up the substance of vagrancy laws.

These vagrancy statutes were popular with the police because they acted as a "catchall" category for undesirables. However, The U.S. Supreme Court rejected such statutes for that reason in *Papachristou v. City of Jacksonville*, due to the ordinance in Jacksonville that read:

> Rogues and vagabonds, or dissolute persons who go about begging, common gamblers, persons who use juggling or unlawful games or plays, common drunkards, common night walkers, thieves, pilferers or pickpockets, traders in stolen property, lewd, wanton and lascivious persons, keepers of gambling places, common railers and brawlers, persons wandering or strolling about from place to place without any lawful purpose or object, habitual loafers, disorderly persons, persons neglecting all lawful business and habitually spending their time by frequenting houses of ill fame, gaming houses, or places where alcoholic beverages are sold or

served, persons able to work but habitually living upon the earnings of their wives or minor children shall be deemed vagrants and upon conviction in the Muncipal Court shall be punished [by 90 days imprisonment, $500 fine, or both]. (*Papachristou v. City of Jacksonville*, 405 U.S. 156 pp. 156–157)

Vagrancy laws placed primary emphasis on police suspicions rather than due process, allowing the police to arrest someone for being part of a category of people rather than for specific conduct (Chambliss & Seidman, 1982). Though vagrancy statutes are in contemporary disfavor, police officers in most jurisdictions now have broad powers to act against public disorder. One example of this power is the use of disorderly persons ordinances, which are open to abuse because of their ambiguity. These tend to hamper police-community relationships because there is not a consensus in the community to enforce such laws, particularly if the police overenforce such ordinances among a particular group of people (Morris & Hawkins, 1970). To freshly empower the police to act vigorously in communities without first securing public consent or at least minimizing public resistance is to invite a potential police-community relations disaster.

Herman Goldstein (1990) said that before the urban unrest of the 1960s, little value was placed on including the community in police decision making. One of the most significant barriers that the police continue to face is legitimacy, or a willingness by the policed to accept police authority (Walker, 1993). Some studies show that when public officials encourage the police to act aggressively, some officers act in an extralegal way (Brown, 1981) or make up the law as they go along (Davis, 1975). Other studies show that negative signals to overenforce the law in some communities can be transmitted down the chain of command directly from the top (Skolnick & Fyfe, 1993).

When laws are broad and amorphous, the police charged with enforcing them may exploit this lack of clarity. Historically, the brunt of police enforcement has fallen on the poor and minorities who, as Bittner (1990) points out, have long been the "preferred target" of the police. Several studies show that the police employ different tactics and standards of enforcement in urban ghettos than other areas (Goldstein 1977; Skolnick, 1968). For instance, the police have often been overzealous in enforcing gambling and other vice statutes in "ghetto" neighborhoods (Cray, 1972), the same areas where roundups and sweeps are among the common police tactics to address street conditions. Though these tactics are ostensibly meant to clean up disorder and crime, they are thinly disguised forms of harassment and abuse of minorities (Friedman, 1993).

Aggressive police tactics have the potential to create division and resentment (Goldstein, 1977; Walker, 1993). Indeed, the Kerner Commission warned that "police misconduct—whether described as brutality, harassment, verbal abuse or discourtesy—cannot be tolerated even if it is infrequent. It contributes directly to the risk of civil disorder. It is inconsistent with the basic responsibility of the police in a democratic society." The Commission also warned about a probable backlash that heavy-handed police tactics might invite. "It has long been recognized that minor crime statutes are often misused. Arrests for minor crimes such as vagrancy, disorderly conduct, use of obscene language, loitering, failure to move, blocking the street or sidewalk, drunkenness, drinking in public and curfew violations constitute about one half of all arrests made in the United States each year." Ominously, the Commission concluded that such arrests create "antagonism in slum communities," and it astutely commented that persons arrested for minor crimes might actually harbor more resentment than those charged with serious offenses (National Advisory Commission on Civil Disorders, 1968).

Regardless of the good intentions to clean up the community, police activity—particularly that which involves aggressive tactics—falls disproportionately upon minorities and minority communities. This is especially obvious when analyzing the application of "zero-tolerance" policing tactics, such as those in New York City.

BROKEN WINDOWS IN NEW YORK

Although it had received widespread attention in the criminal justice community, the Broken Windows theory remained a philosophy rather than a policy until 1989 when a new Transit Police Chief, William Bratton, arrived in New York City.

Selected to head the 4,000 member Transit Police Department—a smaller, separate agency from the New York City Police Department (NYPD)—Bratton came to New York charged with the responsibility of reducing subway crime and, perhaps more importantly, fostering a perception of safety underground for the millions of customers who rode the subways daily. A former high-ranking official in the Boston Police Department, Bratton announced that Kelling would be his chief advisor in his anticrime and antidisorder campaign.

Bratton urged his officers to "get into the game" by encouraging them to aggressively enforce not only state laws and statutes, but to take full advantage of a sweeping set of rules and regulations that the transit authority had promulgated (Bratton, 1998). Those rules and regulations provided that a person could be summonsed or ejected for trivial conduct such as holding subway doors, eating or drinking, falling asleep, taking pictures, or placing packages on seats (see New York Code Rules and Regulations "NYCRR" sections 1050.7–1050.11).

Bratton believed that officers confronting minor offenders sent a signal to the larger mass transit community that lawlessness would not be tolerated. Transit officers would detain, identify, and often conduct warrant checks on even minor wrongdoers. Bratton was agitated by suggestions that the police could become overzealous and justified his tactics by pointing out that major offenders were often apprehended while committing minor infractions (Donohue, 2000a). As Bratton (1998, p. 154) himself said: "Every arrest was like opening a box of Cracker Jack. What kind of toy am I going to get? Got a gun? Got a knife? Got a warrant? Do we have a murderer here?" Transit police officers issued so many summonses that a separate Transit Adjudication Bureau (TAB) was established to rescue the swamped criminal court system. By 2000, TAB was handling a quarter of a million summonses for subway violations annually (Donohue, 2000b). Remarkably, complaints from those detained and summonsed did not generate much media reporting, or perhaps there were too few complaints to justify reporting them. In any event, Transit Chief Bratton had effectively resurrected vagrancy enforcement in the subway; New York courts, like courts in most states, had gotten rid of vagrancy and loitering laws, but Bratton's department substituted subway rules for vagrancy statutes. Moreover, the transit police were skirting New York's demanding stop and frisk law, a law that mandated that the police carefully observe and later articulate in court the grounds for detaining someone. Officers summonsing someone for something as trivial as falling asleep were allowed, at a minimum, to detain, identify, and warrant-screen that individual. The police were permitted to arrest all such offenders and could search them pursuant to arrest. Of course, these regulations put into police hands comprehensive powers—powers that could be exploited improperly.

Crime began dropping in the subways, and Bratton and Broken Windows were given the lion's share of the credit. Some critics have suggested that during Bratton's tenure in the transit police, the Broken Windows approach "morphed" into zero-tolerance policing in which enforcement was emphasized even for trivial offenses (Rosen, 2000). Some have said that Bratton, recognizing the value of massive arrests in identifying and deterring major violators, pushed officers to sanction riders.

Bratton subsequently returned to Boston in 1992, but returned two years later to take a much bigger job—Commissioner of the NYPD.

BROKEN WINDOWS AND THE NEW YORK CITY MAYORAL RACE

The issue of crime and how to reduce it dominated the hard-fought, racially charged, 1993 mayoral campaign in New York City. For months, the press reported that crime was escalating. The tabloids in particular filled their pages with lurid accounts of the many murders in the city (Lardner & Reppetto, 2000). Rudolph Giuliani, a former United States Attorney who had four years earlier been defeated in his bid for mayor, faced David Dinkins in a rematch. Giuliani told audiences that Dinkins was too soft on crime, and often cited cases where a panhandler or "squeegee man" accosted a fearful New Yorker. In the end, Giuliani ousted Dinkins, the city's first African American mayor, from City Hall with the slimmest margin since the municipal elections of 1905 (Jackson, 1995).

The 1993 election exposed the raw racial divisions in the city. A critical subtext to the mayor's race was in the end, who will have control over the police? This is a debate that takes place often in America, in political contests large and small. Because police conduct is so polarizing, any attempt to examine electoral issues where the police are involved ordinarily requires an analysis of racial dynamics.

Upon taking office, Giuliani summoned Bratton back to New York to become his first police commissioner in 1994. As the commissioner, Bratton was responsible for a much larger and more complex organization that was more central than the transit police to the life of the city. Bratton was the point man, selling a brand of aggressive policing to a divided city. This was a difficult task at an emotional time—Giuliani's defeat of Dinkins had a profound effect on the African American community. Few minorities had voted for the new mayor and Giuliani, shunned by minorities at the ballot box, was not inclined to reach out and build bridges (Karmen, 2000). Even Bratton (1998) acknowledged that Giuliani's rise to power was fueled by White concerns that Blacks had "gotten away with too much" under Dinkins. Bratton promised great things, vowing to take back the city "block by block" and inviting the world to watch his progress.

Conspicuously absent from Giuliani and Bratton's rhetoric was any talk of involving the community in achieving consensus, or in identifying priorities. This was unsurprising, though, because Giuliani had mocked community policing as being social work in disguise during the campaign (Purdum, 1993). Instead, both men talked about letting the police set the priorities unencumbered with public sentiment.

Between 1993 and 1997, Giuliani's first term, the NYPD engaged in literally millions of enforcement actions from playing of loud radios to traffic infractions to murders (*Mayor's Management Reports*, 1993–1997). Narcotics officers made hundreds of thousands of arrests for low-level drug (primarily marijuana) offenses, while plainclothes officers stopped, questioned, and frisked additional tens of thousands of people. Ordinary patrol officers and officers in special units issued tickets for, among other things: public drinking, possession of marijuana, disorderly conduct, unleashed dogs, jaywalking, and riding bicycles on the sidewalk. During this period the NYPD swelled to over 40,000 officers due to its merger with the housing and transit forces and, ironically, the addition of several thousand officers funded by former Mayor Dinkins.

Reported crime in the city plummeted during Giuliani's first term (and continued to drop between 1997 and 2001, the period of his second term). Between 1993 and 1997, local and international newspapers heaped praise on the Giuliani-Bratton team, declaring the crime reductions "miraculous" and holding New York out as a model to the nation. Mayor Giuliani brushed aside suggestions that police enforcement would inevitably exact a heavy toll in minority communities. He defended statistics showing that more than 85% of those frisked by officers were non-White by arguing that the police would go where the crime was.

Despite the many praises for the NYPD, there was not universal agreement that they alone were responsible for the declining crime rate. One former high-ranking NYPD official, Anthony Bouza, a retired police chief in Minneapolis, accused police chiefs of riding a national trend in crime reductions and crediting their "nifty" anticrime plans. Bouza was not alone in pointing out that some cities such as Boston and San Diego also had dramatic reductions in crime without resorting to the hard-nosed policies so favored in New York policing (Bouza, 2001).

Some researchers found that crime had actually started to decline under former Mayor Dinkins. There had in fact been a 16% decrease during the last three years of his administration (Barrett, 2000). Two researchers, Stephen W. Raundersbush and Robert J. Samuelson, published a study that cast doubt on the Wilson/Kelling Broken Windows approach. They found that there were complex reasons why some communities had high crime rates while others didn't, factors they labeled "neighborhood structural characteristics" (*Law Enforcement News*, 2001). Even the NYPD's own management team sometimes confessed to having doubts about the causal links between policing, disorder, and crime. "Rapists and killers don't head for another town when they see graffiti disappearing from the subways" wrote Jack Maple, a former deputy police commissioner and Broken Windows architect under Bratton (Maple & Mitchell, 1999).

BROKEN WINDOWS AND MINORITY COMMUNITIES

Without knowledge of American police history, an observer might conclude that the marked reductions in crime would bring great rejoicing in minority communities because these are the neighborhoods that are often disproportionately affected by violent crime. Some minority leaders did acknowledge that the reductions had taken place, although others took exception to the lack of attention given to community crime reduction efforts.

Predictably, however, periodic announcements of crime declines could not negate a fact known only too well by young minority residents and their families: the reductions had come at a great cost to their freedom of movement and their constitutional right to be left alone when going about their business. Resentment about police tactics simmered in minority neighborhoods. After interviewing Mayor Giuliani for a *Nightline* segment, Ted Koppel of ABC television confronted him about the hostility that arose from the aggressive police tactics he promoted. Koppel said that Giuliani evaded the question and Koppel concluded that the mayor was "too smart not to get it" and that his policing policies were designed to please his White constituents (Koppel, 2000).

New York Times polls from 1997, 1999, and 2000 revealed that approximately 80% of African American New Yorkers gave the NYPD negative ratings. In March 1999, 9 out of 10 African American respondents told pollsters that the police "often engaged in brutality against blacks," and "more than two thirds said the policies of the Giuliani administration had caused an increase in police brutality" (Barry & Connelly, 1999). In a separate survey, Latino New Yorkers expressed almost identical levels of concern about being mugged and being brutalized by the police (Hispanic Federation of New York, 1999).

These tensions were exacerbated by three controversial incidents: the 1998 sexual assault on Abner Louima conducted by a police officer, the shooting death of unarmed immigrant Amadou Diallo, and the shooting by an undercover officer of another unarmed man named Patrick Dorismond during a police "buy and bust" operation. After the Diallo shooting, prominent leaders in the African American community as well as others led massive, daily protests at police headquarters to highlight perceived police insensitivity. With tensions running high, the now former Commissioner Bratton began to write and speak about the need for including the community. George Kelling accused New York police officials of transforming Broken Windows policing into a "bastard child"—zero-tolerance policing (*Law Enforcement News*, 1999)—and even Mayor Giuliani seemed stung by the ferocity of criticism directed at him.

A police-community relations meltdown was under way. And it resulted in several studies regarding NYPD operations. New York State Attorney General Elliot Spitzer reported that the Police Department's Street Crime Unit (whose officers killed Diallo) with 1% of the city's police officers searched a total of 40,000 people but ended up arresting only 7,000 of them (Spitzer, 1999). These findings were corroborated by a study made by the Civilian Complaint Review Board (Rashbaum, 2001). In June 2000, the United States Commission on Civil Rights accused the NYPD of engaging in racial profiling of Blacks and Latinos. "The NYPD seems to have avoided learning from the experiences of San Diego and Boston and other places where officials employ approaches to policing that reduce crime and minimize racial tension. Community Involvement seems to be the key," the Commission wrote in its executive summary (United States Commission on Civil Rights, 2000). At the same time, officials of the United States Department of Justice were considering asking a federal court to order the appointment of an outside monitor to oversee NYPD operations.

Between 1994 and 2000, the city paid out a staggering $177 million in false arrest claims (McCoy, 2000)—an amount that totaled the entire operating budget of Bratton's former employer, the Boston Police Department (United States Department of Justice, 1999). The amount was all the more shocking if one considered that civil rights lawyers tend to sue police agencies only in the strongest cases where there are substantial damages. Many less serious cases of abuse are never pursued.

The repercussions of hard-nosed policing surfaced in other places as well. Queens' prosecutors reported a surge in hung juries because jurors were increasingly reluctant to credit police testimony (Rhode, 2000). Bronx District Attorney Robert Johnston's office tallied the lowest conviction rates ever (George, 2000). The *New York Times* reported that federal census takers were receiving hostile receptions in some minority communities, the hostility being linked at least in part to poor police-community relationships (Flynn, 2000a). The Police Department found itself hard pressed to recruit sufficient numbers of potential police officers, due at least in part to the poor opinions many New Yorkers had about their police force (Flynn, 2000b).

So despite the crime drops, for minority New Yorkers the celebrations were, at best, muted—overwhelmed by serious rifts in police-community relationships. Hundreds of thousands of innocent people or people committing minor offenses had crossed paths with the police over the seven years of the Giuliani era, and many—just how many was anyone's guess—had come away with a feeling of anger and bitterness. Of course, whether one called this approach Broken Windows or zero tolerance mattered little to those ensnared in its grasp. This had all been tried before and, predictably, it yielded disastrous results.

THE PROBLEMS WITH BROKEN WINDOWS

Broken Windows was more about political ideology than policing. The proponents of this new watchman-style of policing were not police officers nor did they seem to understand the vagaries and complexities of the urban police. It was the crime crisis of the 1980s that provided an opening for conservatives, without debate, to redefine the police role in a manner that minimized the need for community involvement (Hunter, Mayhall, & Barker, 2000).

The right-wing, business-funded, Manhattan Institute (MI) received much of the credit for imposing these police tactics on the city. Researchers attached to the MI included Kelling, Wilson, and far more radical staffers such as John DiIulio and Charles Murray (co-author of *The Bell Curve*, which ties intellect with genetics). The MI had for years mounted an all-out assault on the conventional wisdom that the accumulated wisdom of policing should dictate police policy. To the MI, this meant that the police were simply hostages to liberal thinking, which emphasized analyzing "root causes" for problems. By repositioning the police department as the central city service, these conservatives hoped to preempt calls for radical urban reform.

Generally opposed to big government and big brother, the MI and other conservatives endorsed multi-billion dollar police buildups and ever-expanding intrusions into the lives of hundreds of thousands of overwhelmingly poor people. If they guessed that these adverse police contacts would fall primarily on minorities, they guessed right; estimates are that more than 80% of those stopped, questioned, and frisked by the NYPD are Black or Hispanic (Edozien, 2001). While income statistics of those frisked have not been gathered, it can be safely assumed that very few White male business executives or wealthy benefactors of the Manhattan Institute found themselves stopped at gunpoint on "suspicion" during the Giuliani era. The MI endorsed these massive and profound (for a democracy) interventions in peoples lives because they believed that the right to be free from unlawful search and seizure was a right less valuable to someone in a poor neighborhood (naturally, the MI has not offered a similar Broken Windows-style catchphrase for combating corporate crime—something like "making suit and tie crimes matter").

That Broken Windows was such a smash hit among right-wing thinkers should have proved cause for concern, but it apparently did not. These conservatives enjoyed little popular support among New York City residents, and less still in those communities where they were encouraging the police to get tough. Because its ideas were so radical, the institute was forced to operate in the shadows through a little-read journal and the editorial pages of the *Wall Street Journal*. Nonetheless, it was reported to have great influence at City Hall, and many of Giuliani's policies were credited to the MI.

When Mayor Giuliani was reelected in 1997, some suggested that this represented a powerful mandate from city residents to continue his police tactics. But as journalist Wayne

Barrett pointed out, Giuliani actually received 172,000 fewer votes than when he first defeated David Dinkins and his electoral mandate, such as it was, represented the votes of fewer than 1 in 10 New Yorkers (Barrett, 2000). The majority of city voters, including hundreds of thousands of minorities, voted on election day to stay home (Barrett, 2000; Kirtzman, 2000).

Under Giuliani's term, the police had become the central institution to deal with all problems related to the city. The police were turning order maintenance situations into law enforcement ones due to the Broken Windows thesis, and this had a negative impact upon the minority communities, which were seen as having high levels of disorder. Were the panhandler and the inebriate really ever the biggest problems in urban America? By developing a new nomenclature, zero tolerance, conservatives found a new way to keep "law and order" center stage.

At the beginning of the new century American cities were confronted with many of the same problems that were identified after the riots by commissions such as Kerner. These include (National Advisory Commission on Causes and Prevention of Violence, 1969, p. 30).

- low income
- physical deterioration
- dependency
- racial and ethnic concentrations
- broken homes
- working mothers
- low levels of education and vocational skills
- high unemployment
- high proportions of single males
- overcrowded and substandard housing
- low rates of home ownership or single family dwellings
- mixed land use
- high population density

How many of these problems could be solved by law enforcement? How many of these problems have, over the past three decades, been substantially mitigated? In reality, some of these problems have become worse. Racial segregation of cities is becoming more pronounced, a sizeable underclass remains, and housing, health care, and education are often substandard or denied outright to many of America's neediest citizens. During the 1960s Congress reacted to revelations of widespread poverty by enacting the "Great Society" programs, which were designed to provide a "safety net" for the poor. With the election of Ronald Reagan as President in 1980, some conservatives such as the MI's Charles Murray advanced the theme that social welfare programs actually "impoverished the poor" (Berman, 1998).

Whether they intended it or not, Wilson and Kelling's Broken Windows article fit nicely into this conservative polemic that de-emphasized the role of government in providing assistance to those who needed it. Herman Goldstein, one of the great American thinkers about policing, warned against policing becoming a panacea in communities that are "starved for social services" (Kaminer, 1995, p. 201).

New York's immense police buildup coincided with the revelation that the city had become the income inequality capital of the United States. Studies show that New York, more than any place in America, has become a city with a relatively small number of people who are earning huge sums, a declining middle class, and ever-growing legions of people who survive on the margins without any hope of quality health care or decent wages or the ability to someday draw from a pension fund. As Barbara Ehrenreich (2001) points out, it is virtually impossible for people to survive on minimum wage employment. Radical academics such as Syd Harring (1983) have long argued that the de facto role of the police is shoring up an economic system that is inherently unbalanced.

Some conservatives such as William Bennett, John DiIulio, and John Walters minimize the extent of American racism, instead emphasizing that the cause of higher minority incarceration rates is "moral poverty" (Bennett, DiIulio, & Walters, 1996). Other conservatives like Wilson, Thomas Sowell, and Edward Banfield tend to "blame individuals, class, cultural factors, or human nature" rather than society for crime (Auletta, 1982).

By emphasizing law and order, Broken Windows, or zero tolerance, New York City and national leaders have ignored history and eschewed government responsibility for improving delivery of services to those in need. Jonathan Kozol, who has spent a great deal of time in New York's borough of the Bronx, writes compellingly of the children he saw at a local public school. In his most recent book, *Ordinary Resurrections*, he documents the depth of despair in that community and describes how difficult it is for children there to climb out of poverty (Kozol, 2000). Naturally, these students and others from low socioeconomic areas are the core police constituency. According to Kozol, the local high school admitted 1,400 freshmen, held onto 90 until senior year, and graduated 65. What ends up happening to these students is not clear, but law enforcement officials will be the last to express surprise when many of them come through the doors of the local precinct wearing handcuffs. This educational Armageddon, while not uniform throughout the city, is not exactly uncommon. A 1999 study by the Community Service Society of New York City reported that the poverty rate for families with children is an appalling 30% (Bernstein, 1999). In the end one is left to wonder whether enhanced policing is really about reducing the level of violent crime or about the promise of an insurance policy to the "winners" in a society that is producing an abundance of "losers."

CONCLUSION

Police chiefs and others in law enforcement should recognize that aggressive policing tactics, although capable of reducing the level of disorder in a community, are not a panacea. These tactics disproportionately affect those in low socioeconomic areas that are, in urban cities like New York, largely minority communities. The reduction of crime is a goal for all police departments, but to do so through aggressive tactics impairs police-community relations. Broken Windows is an insightful philosophy, but in order for it to be translated into a successful strategy it must not be applied disproportionately in minority communities.

REFERENCES

Auletta, K. (1982). *The underclass.* New York: Vintage Publishers.

Barrett, W. (2000). *Rudy: An investigative biography.* New York: Basic Books.

Barry, D., and Connelly, M. (1999, March 16). Poll in New York finds many think police are biased. *New York Times,* p. A1.

Bennett, W., DiIulio, J., and Walters, J. (1996). *Body count.* New York: Simon & Schuster.

Berman, W. (1998). *America's right turn: From Nixon to Clinton.* (2nd ed.) Baltimore: Johns Hopkins Press.

Bernstein, N. (1999, October 7). Poverty rate persists in city despite boom: Twice as high as nation analysis of data shows. *New York Times,* pp. B1, B6.

Bittner, E. (1990). *The functions of police in modern society.* Cambridge, MA: Oelgeschalger, Gunn & Hain.

Bouza, A. (2001). *Police unbound: Corruption, abuse and heroism by the boys in blue.* New York: Prometheus Books.

Bratton, W. (1998). *Turnaround: How Amercia's top cop reversed the crime epidemic.* New York: Random House.

Brown, M. (1981). *Working the street: Police discretion and the dilemmas of reform.* New York: Russell Sage Foundation.

Chambliss, W. & Seidman, R. (1982). *Law, order & power.* Reading, MA: Addison-Wesley.

Clark, R. (1970). *Crime in America.* New York: Simon & Schuster.

Cray, E. (1972). *The enemy in the streets: Police malpractice in America.* Garden City, NY: Anchor Books.

Davis, K. C. (1975). *Police discretion.* St. Paul, MN: West Publishing.

Donohue, P. (2000a, June 25). Hordes of hoods nabbed at turnstile—fare beating suspects run the gamut. *New York Daily News,* p. 4.

———. (2000b). TA doing fine summons crackdown adding millions to the till. *New York Daily News.* June 9 (5).

Edozien, F. (2001, May 19). Rudy crowing over cops low profiling. *New York Post,* p. 3.

Ehrenreich, B. (2001). *Nickel and dimed: On (not) getting by in America.* New York: Metropolitan Books/Henry Holt.

Flynn, K. (2000a, May 16). Who lives here? Who's asking? In a black community, official mistrust hinders the census. *New York Times,* p. B1.

———. (2000b, September 23). City short of police recruits as job loses luster. *New York Times,* p. A1.

Friedman, L. (1993). *Crime and punishment in american history.* New York: Basic Books.

George, T. (2000, July 11). Bronx justice a bust: Boro juries acquit suspects half the time as conviction rate sinks. *New York Daily News,* pp. 22–23.

Goldstein, H. (1977). *Policing a free society.* Cambridge, MA: Ballinger Publishing Company.

———. (1990). *Problem oriented policing.* New York: McGraw Hill.

Green, M. (2000). *Disciplining police: Solving the problem of police misconduct.* New York: Office of the Public Advocate of the City of New York.

Harring, S. (1983). *Policing a class society: The experience of american cities 1865–1915.* New Brunswick, NJ: Rutgers University Press.

Hispanic Federation of New York. (1999). *Hispanic New Yorkers on Nueva York, seventh annual survey—Report 2 police and quality of life.* New York.

Hunter, R., Mayhall, P., and Barker, T. (2000). *Police-community relations and the administration of justice,* 5th Ed. Upper Saddle River, NJ: Prentice Hall.

Jackson, K. (1995). *The encyclopedia of New York.* New Haven: Yale University Press.

Kaminer, W. (1995) *It's all the rage: Crime and culture.* Reading, MA: Addison-Wesley.

Karmen, A. (2000). *New York murder mystery.* New York: NYU Press.

Kelling, G., and Bratton, W. (1994, Summer). Taking back the streets. *City Journal,* 38–46.

Kelling, G., and Cole, C. (1996). *Fixing broken windows: Restoring order and reducing crime in our communities.* New York: Free Press.

Kennedy, R. (1997). *Race, crime and the law.* New York: Pantheon Press.

Kirtzman, A. (2000). *Rudy Giuliani, emperor of the city.* New York: Morrow.

Koppel, T. (2000). *Off camera: Private thoughts made public.* New York: Alfred A. Knopf.

Kozol, J. (2000). *Ordinary resurrections.* New York: Crown Publishers.

Lardner, J., and Reppetto, T. (2000). *NYPD: A city and its police.* New York: Henry Holt & Company.

Law Enforcement News (2001, March 15). If it's broken fix it: Study challenges broken windows thesis on crime and disorder link, p. 8.

————. (1999). Interview with George Kelling. May 15/31 (p. 8).

Maple, J., and Mitchell, C. (1999). *The crime fighter: Putting the bad guys out of business.* New York: Doubleday Publishers.

McCoy, K. (2000, July 16). Police misconduct mess. *New York Daily News,* pp. 6–9.

Morris, N. and Hawkins, G. (1970). *The honest politicians guide to crime control.* Chicago: University of Chicago Press.

National Commission on the Causes and Prevention of Violence (1969). *To establish justice, to insure domestic tranquility.* New York: Award Books.

New York Code Rules and Regulations. Sections 1050.7, 1050.9, 1050.10, 1050.11.

Office of the Mayor, City of New York. (1993–1997). *Mayor's management reports.* New York.

Papachristou v. City of Jacksonville, 405 U.S. 156.

President's Commission on Law Enforcement and Administration of Justice, National Advisory Commission on Civil Disorders. (1968). *Report of the National Advisory Commission on Civil Disorders.* Washington, DC: U.S. Government Printing Office.

Purdum, T. (1993, October 24). Giuliani campaign theme: Dinkins isn't up to the job. *New York Times,* p. B1.

Rashbaum, W. (2001, June 14). Police review board study. *New York Times,* p. B6.

Rhode, D. (2000, March 9). Jurors trust in police erodes in light of Diallo and Louima. *New York Times,* p. B1.

Richardson, J. (1974). *Urban police in the United States.* New York: Kennikat Press.

Rosen, J. (2000, April 10). Excessive force: Why Patrick Dorismond didn't have to die. *The New Republic,* p. 24.

Rubinstein, J. (1973). *City police.* New York: Ballantine Books.

Shipler, D. (1997). *A country of strangers: Blacks and Whites in America.* New York: Alfred Knopf.

Silberman, C. (1964). *Crisis in black and white.* New York: Vintage Books.

Skolnick, J. (1968). *The police and the urban ghetto: The ambivalent force.* Hinsdale, IL: Drysden Press.

Skolnick, J., and Fyfe, J. (1993). *Above the law.* New York: The Free Press.

Sparrow, M., Moore, M., & Kennedy, D. (1990). *Beyond 911: A new era of policing.* United States: Basic Books.

Spitzer, E. (1999). *The New York City Police Department's 'stop and frisk' practices: A report to the people of the State of New York from the Office of the Attorney General, New York.* New York: Office of the Attorney General.

Task Force Report on the Police, The President's Commission on Law Enforcement and Administration of Justice. (1967). *Task force report: The police.* Washington, DC: U.S. Government Printing Office.

United States Commission on Civil Rights. (2000). *Police practices and civil rights in New York City.* http://www.usccr.gov/nypolprc/html.

United States Department of Justice. (1999). *Data for individual and local agencies with 100 or more officers.* Washington, DC: U.S. Department of Justice, Office of Justice Programs.

Walker, S. (1999). *The police in America.* New York: McGraw Hill.

————. (1993). Broken windows and fractured history. In R. Dunham and G. Alpert (Eds.)., *Critical issues in policing.* Prospect Heights, IL: Waveland Press.

Wilson, J. Q., and Kelling, G. (1982). Broken windows: Police and neighborhood safety. *Atlantic Monthly, 249,* 29–38.

Young, A. (1996). *An easy burden: The civil rights movement and the transformation of America.* New York: Harper Collins.

7

Managing Ambiguity

The Role of the Police Middle Manager in Brokering Police-Minority Community Relations

T. Kenneth Moran and Raymond Manus

❖

Discretionary police conduct and marginalized communities are a volatile combination. Police agents are routinely drawn into ambiguous situations to make difficult discretionary decisions based upon incomplete facts while under pressure for immediate action. Collectively these decisions determine who gets protection, who gets service, who gets policed, and who gets ignored. Properly employed, discretionary decisions promote the general welfare of the policed. Misguided discretion denies justice, contributes to community conflict, and undermines the Rule of Law. This type of discretion is often evident when police are deployed in high crime (often, minority) areas to engage in proactive, aggressive tactics. It is unfortunate, but not totally unexpected, that a poor discretionary choice produces bad results, typically in minority neighborhoods. Discretionary police actions have contributed to the unfair treatment of minorities in this nation. There is no denying that police stop a disproportionate number of Black and Hispanic citizens, often without legal cause (Butterfield, 1990).

This chapter contends that the police will be most effective when they operate with the full cooperation and consent of the community. Community-police partnerships build mutual trust and respect, enabling the collective to do more than the sum of their individual efforts. These partnerships depend upon commitment from participants to position the good of the community ahead of an individual's comfort. Committed individuals arrange their personal schedules and participate in the solution of identified problems. The community works with the police, sharing information, identifying problems, proposing solutions, and evaluating results. The police on their part must be willing to participate as full partners with the community. Several researchers have shown that effective police/community partnerships have driven down crime and improved quality of life in a number of communities (Goldstein, 1977; Silverman, 1999; Trojanowicz, 1990; Wilson & Kelling, 1982).

From our perspective, success or failure of policing programs is determined to a great extent by the ability of middle manager police officials to balance the often contradictory forces placed upon them by their supervisors, the political system, and the community. We focus on the middle managers because we believe that they are the key conduits of policy making from the police hierarchy to the community. The purpose of this chapter is to examine the institutional forces that lead to the differing needs of the police department, the community, and the political system, using the Diallo tragedy as a prime example of what occurs when the police-minority community partnership breaks down.

INSTITUTIONAL FORCES

The trifurcated task for the police middle manager is to balance crime control, the protection of individual rights, and the often-conflicting demands of local communities and political leaders. The supervisor must simultaneously control discretionary police actions, react to political pressures for immediate results, and address the legitimate concerns of minority communities. Police managers must ward off those community demands that are inconsistent with the police role, demands that would violate the Constitution or advance one group at the expense of another (McCarthy, 1990; Matuila, 1982). This balancing act requires prompt correction of inappropriate police responses and, conversely, negotiating and explaining to the community at large that there are distinct limits to what constitutes an appropriate response.

The role of the police officer has evolved from the simple crime fighter to a new crime prevention specialist analyzing the social problems contributing to crime and disorder. In earlier times, numerous laws reflected Puritan values, and the police enforced laws protecting the sanctity of the Sabbath and public virtue from the vices of vagrants and disorderly persons. Many of these laws have since been declared unconstitutionally vague. The urgent need to deploy the police to suppress riots or insurrection likewise has diminished with the passage of years. The police have been redirected to proactive rather than reactive forms of social control (McQuillan, 1994).

The public's fear of violent crime has encouraged these proactive patrol strategies (Silverman, 1999). Additionally, policing experts have developed the proposition that the best way to curb crime is to eliminate disorder within a community (Wilson & Kelling, 1982). Putting Wilson and Kelling's "Broken Windows" philosophy into policy, police began to aggressively enforce minor violations hoping to find habitual and/or serious criminals. This increases confrontations between the police and the public, most often in minority neighborhoods. As part of the aggressive tactics, police officers have been instructed to stop and question "suspicious" persons fitting some unchallenged profile or appearing in a high crime area. These patrol tactics seem to engender fear in both the officer—who wants to find the violent criminals—and the citizen—who knows he or she has done no wrong but must submit to the directions of the officer. The individuals who are most frequently stopped in this questionably unconstitutional manner are minorities

(Blumner, 1998; Celona & Neuman, 1999; Mollen, 1994; Wisconsin Advisory Committee, 1994).

The public is repeatedly reminded that police frequently exercise force in minority neighborhoods. The civil rights movement and the activist Supreme Court decisions of the 1960s combined to dismantle legal discrimination, but that design has not fully filtered down to the discretionary decisions routinely made by individual agents of government.

While the Court in the 1960s struck down laws supporting police powers (e.g., in cases such as *Mapp v. Ohio, Escobedo v. Illinois*), it also broadened some forms of police authority by legitimizing the use of discretion. Originally, police could arrest only when they observed an offense in their presence. Since the ruling in *Terry v. Ohio* in 1968, the police are able to stop and question individuals if they have reasonable suspicion that crime is "afoot"—a colorful phrase that encompasses offenses about to happen, currently ongoing, or recently completed. Reasonable suspicion is defined from the officer's perspective and greatly expands their discretionary authority.

Police authority is an authority to use force, including deadly physical force. With this authority comes a significant burden: the requirement to use force only when necessary, and to the extent reasonable, to achieve a public good. When right and wrong are clearly understood, the decision to exercise force is relatively straightforward. Public good, however, is not always clearly defined, and a judicial determination of reasonableness often takes place long after the police have exercised force. Making the discretionary decision to use force even more complex, the police must act when two rights are in conflict and there is no clear wrong or correct. The question then rises of when an officer should be held accountable for inappropriate use of discretionary power (U.S. Commission on Civil Rights, 1981; Walker, 1968).

As a matter of routine, discretionary decisions produce results. Individual officers make decisions and take action based upon reasonable cause to believe that a crime is about to take place or in fact has taken place (Article 140 NYCPL). While a police mistake in this connection can carry a great deal of personal or public harm, they are under no burden to be absolutely right. Police agents legally exercise the minimum level of force consistent with their *perception* of the threat presented. Police supervisors observe police officers in a variety of situations and evaluate their conduct, examine reasonableness, ask clarifying questions, and take corrective actions as necessary (Flanagan, 1987; Stahl, 1974).

Most attempts at fixing accountability for police conduct have focused upon upper management or the line officers themselves. Upper management sets the tone, and the street officers engage in practices that produce results (Inciardi, 1996; Wilson, 1968). The top-down approach assumes that the officers who have to translate official policy into action will embrace the vision from the top. This is not always the case, as evidenced by the Knapp Commission:

> The pervasive failure in the Department to hold commanders and supervisors responsible for the actions of their subordinates has been a managerial failure, not an ideological one. Department rules have long emphasized command accountability. However, during the many years when the corruption that led to the creation of this Commission was growing, the Department never succeeded—despite the efforts of some police commissioners—in translating dogma into operating routine. (Knapp, 1972, p. 232)

For over 30 years, the focus on the line officer typically promotes diversity in recruitment, hiring, and training (Katzenbach, 1968; Kerner & Lindsay, 1968; Saunders, 1970).

Considering that the average tenure of top administrators may be as short as 30 months, middle managers actually have more of an impact on the behavior of line personnel than police commissioners. For example, police officers with just 10 years in service with the New York City Police Department have had to adapt to the leadership of five different Police Commissioners: Lee Brown, Ray Kelly, Bill Bratton, Howard Safir, and Bernard Kerik. Each of these leaders had taken a lifetime to develop their unique vision of policing, and there is a significant difference in their styles and their policies.

Given the greater demands that are now being placed upon the role of the police officer, it is most appropriate to examine the role of the middle manager rather than the Commissioner or Chief. These sergeants or lieutenants began their career as police officers and now direct and control the conduct of patrol officers. As the first-line supervisors, they are in position to manage the often-conflicting demands made upon police officers (Wilson, 1968; Spriegel, 1957).

The demands of the local political system and the expectations of competing communities often involve the police in activities beyond crime fighting (Wilson, 1976). The police enforce local laws and ordinances that reflect the will of the dominant political culture. Some of these laws have been unpopular and difficult to enforce; the police responded by making arrangements with violators to control public conduct. The expansion of the police role at times introduces the police into illegal actions, where they protect activities such as gambling and prostitution (Reppetto, 1978; Sherman, 1974). Much of what the police do today is not simply grounded in law, but in traditional practices, and the danger is that these practices do not stand up to a judicial examination of due process (Guart, 1996; Goldstein, 1977).

For example, when voters select an administration promising to be tough on crime, you can expect the mayor to choose a commissioner who focuses upon crime reduction through the development and implementation of proactive police strategies (McQuillan, 1994). While the victor gains enough support to occupy the office, there are a significant number of people who do not share this enthusiasm for strict enforcement. Generally, the minority community understands that the service role of the police will change, often resulting in overzealous law enforcement in high-crime communities (Krauss, 1994). Such policing tactics lead to discontent in these communities, resulting in conflict and often force. When the police incorrectly apply force or discretionary tactics, the community will use these errors by the police to embarrass the incumbent mayor.

Some official policies actually work against good community relations. The New York City Police Department paints "Courtesy, Professionalism, and Respect" on the doors of their marked radio motor patrol cars and then plants quite a different message in the minds of the police officers by directing them to "take back the streets" (Bratton, 1998). In taking back the streets, the agency decides which laws will be enforced, which neighborhoods will be policed, and which infractions will be tolerated with minimum community input. This creates additional tension as the "good" sons and daughters are routinely stopped and questioned with little or no legal justification. The minority teenagers and their parents properly feel harassed by proactive police tactics that single them out for special attention (Cooper, 1999; Blumner, 1998). Defenders of the police conduct use statistics to justify the focus on minorities, pointing out the large number of crimes committed by minorities against minorities (Roane, 1999). Those same statistics can be used to demonstrate that the scrutiny of minority communities yields more crimes reported to the police and, hence, a rationale for more police activity. Relying exclusively on official crime report data one would believe upscale individuals do not use illegal drugs, drink alcohol, abuse family members, or attend loud parties. It comes as no surprise that police find the offenses they look for, and do not observe conduct they choose to ignore. Either way, aggressive "quality of life" policing tactics often yield poor relations between the police and minorities. The problem of brokering this issue falls in the lap of the precinct middle managers, who must find a state of equilibrium between the two groups.

Sergeants and lieutenants recognize that the police cannot solve all problems. The police manager must work with local communities to broker competing demands, developing strategies that do not depend upon extralegal conduct on the part of the police. There will be times when the police middle manager will have to resist pressures from superior officers within the police organization itself. No matter how just the ends, the police manager who encourages unethical means does a disservice to the public, to the individual officer, and to the Rule of Law (Weiss, 1999).

Most discretionary decisions are invisible to the general public (Davis, 1976; Moran, 1978). Police officers routinely apprehend criminals, assist victims of violence, and investigate suspicious conduct without attracting significant public attention. The collective results of these discretionary decisions, some good, some neutral, and some bad, will contribute to the overall quality of life. A bad decision may be better than no decision when action must be taken to prevent a minor conflict from escalating. Even bad decisions will normally escape public attention as the police manager or judicial review corrects the error. Occasionally routine police conduct will produce tragic results that awaken the apathetic public and attract scrutiny. The death of Amadou Diallo illustrates what can go wrong when the police-minority community partnership fails.

ROUTINE POLICE CONDUCT: TRAGIC RESULTS

At approximately 12:45 A.M. on February 4, 1999, four plainclothes officers assigned to New York City's Street Crime Unit (SCU) fired 41 shots, of which 19 struck and killed an unarmed man. The unarmed man was Black; the four New York City police officers were White. The media assembled additional data. The management of the elite SCU considered a high number of arrests to be an asset. The unit's 424 members are proud of their motto, "We Own the Night," and while they make up less than 1% of the police force they were responsible for 40% of the guns seized. Armed with 16-shot, semiautomatic 9 mm handguns, they wear street clothes to blend into the neighborhoods (De La Crux, 1999). Their work is dangerous; four officers have been killed while serving with the unit. The Street Crime Unit helped to reduce shootings from 2,500 in 1993 to less than 1,000 during a similar six-month period in 1998. During 1998, the unit stopped and frisked 45,000 persons, seizing 2,072 guns (De La Crux, 1999). The print media also reported that ". . . prosecutors, speaking on the condition of anonymity, have noted that the unit's mission of searching out crimes instead of responding to them had left some of their arrests vulnerable to complaints of unlawful search and seizure. Cases have been thrown out because officers chased suspects without probable cause, only then finding a gun or other illegal item" (Roane, 1999).

The facts of the Diallo case were presented to the public, producing two decidedly different interpretations of the data. A large section of (the predominantly White) society extracted data to suggest that the shooting was an accident; an isolated incident and an unfortunate by-product of a disorderly society where the police occasionally had to use deadly force. In this view, it was basic police practice with a tragic outcome. Minorities, on the other hand, extracted the data that presented this conduct as another example of the abuse of authority they routinely received at the hands of the police; it was part of a pattern of police abuses and a blatant denial of their individual rights. This was an example of police abuse of power with an outcome that should have been anticipated and avoided.

One year after the death of Mr. Diallo, the four officers were tried by a jury of their peers and acquitted of all charges. While it was legally decided that they had committed no crime, the fact remains that government agents were responsible for the death of an innocent person. Numerous questions remain as to how routine police conduct turns to tragedy. At the time of the shooting, these officers were reacting to the numerous pressures from the public, political leaders, and the culture of the police organization as they exited their unmarked vehicle to investigate conduct in a low socioeconomic neighborhood. These officers, like so many others, had been repeatedly rewarded for their proactive approach to crime reduction. Somehow the encounter that started as a fairly normal stop and inquiry—the officers were searching for a rapist who fit the description of Mr. Diallo—escalated to the point of deadly force against an unarmed man.

Community Pressure

To better understand the police and supervisory issues related to the dangerous situations encountered by police officers, it is necessary to look beyond a specific event. In the case of the officers who shot Amadou Diallo, it may be useful to go back to when these four officers were assigned to the police academy for their initial training. A fair starting point would be the year 1990, when crime was rampant and an outraged public demanded relief from the everyday occurrence of random violence. Not everyone was a victim of a homicide, rape, or violent assault—far from it. But there were a large number of vicarious victims—persons who were related to or knew the victims—and those who could see themselves as future victims. Fear became a significant factor in where people would go, what they would do, and how they acted. When victims called the police and expected a prompt response to their emergency, they found the police had inadequate resources to keep pace with the increasing demands for service (James, 1994).

Fear of crime had become a rallying point, drawing individuals together to demand action from their elected representatives. Taxpayers accepted an increased burden of $1.8 billion to provide additional police protection. The "Safe Streets, Safe City" legislation promised to provide relief, reduce the fear of crime, and build a partnership between the police and the community. This legislation, which was very specific when providing the funds for additional police personnel, was not at all helpful in the description of "community." Communities had no specific geographical boundaries, distinctive characteristics, nor identifiable traits. This lack of definition encouraged individuals to form groups, claim community status, identify selected problems, and participate in the partnership with the police to receive special services. Membership in a community was attributed more by affiliation and personal choice rather than by legislative design or criteria. The power and influence of groups varied widely, as did their demand for police services. This put pressure on political leaders, who had considerable influence over the allocation of resources to the police in their battle against crime (Girgenti, 1993).

Political Pressure

Politics is the process by which representatives of the people allocate public resources and set priorities. Citizens pay taxes and expect services. The more services provided, the more taxes required. When anticipated revenue is scarce, community services must compete for limited resources. It is the responsibility of elected officials to determine which services will be funded and which will be deferred.

In 1990, the mayor of New York City appropriately appointed a police commissioner who shared his views on policing the city. The administration promised to make community policing the dominant philosophy of the New York City Police Department. The police would build partnerships and solve problems. Local police commanders were invited to "get on board the train" before it left the station, leaving them behind. The administration criticized the incident-driven approach of traditional policing and would direct the police to look beyond the symptoms to find the roots of police problems. Arrests and summonses were deemed to be less important, and the police would be directed to find and fix the underlying conditions that produced the call for help. With the cooperation of the community, the police would find alternatives to arrest, solve problems, and reduce the need to call the police for assistance (Brown, 1991).

This official policy was presented to the command staff in the police department and taught to all new recruits. The public was concerned about crime and the administration responded with community policing. Upper management worked diligently to produce mission and value statements, while police officers were taught diversity and verbal judo. The administration promised that the "beat cop is back" and touted the "staffing needs of the New York City Police Department" (Brown, 1990) to describe a force deployed to serve local needs. Another report (Brown, 1991) accompanied this, detailing the methodology necessary to coordinate the efforts of various components to provide "Safe Streets, Safe City." This official policy relied heavily upon the discretionary performance of the individual police officers.

The initial political response to the public's fear of crime was a high-profile program. While dedicated funding had been provided in the adopted budget, the actual hiring was treated as flexible on the part of elected officials. Other special interest needs had to be addressed, and when the administration looked to find funding, the delayed hiring of police officers provided ready cash (Laird, 1993).

There was a lack of political commitment to bring the street cop to all communities, however, and this became apparent. As a result, the public chose a new administration at the next election (Silverman, 1999). Changing administrations can be a significant factor in pressures brought to bear on police practices. Political rhetoric prior to the 1993 mayoral election accused the police of being brutal, incompetent, and corrupt. The challenger attacked the incumbent as being soft on crime and failing to support the police force (Krauss, 1994; Girgenti, 1993). Opinions formed at that time linger today in the minds of both the police and the public, and resurface during routine police actions. The new administration had an entirely different vision for the deployment of the police and imposed new pressures (Mitchell, 1994). The concept of a beat cop building partnership with communities was transposed to a super crime fighter with a singular mission of driving down crime. The cautious, time-consuming, problem-solving approach to disorder was replaced with a mandate for aggressive, immediate, zero-tolerance enforcement. Specific strategies were developed at the direction of headquarters to address violent crime, and local precinct commanders were put on notice to drive crime down in their areas (Silverman, 1999). Precinct commanders soon learned that if crime patterns did not improve they would lose their jobs. Hence, pressure was placed on the police middle managers to emphasize aggressive police tactics (Celona & Massarella, 1998; Heilbroner, 1989).

At this time, there was little evidence to suggest that the middle management brokering role was even wanted any longer. Getting guns off the street became the number one strategy in March 1994, and the pressure leading up to the February 1999 shooting of Mr. Diallo started to intensify (Celona, 1994). The SCU, originally designed as a decoy operation with police acting as surrogate victims to capture and convict habitual violent offenders, was revamped. Politically, the gun became the target, not the violator, and conviction was less important as long as the gun was removed from the street. Individual rights could be manipulated as long as crime was going down, and political voices would cry "Junk Justice" when judges suppressed evidence gathered by illegal searches (Guart, 1996). The SCU grew in scope and intensity, and it was at this time that superiors began to encourage the unit's officers to stop, question, and frisk individuals to find guns. They were deployed in targeted, high crime areas that were known to have guns, and the officers were rewarded when they found and confiscated them. These latent political pressures contributed to both the expectation and perception that a Black man, standing in the doorway to his Bronx home holding his wallet, had a gun.

Today, political decisions may run contrary to the expectations of many people in minority communities. Political pressure rewards aggressive, proactive police conduct, emphasizing full enforcement with zero tolerance for offenders, no matter how minor the offense (Newfield, 1994). Pressure for results at weekly COMPSTAT meetings (comparing reported crime statistics from a previous period to current data) creates a climate that tolerates innovative methods to circumvent constitutional safeguards. Those individuals receiving the benefits of this enforcement do not mind the reduction of constitutional rights for others; those whose constitutional rights are violated because of their race, customs, traditions, or neighborhood realize not all communities get similar scrutiny and voice their displeasure.

The voices of the aggrieved minorities who live with reduced constitutional rights have not been heard since the inception of zero-tolerance policies. Prime-time newscasts, national magazines, and local newspapers focused on the winners in the war on crime. The voices of minorities are ignored as routine police conduct, measured exclusively by crime reduction, is viewed as contributing to the greater public good. The concerns of the powerless are overlooked as the police position their juggernaut to impose full enforcement in their communities. When the use of deadly force did occur against an unarmed man, the frustrated voices of the minority community were heard—briefly (Cooper, 1999).

Police Organizational Pressures

Police discretion is greatly influenced by the police culture—a system of shared values, traditions, and experiences (Moran, 1978). Formal instruction at the academy and designated training sessions describe the official policy of upper management. Sergeants and lieutenants present this material to the police recruits. The dynamic nature of police work constantly presents new challenges for police officers and new solutions are being applied. The new material is compared to the preexisting practices and may be accepted, rejected, or given a chance to work. It is not uncommon for the police culture to "forget what they taught you in the academy, here's how we do it in the streets" (Reuss-Ianni, 1983).

By design, police organizations are bureaucratic structures with division of labor, lines of authority, unity of command, and adherence to a variation of the exception principle (Iannone, 1970; Shanahan, 1985). Police work requires the officer at the bottom of the organizational chart to make critical decisions and take necessary action. The absence of time to confer with others, research legal precedents, and review alternatives requires an officer to make decisions based upon his or her own knowledge, experiences, values, and judgment.

Police firearm training encompasses both tactical instruction on how to shoot and legal instructions on when to shoot. Several researchers (e.g., Fyfe, 1982) have demonstrated that relatively few police-citizen encounters rise to a level that would justify deadly force. In many cases where deadly force might have been justified, police agents found an alternative means to contain criminals. Though most city police departments exercise a great deal of restraint, there is no guarantee that all police officers will exercise restraint under all conditions.

Police work has an ever-present element of danger, and the death or injury to an officer will have a great influence on police practices. Police reconstruct the factual events surrounding the killing of an officer by a person with a knife, an unexpected movement producing a weapon, or a routine assignment turning into an ambush. The impact of unique events far outweighs their frequency, and these exceptional cases provide a latent component to decision making in crisis situations. Issues of law and legal liability may drive official policy, but police officers are more likely to be motivated by basic survival instincts.

Department policies, procedures, and guidelines provide the standard operating procedure for the members of the New York City Police Department. These policies direct the activities and influence the alternatives available to the members of the SCU. Even a cursory examination of these policies shows that the organizational pressure placed upon members of the police force shifted dramatically from a policy under Mayor Dinkins that emphasized cooperation with minority communities to a policy that virtually ignored the minority community under Mayor Giuliani (Halper, 1998).

When the Giuliani administration implemented a system of increased enforcement to find illegal guns, the police organization employed a fourfold increase of officers in the SCU (De La Crux, 1999; Halper, 1998). More significantly, this enlarged force would not simply consist of decoys, but practice agents who would hide from the public, look for illegal weapons, and investigate suspicious conduct. The members were encouraged to confront potential violators, and they were rewarded when they produced results. The publicized strategy to get guns indicated that between 43% to 55% of felony weapons charges resulted in convictions. With special focus and minimal additional training, SCU officers accomplished their task of seizing a large number of guns and arresting a large number of perpetrators (De La Crux, 1999; Halper, 1998).

Using arrest to measure performance, however, encourages officers to make easy arrests (Knapp, 1972). Police officers could arrest upon "reasonable cause to believe," and cases that failed to meet a "beyond a reasonable doubt" standard would return the accused to the street. This does not matter to the members of the SCU, however, because career advancement in the police department relies upon the number of arrests with no consideration of the outcome of the arrest (Knapp, 1972).

SCU officers used authorized weapons and jacketed ammunition that could pass through a man—an unexpected movement brought tragic consequences. Like most shootings involving police officers, the Diallo shooting took place at close range and was over in a matter of seconds. This time, however, the four officers averaged over 10 shots each. Just two of the shots struck vital areas that would produce an immediate termination of the perceived threat.

THE SCU AND "HIGH CRIME" NEIGHBORHOODS: LESSONS LEARNED

Labeling an area as "high crime" has a host of negative connotations, including decreased property values, banks redlining, increased insurance rates, and diminished quality of life. Many communities resent the deliberate stereotype and resist the label that makes them somewhat different from their neighbors, subjecting them to different treatment. The "high Crime" label influences the level of resources given to the community and the strategies employed by the police in that community, and produces pressure for police to clean up the neighborhood. It also creates a "mind-set" that these communities should be acted upon by the police rather than engaged in a mutual problem-solving enterprise. These communities often become isolated from the police department (Silverman, 1999).

In New York City, there is a conflict between the official position of the department—promoting courtesy, professionalism, and respect—and the macho image that influences the practices of the unit. The unit takes pride in *ownership*, while the official policy promises partnership. The motto "We Own the Night" seems to be a refrain taken from Commissioner Bratton's promise to take back the city street by street (Bratton, 1998). This war-like call, reminiscent of Winston Churchill, is hardly conducive to effective collaboration between the police and the community. To take back a city street by street is almost like declaring war in the high crime communities. People generally do not feel appreciated when they are in a war zone, and the New York City minority communities are no exception (Cooper, 1999; Girgenti, 1993).

The SCU's preoccupation with reducing the crime rate resulted in not only the loss of a sense of partnership between the police and minorities but also an ever-widening gulf of suspicion and, ultimately, rage against the police. Under Commissioner Bratton, commanders who could not solve the crime problem in the precinct would lose their jobs. Headquarters paid little or no attention to the quality of trust and support that existed between the precinct and the community. Under these circumstances, commanders pressured the middle managers to solve the crime problem through aggressive tactics. At a minimum, the middle manager's brokering role was diminished. There is no evidence to suggest that these managers provided the feedback to their commanders concerning the negative effect that this proactive policy was having on the community. It is possible that the middle managers preferred the aggressive tactics and, as such, they did not give feedback to the commanders. Whatever the case, in a short period of time the police lost support of the minority community—though minority community is difficult to define in New York City.

The city's population consists of approximately eight million residents and a significant mix of commuters, visitors, and persons passing through the city on a daily basis. There is no single, identifiable language, culture, tradition, or value system to bind people together. This collection of individuals has been described as a mosaic, each contributing to the value of the whole. This diverse population shares limited space on streets, highways, and mass transportation, contributing to ongoing congestion and inviting conflict. Order in this chaotic environment derives from consent to the Rule of Law to resolve conflict. The degree of order is directly attributable to the degree individuals accept the Rule of Law and respect the rights of others. When people withdraw their consent, order breaks down and crime flourishes.

Police officers working in a community feel the support, or lack of community support, as they perform various tasks. Individual police officers do not get to choose the community they serve nor the victims that require assistance. Some may applaud the police for rendering aid at the scene of an accident while others may condemn them for failure to prevent the accident from happening. The unsuccessful crime prevention practices that earn an area a high crime designation may invite hostility from some members of the community. Those who have been victimized by the threat of violence might desire greater police protection. The aggressive patrol tactics, however, may offend the very same citizens they are designed to protect. Police managers have learned by experience that during most police-citizen encounters, the individual members of the community exist as disinterested bystanders, not identifiable members of a specific group. Police officers interact primarily with victims and offenders. It is not uncommon for officers to empathize with the victims of crime and develop a dim view of offenders. The desire to protect the innocent from injury encourages an officer to be quick to identify potential aggressors and, once identified, act quickly to prevent injury to the officer or the public.

The pressure from the community to protect the "good" people may at times come in conflict with constitutional safeguards when police officers are tempted to take shortcuts in their duties. This follows the two models of policing described by Packard (1968): due process and crime control. By overstepping constitutional boundaries in their duties, the police follow the crime control model of policing, which states that the interests of justice are more important than individual rights. The due process model opposes this, following the premise that individual rights must be upheld at all times. The police manager recognizes that the community rewards crime control efforts when the outcome of an interaction is good (i.e., the perpetrator is arrested and brought into custody). However, the community values the necessity of due process rights when the outcome is poor (i.e., deadly force is used against an innocent minority).

Police officers, by definition, have the right to use coercive force if necessary to control a situation, although they "must resolve the contradiction of achieving just ends with coercive means" (Muir, 1977, p. 4). Police officers represent the coercive authority of the state, and every police intervention, even those that seem insignificant, has the potential to be perceived as a threat to the parties involved. Diverse populations bring different language, traditions, cultures, and expectations to an encounter with the police. The police, in turn, respond to crises by bringing the values and traditions of the police culture and an expectation that the public will submit to their lawful authority (Goldstein, 1977). The police officer is the agent who exercises discretionary judgment to enforce laws. A miscalculation on the part of the police can produce tragic results in the community.

THE BUREAUCRACY OF MIDDLE MANAGEMENT

Often, upper management directives that reflect the dictates of the legal and political community will modify the middle managers' decisional arena. Unfortunately, middle managers are unable to oversee the actions of all officers who are in the field using their discretionary powers on a daily basis. Judicial policies acknowledge the police should act when they "reasonably believe" that a crime is afoot. Legislated policies authorize the police to exercise coercive force—an ambiguous term that includes deadly physical force if it is the minimal amount of force necessary to protect the officer or the public. The police are asked to solve social problems in the community, all the while equipped with deadly weapons, and middle management should, as a result, pay careful attention to the routine conduct of police agents.

The police today have been given increased responsibility to meet current needs, yet their legal authority has not been expanded to meet their new roles. Many of the current policing tactics and strategies were developed through a trial and error process under an organizational model that emphasized discipline and control (Stahl, 1974; Wilson, 1968). Diminishing bureaucratic controls and encouragement of greater discretion on the part of individual police officers have accompanied expanding police responsibilities. The expansion of the police role requires even greater attention on the part of the police manager (Silverman, 1999; Trojanowicz, 1990).

A tragic event typically raises a number of legitimate issues, finger-pointing, and damage control (McFadden & Roane, 1999; Wolff, 1993). The police immediately present statistics about crime reduction and the profiles of victims of violence as minorities. Statistics indicate that New York City police officers exercise significant restraint and that shootings by police officers have been going down; as such, the four officers involved in the shooting death of Mr. Diallo are set apart from the larger police organization. Policy makers defended the police agency by implying that the four police agents involved were rogues, and a "few rotten apples" could be found in any large organization. Assuming all of these claims are true, the public is still no closer to understanding how four officers shot an innocent man. That understanding can only be reached by further inquiry into the known data.

The police department acknowledged that the SCU stopped 45,000 individuals and seized 2,072 guns. By extension, for every 100 persons stopped the Street Crime officers found 5 individuals in possession of illegal weapons and 95 without weapons (De La Crux, 1999). These officers were specially trained and strategically deployed in high crime areas with specific instructions to find illegal weapons. The officers prepared an official department record in each of those 45,000 stops. These records provide information concerning the date, time, location, description of the person stopped, and the specific conduct contributing to the articulation of suspicion required to justify the initial stop. Each of these records had to be reviewed and signed by a superior officer shortly after the encounter. Police managers were in the position to know when SCU officers conformed to constitutional standards during stops, when the stops were questionable, and when the officers seemingly abused their authority.

Those who defend the police conduct indicate that the SCU officers do more than seize illegal weapons, claiming that the use of simple statistics distorts their proper police role. They offer as evidence the reduction of crime while ignoring the stops where no official report was prepared and all the times when arrests were dismissed due to illegal searches and seizures. They reject the obvious conclusion that many persons stopped by the police did not even meet the minimum standard of reasonable suspicion that crime was afoot. They imply that fitting a description or being in the wrong place at the wrong time is sufficient reason to stop a person. They have substituted "fitting a profile" for "reasonable suspicion" as a legitimate rationale to overcome the constitutional protection of the Fourth Amendment (Meyers, 1999).

Many SCU arrests do not survive a defense motion to suppress evidence resulting from an illegal search and seizure. In cases where the evidence is thrown out under the Exclusionary Rule, the otherwise guilty defendant has his or her rights protected by judicial review. An apathetic public and the police culture applaud one another with the knowledge that the gun is off the street and will not be used to kill someone in the community. This simplistic view ignores the fact that the police routinely confront individuals in such a manner, but often there is no contraband and, subsequently, there is no arrest. Questionable police action might even be treated positively on the officer's evaluation and included in the agency's arrest statistics. Questionable organizational policies and practices were readily ascertainable throughout the 1960s, resulting in the formation of commissions to investigate the actions (Kerner & Lindsay, 1968). There were signs indicating that police conduct contained a significant potential for tragedy, but these signs were routinely ignored by local communities, the political leadership, and, most importantly, the police organization itself. The convenient fact that police officers repeatedly engaged in virtually identical conduct without shooting innocent individuals may have lulled everyone to believe "if it ain't broke, don't fix it." Crime was going down dramatically, and quality of life was going up.

Common Data, Diverse Opinions

Even with sufficient time to reconstruct the moment prior to the first shot in the Diallo tragedy, and the discovery of facts unavailable to the officers at that time, there is still no agreement as to what actually occurred during the few seconds that shots were fired. This is not unusual, however. Reasonable people often view the same facts and draw different conclusions in cases—consider the number of five-to-four rulings by the Supreme Court. Different members of the public may form entirely different opinions regarding a police action. Police managers may respectfully disagree with those opinions, but they should realize those opinions and the emotions attached to them are legitimate concerns to be addressed.

Police managers understand that pressure from the community for immediate action may produce unintended results. Police practices that might help one community may violate the rights of individuals who are not part of that community. Poor judgment choices, or decisions without all pertinent facts, are prone to error. The police manager has the responsibility and authority to correct any such error. When minor police errors are overlooked or deliberately ignored, a simple mistake may become a major inconvenience, or injury, to an individual. Many of the complaints of police conduct surface long after the occurrence and are far removed from the facts in the case. Police managers must make timely corrections and not simply defer judgment to Civilian Complaint Review Boards or judicial process. Civilian Complaint Review Boards, operating with limited authority and resources, may make a valiant effort to find the truth, but their investigations are often too little, too late (Meyers, 1998). Expecting a prosecutor to correct police misconduct is an abdication of the manager's responsibility. Neither of these processes is a proper substitute for timely correction.

RECOMMENDATIONS: HOW MIDDLE MANAGEMENT CAN EFFECTIVELY MANAGE

Based on the information presented in this chapter, we offer five recommendations to middle managers in order to better supervise the officers under their direction. These should not be acknowledged after an emotionally charged incident occurs, inflaming the community. Rather, these are techniques that can be used to improve police-community relations on a daily basis, particularly in minority communities that are often marginalized by the police.

Recognize the real problem goes beyond race to routine police management practices. The police department must admit its mistakes before any meaningful correction will take place (Meyers, 1998). Middle managers, because of their unique relationship with the community and officers who are in the community on a daily basis, can provide valuable data in this connection. Effective partnerships with minority communities can yield data on the damage that police practices are doing to public support for the police. Precinct supervisors can use this data to alert headquarters of potential problems that are emerging from departments' law enforcement strategy.

Reduce pressures to employ extralegal tactics to "fight crime." Sergeants and lieutenants have to make sure police officers recognize the distinction between acting upon suspicious conduct versus harassing individuals simply because they fit a profile of convenient character traits or happen to live in an area the police organization considers to be violent or dangerous (Blumner, 1998). It would also be helpful to remind patrol officers that they have sworn to uphold the constitutions of their state and the United States, as well as the substantive law on crime.

Relax the rhetoric, facilitate understanding, and avoid the diversions of blame and denial. It is necessary to examine the Diallo case in the context of routine police work, including the contributing factors and identification of problems, in order to draw reasonable conclusions. The search for the truth should not be hindered by a preoccupation with protecting the bureaucracy nor limited to any one specific event. It is important to understand the assorted pressures on police officers to produce results and to recognize that the best way to minimize the risk to innocent bystanders is not to wait until the first shot has been fired but to take steps required to reduce confrontations.

Restore the hierarchical chain of accountability. Accountability should be restored from the individual actor, to the immediate supervisor, to the commander, to the appointed commissioner, to the elected mayor, and to the voters. The greatest strength of a hierarchical organization is the ability to accomplish an assigned task. Individual police agents are provided with the knowledge and tools necessary to accomplish the police mission. Responsibility and commensurate authority is fixed to the rank, while accountability resides with the incumbent. The roles of commander, lieutenant, and sergeant are clearly defined with responsibilities specifically stated. The role of the police officer must be more clearly defined and responsibilities more narrowly stated. Special practice patrol tactics, with agents not immediately identifiable as police, impose greater accountability on the middle manager. Individuals respond differently to stressful situations along a continuum of avoidance to caution to preemptive strike. Officers who practice avoidance are not normally the first choice for aggressive patrol units; officers who favor preemptive strike may not be the best choice. Police managers should explain the rationale to select officers and the procedures to guide police conduct. Once the officers are selected and deployed, police managers must be alert for early signs of inappropriate practices and provide consistent discipline, both positive and negative when necessary, to focus discretionary practices toward the achievement of a common good (Campbell, Sahid, & Stang, 1970).

Establish criteria to reward meritorious community police work. The reliance upon arrest and summonses while ignoring services rendered to the public invites the police officer to engage in activity with little thought of community needs. Ambitious police officers under the present award system would often ignore minority discomfort with aggressive police tactics. Their future lies with "good" numbers. The road to promotion is not paved with good relations with minority communities but with high arrest and summons numbers. Adding a reward system for good police-community relations can encourage police officers to balance their crime control function with the need to police with the consent of the governed.

CONCLUSION

This chapter provides an analysis of the institutional forces that lead to the differing needs of the police department, the community, and the political system. We have tried to illustrate that tragedies, such as that which befell Mr. Diallo, can be linked to a breakdown in the police-minority community partnership. While the four officers who shot Mr. Diallo bear the ultimate moral responsibility for his death, they are not solely accountable. It is the senior police hierarchy and their political overseers who are also blameworthy because they created the aggressive law enforcement philosophy that the four SCU officers followed. Additionally, there is not much evidence that the police middle managers employed their brokering role of balancing crime control and protecting Constitutional rights. This results in distrust, isolation, and, ultimately, rage on the part of the marginalized minority community, enhanced by poor communication and a patent inability of the police to address the grievances of the minority community. It is possible that relations between the police and minority communities can be greatly improved when each side rekindles a partnership based on mutual respect and participation in problem solving.

REFERENCES

Blumner, R. (1998, May 8). Arrested because the cop doesn't like your looks. *New York Post*, p. 31.

Bratton, W. (1998). *Turnaround: How America's top cop reversed the crime epidemic in New York.* New York: Random House.

Brown, L. (1990). *Report to the mayor: Staffing needs of the New York City Police Department.* New York City Police Department.

Brown, L. (1991). *Policing New York City in the 1990's: The strategy for community policing.* New York City Police Department.

Butterfield, F. (1990, December 20). Massachusetts says police in Boston illegally stopped Black youths. *New York Times,* B16.

Campbell, J., Sahid, J., & Stang, D., (1970). *Law and order reconsidered.* New York: Bantam.

Celona, L. (1994, March 8). City police taking aim at handguns. *New York Post.*

Celona, L., & Massarella, L. (1998, June 11). 'Collar' shortage puts Queens' cops in doghouse. *New York Post,* p.12.

Celona, L., & Neuman, W. (1999, April 12). NYPD to bare 'stop & frisk' data. *New York Post*, p. 19.

Cooper, M. (1999, March 16). Dinkins among 14 arrested in protest of police shooting. *New York Times,* p. B8.

Davis, K. (1976). *Discretionary justice: A preliminary inquiry.* Chicago: University of Illinois Press.

De La Crux, D. (1999, February 6). Elite street crime unit under scrutiny following police shooting. Associated Press state and local wire.

Flanagan, T. (1987). *Constitutional criminal law: New York City Police Department legal policy.* New York City Police Department.

Fyfe, J. (Ed.). (1982). *Readings on police use of deadly force.* Washington, DC: Police Foundation.

Girgenti, R. (1993). *A report to the governor on the disturbances in Crown Heights.* New York State Division of Criminal Justice Services. Albany, NY: Office of Justice Systems Analysis.

Goldstein, H. (1977). *Policing a free society.* Cambridge: Ballinger.

Guart, A. (February 7, 1996). Prosecutors: Drug judge is second-guesser. *New York Post,* pp. 6, 12.

Halper, A. (1998). *New York City Police street crime unit.* Washington, DC: U.S. Department of Justice.

Heilbroner, D. (1989, December 19). Collars for dollars. *New York Times.*

Iannone, N. (1970). *Supervision of police personnel.* Englewood Cliffs, NJ: Prentice Hall.

Inciardi, J. (1996). *Criminal justice.* New York: Harcourt Brace.

James, G. (1994, February 7). Police to carry more rounds for semiautomatic weapons: Commissioner acts on concerns by officers. *New York Times,* pp. B1, B3.

Katzenbach, N. (1968). *Challenge of crime in a free society.* New York: Avon.

Kerner, O., & Lindsay, J. (1968). *National Advisory Commission on Civil Disorders: U.S. Riot Commission Report.* New York: Bantam.

Knapp, W. (1972). *The Knapp Commission Report on police corruption.* New York: George Braziller.

Krauss, K. (1994, January 25). Memos fault community policing. *New York Times,* p. B2.

Laird, R. (1993, April 15). Millions for cops who still aren't there. *New York Daily News,* p. 39.

Matulia, K. (1982). *A balance of forces.* Washington, DC: National Institute of Justice.

McCarthy, S. (1990, October 22). Off-target targets of drug war. *New York Newsday,* pp. 6, 27.

McFadden, R., & Roane, K. (1999, February 6). U.S. examining killing of man in police volley. *New York Times.*

McQuillan, A. (1994, January 24). Bratton plan targets lazy cops: Says he'll 'kick butt.' *New York Daily News,* p. 18.

Meyers, M. (1999, April 13). Yes, Jesse, it's open season—on the NYPD. *New York Post,* p. 33.

Meyers, M. (1998, September 1). It's past time to admit the NYPD has a problem. *New York Post,* p. 29.

Mitchell, A. (1994, January 25). Giuliani urges street policing refocused on crime. *New York Times,* pp. A1, B2.

Mollen, M. (1994). *Commission to investigate allegations of police corruption and the anticorruption procedures of the police department.* New York.

Moran, T. (1978). Toward more effective control of police discretion: The cooperative model. *Journal of Police Science and Administration,* 6(3), 253–263.

Muir, W. (1977). *Police: Streetcorner politicians.* Chicago: University of Chicago Press.

Newfield, J. (1994, September 13). Taking back the streets: Cops make village livable again with 'zero tolerance and total enforcement.' *New York Post.*

New York Criminal Procedure Law (NYCPL). Article 140: Arrest without a warrant. Flushing, NY: Looseleaf Law Publications, Inc.

Packer, H. (1968). *The limits of the criminal sanction.* Palo Alto, CA: Stanford University Press.

Reppetto, T. (1978). *The blue parade.* New York: The Free Press.

Reuss-Ianni, E. (1983). *Two cultures of policing.* New Brunswick: Transaction.

Roane, K. (1999, February 6). Elite force quells crime, but at a cost, critics say. *New York Times,* B6.

Roane, K. (1999, December 2). Safir attacks state finding of racial inequity in searches. *New York Times,* p. B3.

Saunders, C. (1970). *Upgrading the American police.* Washington, DC: The Brookings Institution.

Shanahan, D. (1985). *Patrol administration: Management by objectives.* Boston: Allyn and Bacon.

Sherman, L. (1974). *Police corruption: A sociological perspective.* Garden City: Anchor.

Silverman, E. (1999). *NYPD battles crime.* Boston: Northeastern University Press.

Spriegel, W. (1957). *Elements of supervision.* New York: Wiley Press.

Stahl, O. (1974). *Police personnel administration.* North Scituate, MA: Duxbury Press.

Trojanowicz, R. (1990). *Community policing: A contemporary perspective.* Cincinnati: Anderson.

U.S. Commission on Civil Rights. (1981). *Who is guarding the guardians?: A report on police practices.* Washington, DC: Government Printing Office.

Walker, D. (1968). *Rights in conflict: The Walker report.* New York: Bantam.

Weiss, M. (1999, March 16). Ends justified means for top brass at 1 Police Plaza. *New York Post,* p.16.

Wilson, O. (1968). *Police administration.* New York: McGraw-Hill.

Wilson, J. (1976). *Varieties of police behaviors: The management of law and order in eight communities.* New York: Atheneum.

Wilson, J. Q., & Kelling, G. (1982). Broken windows: Police and neighborhood safety. *Atlantic Monthly,* 249, 29–38.

Wisconsin Advisory Committee to the United States Commission on Civil Rights. (1994). *Police protection of the African American community in Milwaukee.*

Wolff, C. (January 31, 1993). Police tactics in shootout are debated: Kelly orders review of hostage guidelines. *New York Times,* pp. 35–36.

8

The Effects of Officer and Suspect Ethnicity in Use-of-Force Incidents

Miami-Dade County, Florida[1]

Roger G. Dunham and Geoffrey P. Alpert

❖

In the early morning hours of December 19, 1979, an African American insurance sales-man named Arthur McDuffie was riding his motorcycle in Miami, Florida. According to the police reports, Mr. McDuffie "popped a wheelie," accelerated quickly, and "flipped the bird" to a police officer who was watching him. The police officer, who was Anglo, gave chase and was joined by more than a dozen police cars and officers. The pursuit lasted over eight minutes and reached speeds over 100 miles per hour. To end the pursuit, police officers blocked Mr. McDuffie's path. Mr. McDuffie decided to end his flight and stopped his motorcycle. Because there had been a radio call about a chase of a "Black motorcy-clist," police officers continued to arrive at the scene. Interestingly, all of the officers who responded to the call were Anglo officers. No fewer than six officers jumped on Mr. Mc-Duffie and, as reported by Porter and Dunn (1984, pp. 33–35), "in three minutes it was all over: McDuffie lay immobile, his head split open and his brain swelling uncontrollably. He died four days later."

The initial police reports indicated that McDuffie had been hurt falling off his mo-torcycle. Several of the officers altered the evidence to make it consistent with the con-

[1] Support for this research has been provided, in part, by the National Institute of Justice Grant 98-IJ-CX-0018. Opinions stated in this paper are those of the authors and do not necessarily represent the official posi-tion of the National Institute of Justice.

trived story that McDuffie had fallen. One of the commanders at the Liberty City substation became suspicious after reading numerous inconsistencies in the officers' reports. McDuffie's mother believed that the officers killed her son because he was Black (Porter & Dunn, 1984, p. 36). The officers were indicted for manslaughter, and the trial was moved to Tampa. In April 1980, an all-Anglo jury was selected to hear the charges against the officers. In May, after only deliberating two hours and forty-five minutes, all the officers were acquitted. Shortly after the verdict was announced, one of the ugliest incidents in racial violence in the United States rocked the Miami area and sent shock waves across the country. As a consequence of the three days of rioting, 18 deaths and millions of dollars of damage were recorded. Beyond the deaths and physical damage, the scars left by the senseless police beating were deeply embedded on members of minority communities.

The circumstances surrounding the Arthur McDuffie case are eerily similar to the events in 1992 in Los Angeles concerning Rodney King. These scenarios are the typical method by which the public learns about police use of force against ethnic minorities. Certainly these incidents and the recent cases involving the New York City and Los Angeles Police Departments deserve public and media scrutiny and attention from police recruiters, trainers, and supervisors. However, contrary to popular belief, the senseless beatings of Arthur McDuffie and Rodney King may not reflect the routine scenario that occurs when Anglo officers arrest ethnic minorities.

POLICE USE OF FORCE AND ETHNIC DIVERSITY

One method of studying police abuse of force against minorities is to review and analyze complaints of police abuse made by minority citizens. Most of this literature focuses on alleged abuses of authority by Anglo officers against minority suspects (for a review of this literature, see Walker, 2001, and Locke, 1995). This line of inquiry serves an important purpose of demonstrating persistent and widespread abuse of police authority and draws attention to the need for organizational change within police organizations and a need for more effective citizen oversight of police activities. While there are many examples of these alleged abuses and they merit the attention they have received, this line of inquiry does not address another important question. What is the extent of these abuses and what proportion of all use-of-force incidents include excessive force (Worden, 1995)? In other words, the question that surfaces is whether the types of beatings experienced by Arthur McDuffie and Rodney King are typical of police use of force against minority suspects or whether these abuses occur only infrequently. The only way to address this second question, the extent of abuse of force, is to study all known uses of police force against citizens and to assess the differences between force used on minorities and nonminorities.

While there are problems in getting police departments to release this type of data and some methodological problems analyzing it, an increasing number of studies have been conducted assessing general patterns of use of force within police departments (for a review, see Locke, 1995). It is very difficult, if not impossible, to uncover the officers' motivations for use-of-force decisions, but general patterns of police behavior can be examined to reveal disparities in force used against minority and nonminority suspects. Using this methodology, it is difficult to determine abuse of authority or excessive force; however, it is possible to answer questions concerning patterns of use of force against minority and nonminority suspects. One consistently reported finding is that members of minority populations compared with nonminority populations are disproportionately represented among those subjected to the use of deadly force (Locke, 1995). Of course, this finding raises the question of why minorities receive disproportionate force when compared with others. Obviously, racial discrimination due to hatred and fear is a natural conclusion, and it certainly accounts for some of the disparity, but this source of data does not allow assessment of officers' motives for their use-of-force decisions. However, we can rule out other reasons for the disparity and see if minority differences persist.

This is exactly the logic behind multivariant analyses that control for the seriousness of the offense, resistance by the suspect, and any other known contextual factors surrounding the use-of-force incident. Because most studies rely on data from individual police departments, it is little wonder that results differ when contextual effects are controlled when assessing use of force. Binder and Fridell (1984) reviewed studies on police shootings and concluded that any patterns of racial disparity in police shootings were due to confounding variables that support alternative interpretations. These studies indicate that circumstances surrounding the incident account for any race differences (e.g., suspect resistance, severity of the threat to the officer, severity of the offense). Other studies find a residual race effect after controlling for all known contextual variables (e.g., Worden, 1995; Meyer, 1980). These studies suggest racial discrimination, even after controlling for alternative variables. Variations in findings may be due to research methodologies, including available data or differences between the cultures of the police departments studied.

The purpose of this chapter is to assess the patterns of force by police for different levels of resistance by suspects while accounting for the ethnicity of officers and suspects. To accomplish this, we will discuss some of the findings of a multiyear study of use of force in a large metropolitan police department in Miami-Dade County, Florida.

THE STUDY

The Miami-Dade use-of-force data set comes from an agency that employs approximately 3,000 sworn officers and includes information from official Control of Persons Reports from the years 1996, 1997, and 1998. These reports are more reliable than most coming from police departments because they are not just from the attending officer's point of view. The reports are a compilation of interviews with each suspect and available witnesses, in addition to the attending officer. The officer's supervisor, after talking to the officer, suspect, and available witnesses, compiles a report including all accounts (Alpert & Smith, 1999). The department's computerized data were used to create the majority of the data set. In addition, police narratives were read and information was coded onto the data set that allowed us to conduct some validity checks of the computer accounts.

It is important to remember that the reports are only made when the officer uses force or a suspect complains of an injury, so the study population ideally includes all incidents involving force by an officer. The cases to be included in our analysis numbered 1,038 (see Table 1).

The findings from our analysis of the Miami-Dade Police Department Control of Persons Reports are described in the following order. First, a brief description of the suspects'

TABLE 1   Year of Incident

Year	Use-of-Force Cases	Percentage of Cases
1996	362	34.9%
1997	348	33.5%
1998	328	31.6%
Total	1038	100%

and officers' characteristics will be followed by the analyses of the officers' characteristics and use of force. Second, an examination of how the suspect's ethnicity is related to the suspect's behavior during the incidents will be presented. Third, a series of analyses are reported on the role of officer and suspect ethnic matches in force incidents, and how these matches affect the interaction process. Finally, we have presented an analysis of the "Force Factor," a measure of officer force relative to the level of suspect resistance.

Suspects' and Officers' Characteristics

Suspects ranged in age from 12 years old to 85 years old. The mean age is 29.6 years. Forty-four percent of the suspects are Black, 32% are Latino, and 24% are Anglo. Ninety percent of the suspects are male and 10% are female. Thirty percent of the suspects were impaired by alcohol or drugs at the time of the incident. Twenty-two percent were impaired with alcohol, and the remainder were impaired with a variety of illegal drugs.

The age of the officers ranged from 20 years old to 60 years old. The mean age is 33.1 years. Most officers are Anglos (60%), but 26% are Latinos and 14% are Black. Ninety-two percent of the officers are male and 8% are female. Most of the officers were patrol officers (92%) and 5% were sergeants. The majority of the officers were assigned to the Uniform Unit (85%), 4% were assigned to General Investigation, and 4% to K-9 Patrol. The remaining 7% were scattered throughout a number of other units.

The Relationship Between Officers' Characteristics and Use of Force

In a perfect police department, with perfect officers and perfect training, officer characteristics would not be related to officer behavior. All officers would respond to the same situations in the same way, according to the rules, the regulations, and the policies of the department. In the real world, officers' characteristics often do make a difference in how officers respond to different situations. In the cases examined in the present study however, officers' characteristics did not make much of a difference in whether or not force was used nor in the level of force used. More specifically, there were no statistically significant differences in the level of force used by male and female officers. Further, the ethnicity of the officer did not affect whether force was used or the level of force used. Officer age differences were statistically significant, but the differences were small and may simply reflect the differences in assignments of younger versus older officers.

The Relationship Between the Suspect's Ethnicity and Behavior

The next few analyses examine whether there are variations in the behavior of suspects from different ethnic groups during the arrest situation. When comparing the initial behavior of suspects from different ethnic groups, Blacks were slightly more likely to be calm (26%) than the average, and Anglos were slightly less likely (17%) to be calm (see Table 2). Further, Black suspects were significantly less likely to be erratic in their initial behavior (17%) than Anglos (29%) and Latinos (25%). Baker Act or Exparte refers to suspects who displayed mental problems. Further, Black suspects were significantly less likely to be impaired during the arrest situation (17%) than both Anglos (45%) and Latinos (37%) (see Table 3).

TABLE 2   Suspect Ethnicity and Initial Behavior in Force Situations

Suspect's Ethnicity	Calm	Visibly Upset	Erratic	Highly Agitated	Baker Act/ Exparte	Total
Anglo	43	66	71	68	—	248
	(17%)	(27%)	(29%)	(27%)		(100%)
Black	117	115	76	137	2	447
	(26%)	(26%)	(17%)	(31%)	(.4%)	(100%)
Latino	68	77	83	99	3	330
	(21%)	(23%)	(25%)	(30%)	(.9%)	(100%)
Total	228	258	230	304	5	1025
	(22%)	(25%)	(22%)	(30%)	(.5%)	(100%)

Chi Squared = .007

TABLE 3   Suspect Ethnicity and Impairment by Alcohol or Drugs During Force Situations

Suspect's Ethnicity	No Impairment	Impairment	Total
Anglo	124	101	225
	(55%)	(45%)	(100%)
Black	343	68	411
	(84%)	(17%)	(100%)
Latino	191	110	301
	(64%)	(37%)	(100%)
Total	658	279	937
	(70%)	(30%)	(100%)

Chi Squared = .000

None of the measures of resistance resulted in significant differences between ethnic groups. This included a general measure of the level of resistance as assessed by the officer's supervisor after interviewing the officer, suspect, and available witnesses. The general categories of this measure are as follows:

1. Cooperative/No Resistance
2. Verbal Noncompliance/Passive Resistance/Psychological Intimidation
3. Defensive Resistance/Attempted to Flee
4. Active Resistance (without a weapon)
5. Aggravated Active Resistance (used weapon—nondeadly)
6. Active Resistance (with a deadly weapon)

Another more specific measure of suspect resistance, specifying the type of behavior during resistance (e.g., kick, punch, stab, shoot), also resulted in no significant ethnic differences.

The findings in Table 4, while not quite reaching the typical standard for statistical significance, do indicate that over the three-year study period that Black suspects were slightly more likely to inflict injuries on officers (44%) than Anglo (37%) or Latino (39%) suspects. Further, Black suspects were slightly *less* likely to be injured by the officer (76%) than Anglo (82%) or Latino (80%) suspects (see Table 5).

Officer and Suspect Ethnicity

For this analysis, the force situations were categorized according to the ethnic matches between officers and suspects. Officers and suspects were placed into three major groups: Anglos, Blacks, and Latinos. This created nine ethnic matches. The data in Table 6 compare officer/offender ethnic matches with the degree of resistance of the offender. It appears that Black officers using force to arrest either Anglo or Latino suspects are the most likely to receive some resistance (100% resisted). Similarly, Latino officers arresting Black or Latino

TABLE 4   Suspect Ethnicity and Officer Injury During Force Situations

Suspect's Ethnicity	No Injury	Injury	Total
Anglo	158	91	249
	(64%)	(37%)	(100%)
Black	253	195	448
	(57%)	(44%)	(100%)
Latino	203	128	331
	(61%)	(39%)	(100%)
Total	614	414	1028
	(60%)	(40%)	(100%)

Chi Squared = .15

TABLE 5   Suspect Ethnicity and Suspect Injury During Force Situations

Suspect's Ethnicity	No Injury	Injury	Total
Anglo	46	203	249
	(18%)	(82%)	(100%)
Black	106	339	445
	(24%)	(76%)	(100%)
Latino	66	264	330
	(20%)	(80%)	(100%)
Total	218	806	1024
	(21%)	(79%)	(100%)

Chi Squared = .20

TABLE 6   Officer/Suspect Ethnic Matches and Resistance by Suspect

Officer/ Suspect	No Resistance	Passive Resistance	Attempted to Flee	Actively Resisted	Resisted Arr./Incite	Assaulted Officer
Ang/Ang	7 (4%)	16 (10%)	27 (17%)	73 (46%)	4 (3%)	31 (20%)
Ang/Blk	4 (2%)	17 (7%)	68 (28%)	97 (40%)	13 (5%)	43 (18%)
Ang/Lat	9 (5%)	12 (6%)	53 (27%)	73 (37%)	3 (2%)	50 (25%)
Blk/Ang	—	1 (5%)	5 (23%)	6 (27%)	2 (9%)	8 (36%)
Blk/Blk	3 (3%)	3 (3%)	30 (33%)	35 (39%)	2 (2%)	17 (19%)
Blk/Lat	—	3 (13%)	6 (26%)	8 (35%)	2 (3%)	4 (17%)
Lat/Ang	1 (2%)	8 (14%)	18 (31%)	19 (32%)	2 (3%)	11 (19%)
Lat/Blk	1 (1%)	6 (6%)	31 (30%)	36 (35%)	6 (6%)	24 (23%)
Lat/Lat	1 (1%)	10 (11%)	24 (27%)	36 (40%)	5 (6%)	13 (15%)
Total	26 (3%)	76 (8%)	262 (27%)	383 (39%)	39 (4%)	201 (20%)

Chi Squared = .044

suspects received resistance in 99% of the incidents. Also there are differences in the levels of resistance. For example, the ethnic match resulting in the greatest likelihood of the offender assaulting the officer is when a Black officer is arresting an Anglo suspect (36%). Contrast this to the likelihood of an assault when a Latino officer is arresting a Latino suspect (15%), or when a Black officer is arresting a Latino suspect (17%).

In Table 7, officer/suspect ethnic matches are compared with the level of force used by the officer. First, looking at whether force was used in these situations, it appears that Anglo officers used force consistently across all groups of suspects (about 97% of the time).

TABLE 7   Officer/Suspect Ethnic Matches and Level of Force
Used by the Officer

	No Force	Minimal Force	Force w/Hands	Force Other
Ang/Ang	4 (3%)	43 (27%)	81 (51%)	30 (19%)
Ang/Blk	6 (3%)	38 (16%)	135 (56%)	61 (25%)
Ang/Lat	6 (3%)	57 (29%)	95 (48%)	42 (21%)
Blk/Ang	1 (5%)	3 (14%)	14 (64%)	4 (18%)
Blk/Blk	5 (6%)	12 (14%)	47 (53%)	25 (28%)
Blk/Lat	1 (5%)	4 (18%)	16 (73%)	1 (5%)
Lat/Ang	1 (2%)	16 (27%)	30 (50%)	13 (22%)
Lat/Blk	4 (4%)	18 (17%)	55 (53%)	27 (26%)
Lat/Lat	—	31 (35%)	40 (46%)	17 (19%)
Total	28 (3%)	222 (23%)	513 (52%)	220 (22%)

Chi Squared = .021

Black officers were fairly consistent in using force about 94% or 95% of the time. However, Latino officers were more variable in their use of force. They used force 100% of the time when the suspect was Latino, but only 96% of the time when the suspect was Black. Comparing across all groups, force was used most often when the officer was Latino and the suspect was Latino (100%) and when the officer was Latino and the suspect was Anglo (98%). Force was used the least often when the officer was Black and the suspect was Black (94%). Force with hands was used most often when the officer was Black and the suspect was either Latino (73%) or Anglo (64%). The explanation may be that suspects were reporting injuries when officers were reporting no force at differential rates. Force other than hands, which is a greater level of force than force with hands, was used most often when the suspect was Black regardless of the ethnicity of the officer.

Officer Force and Suspect Resistance: The Force Factor

The discussion will now turn to more complex analyses using a measure that simultaneously accounts for officer force and suspect resistance. Most of the prior research on the use of force by the police has focused on the most force used or the highest level reached in an encounter. A problem with these measures is that they do not account for the level of resistance by the suspect. Obviously, a measure of force without controlling for the level of resistance is quite limited. Alpert and Dunham (1997) have devised a measure combining the level of the suspect's resistance with the level of the officer's force called the Force Factor. The Force Factor is employed in the present analysis to change the focus of the discussion to the level of force used by the police *relative* to the suspect's level of resistance. To calculate the Force Factor, one must measure the suspect's level of resistance and the officer's level of force, both scaled in the same manner. These measures were discussed earlier.

Even though the Force Factor is a relative measure of force, in situations where the level of police force is greater than the level of resistance, there is no automatic implication that the level of force was excessive or improper. For example, an officer may justifiably use more force than a suspect to gain control of some situations. Similarly, it is possible that a suspect's resistance may exceed the level of force used by the officer. A Force Factor representing such a disparity does not necessarily mean that the officer's level of force was too weak or improper. A weaker use of force by the police could represent an incident in which a suspect shoots an officer who was unable to respond. Similarly, a negative number could represent a suspect who attacked an officer but who was controlled with a minimum of police force. In spite of the fact that no automatic implication of impropriety can be drawn from Force Factor scores with considerable disparity between force and resistance, these instances should be "red flagged" for evaluation. It is the Force Factors that reflect the greatest differences between force and resistance that are the most interesting and important in an analysis.

Miami-Dade Police Force Factor

In this data set we recoded the level of suspect resistance and officer force from the Control of Persons Reports into six ordinal categories. Recall that the reports are completed by supervisors after interviewing officers, suspects, and witnesses (when available). The levels of force mirror the continuum of force taught in most police academies. Clear categories of activities emerged from an analysis of the reports. The suspect's actions began with no force or compliance and increased to verbal noncompliance or passive resistance. These actions included arguing with the officer or refusing to obey her or his orders. There were a few cases of suspects threatening officers and challenging them to start a fight. The next level of resistance was defensive and included attempts to flee. We termed the next level Active Resistance, which was a fight without the use of any weapons. When a weapon excluding a firearm was introduced the level was called Aggravated Active Resistance. When a firearm was used it reached level six (i.e., Active Resistance with a deadly weapon).

The officer's use of force was coded in a similar fashion to the actions of the suspect. For example, when an officer attempted to apprehend a suspect but only used hands and feet defensively or to fend off an attack, it was coded into level three. When the officer used hands and feet in an aggressive manner to control the suspect, it was coded as level four. When an intermediate weapon such as a baton or PR-24 was used, the action was coded as level five. If an officer used a firearm, it was coded as level six.

Officer Force:
1. Police Presence/Verbal Direction
2. Strong Verbal Order (minimal contact)
3. Forcibly Subdued—Hands or Feet (defensive use—open hand)
4. Forcibly Subdued—Hands or Feet (offensive use)
5. Forcibly Subdued—Intermediate Weapon
6. Deadly Force

The Force Factor is calculated by subtracting the level of resistance (1–6) from the level of police force (1–6): Force − Resistance = Force Factor. The range of the Force Factor is from minus five to plus five. A zero is interpreted as commensurate force for the level of resistance. For example, no resistance and no force would be 1 − 1 = 0. If the level of force is higher than the level of resistance, then the Force Factor is positive, one point for each level of discongruence, or a maximum of 5. If the level of force is lower than the level of resistance, then the Force Factor is negative, one point for each level of discongruence, or a maximum of −5. The distribution of scores on the Force Factor for the Miami-Dade data is close to a normal curve but slightly skewed to the negative side, indicating the use of less force than resistance.

The Force Factor and Ethnic Matches Between Officers and Suspects

While the overall relationship between ethnic matches between officers and suspects and the Force Factor scores is not statistically significant, there are some differences in mean scores that are large enough to be interesting (see Table 8). Black and Latino officers arresting Anglo suspects employ lower levels of force in relation to the level of resistance than other ethnic matches, and Black officers use even lower levels of force against Anglo suspects than Latino officers. The highest level of officer force in relation to suspect resistance occurs when Latino officers arrest Latino suspects (− .04). The other ethnic matches in which a higher level of force was used in relation to the level of resistance are Black officers arresting Latino suspects and Latino officers arresting Black suspects. It is interesting to note that most of the variation in levels of Force Factor scores occurs among minority officers. All the highest and lowest means, signifying deviations from the overall mean, occur among incidents with Black or Latino officers. Anglo officers tend to use about the same amount of force for given levels of resistance in each ethnic category (ranging from −.23 to −.29).

TABLE 8   Force Factor Means and Standard Deviations for Ethnic Matches Between Officer and Suspect

Officer/Suspect	Mean	Standard Deviation	Cases
Anglo/Anglo	−.26	.91	113
Anglo/Black	−.23	1.03	166
Anglo/Latino	−.29	.87	109
Black/Anglo	−.64	.67	11
Black/Black	−.28	.96	65
Black/Latino	−.15	.69	13
Latino/Anglo	−.38	.89	34
Latino/Black	−.15	.90	74
Latino/Latino	−.04	1.16	56
Group Totals	−.24	.96	641

Chi Squared = .598

Black officers have a greater range (from $-.15$ to $-.64$) and tend to treat Anglo suspects with less force than the average and Latino suspects with more force. Latino officers also have a greater range of scores than Anglo officers (ranging between $-.04$ to $-.38$). Latino officers use significantly less force for a given level of resistance when arresting Anglo suspects and more when arresting Black and Latino suspects (see Table 8).

CONCLUSION

An examination of the level of force used by police officers against suspects during arrest situations shows remarkably similar levels of force used against suspects of different racial and ethnic backgrounds. Further, officers utilize comparable levels of force regardless of their ethnic backgrounds. It is significant that only a few patterns of ethnic differences exist in the administration of force and that those differences were usually quite small. This speaks well for the training and supervision of officers in the agency under study. Of course, this does not mean that abuse of force does not exist in individual incidents. It simply means that our analyses of police data did not uncover patterns of abuse.

In spite of this overall consistency in administering force, the few ethnic differences found are interesting and can be interpreted using several rationales. For example, the data from this study show that minority officers have more variation in levels of force administered to suspects from different ethnic groups than Anglo officers. On the average, Anglo officers administered similar levels of force whether the suspects were Anglo, Black, or Latino. In contrast, Black and Latino officers were more likely to vary the levels of force used against suspects from the different ethnic groups. This variation manifests itself in two directions (lower and higher than average levels of force) depending on the ethnicity of the suspects. Some of the variation is the result of Black and Latino officers treating Anglo suspects with *lower* than average ratios of force to suspect resistance. However, there is nearly as much variation resulting from minority officers administering *higher* than average ratios of force when arresting minority suspects. This variation can be explained by the "deference-exchange" theory. Sykes and Clark (1975) have referred to police-citizen interactions as a "deference exchange," which is governed by an asymmetrical status norm with the police being the dominant figure. In fact, police officers often feel threatened if citizens do not give enough deference to their authority, arguing that they "live and die" by their authority. In the deference exchange, the demand for respect by officers is balanced by the willingness to give homage by the suspects. It should be noted, as Locke (1995) points out, that the "deference exchange" notion serves as a possible explanation for police behavior, not necessarily as a justification. Our results suggest that minority officers, whether Black or Latino, require less deference from Anglo suspects or are at the least more tolerant (or fearful of repercussions) of a lack of respect if the suspect is Anglo. This possible explanation could account for the lower levels of force used for specific levels of resistance in these police-citizen interactions. Similarly, Anglo suspects resist at higher levels when the arresting officer is Black than when the arresting officer is Anglo or Latino. According to the "deference-exchange" theory, it appears that Black officers are given less deference by Anglo suspects than other officers. In turn, they may expect less respect, which results in Black officers administering lower levels of force for a given level of resistance. The deference exchange is affected by attitudes and expectations of actors on both sides of the interaction.

The "deference exchange theory" can also explain our findings concerning the higher levels of force for given levels of resistance among minority officers arresting minority suspects. Minority officers may be influenced by the police subculture to have less respect for minority suspects. In turn, this could create a lower tolerance level for any resistance by minorities and explain why they use higher levels of force relative to suspect resistance than other officers. Further, minority officers may not fear being charged with prejudice. Hubert Locke (1995) raises another potential implication of the higher rates of force used by minority officers on minority suspects. He notes that these higher levels of force suggest that Anglo officers are not racially discriminatory because they use less force on minority suspects than minority officers. To the contrary, it could be argued that both nonminority and minority officers are discriminating against minority suspects. In fact, all officers may view minority suspects as less likely to complain about excessive force, or at least less likely to complain successfully.

One further twist in the "deference exchange" interpretation involves the suspects' side of the interaction. If minority citizens have more negative (including hostile) attitudes toward the police than Anglo citizens, they could upset the "deference exchange" in a fashion that results in higher force/resistance ratios for minority suspects. Further, an escalating negative relationship between the two groups could result in patterned discriminatory treatment with respect to force. Ideally, but perhaps unrealistically, all police officers should be professional and use force only when necessary and use only the amount of force necessary to control a suspect, regardless of any interethnic hostility. Our findings suggest that racial/ethnic identity of actors on both sides of the interaction (police and citizens) may affect the perceived "need to control" and the amount of control deemed necessary.

In spite of these few ethnic differences, force is administered quite consistently among ethnic matches when resistance is taken into account. This overall conclusion is consistent with the findings of Alpert et al. (forthcoming) where they assess the relative influence of legitimate and illegitimate criteria for deciding the level of force to control suspects. The block of "legitimate" variables is comprised of (1) the type of call for service the officer received, (2) the initial behavior of the suspect, (3) the suspect's level of resistance, and (4) whether or not the suspect was high on alcohol or drugs. The "illegitimate" variables include suspect characteristics (age, gender, and ethnicity), officer characteristics (age, gender, ethnicity, date of hire), and ethnic matches between officers and suspects (i.e., Anglo - Anglo, Black - Latino, etc.). In this analysis only the variables deemed legitimate criteria for assessing the level of officer force should be significant in effecting the force/resistance ratio. It is of considerable interest that when controlling for the legitimate criteria for using force, the ethnicity of the suspect is not related to the level of force used against a suspect. Further, it is noteworthy that when controlling for the legitimate criteria for using force, the ethnicity of the officer had no significant effect on the level of force used in the incident. Finally, there were no ethnic matches between officers and suspects that had statistically significant differences on the Force Factor when compared with other ethnic matches. Apparently, when controlling for legitimate criteria for choosing which level of force to use when subduing a suspect, neither the ethnicity of the officer nor that of the suspect has an effect on the level of force used.

Caution should be used when generalizing our findings to other police departments. The Miami-Dade Police Department is a progressive department with excellent data collection techniques, training, and supervision. Other agencies with different policies and training may experience more variation in use of force. Further, our findings should not be used to argue that excessive force does not exist or that racial prejudice is not a factor in some cases because our research was designed to assess overall averages rather than discover individual cases involving abuse of force or racial prejudice. Further, mistakes are often made in regard to the amount of resistance reported by officers in many agencies.

REFERENCES

Alpert, G., Dunham, R., Smith, M., Kenney, D., & Madden, T. (forthcoming). *The force factor: Measuring police use of force relative to suspect resistance. A final report to the National Institute of Justice.* Washington, DC: National Institute of Justice.

Alpert, G. P., & Dunham, R. (1997). The force factor: Measuring police use of force relative to suspect resistance. *Police Research and Evaluation Series.* Washington, D.C.: Police Executive Research Forum.

Alpert, G. P., & Smith, M. (1999). Police use-of-force data: Where we are and where we should be going. *Police Quarterly, 2,* 57–78.

Binder, A., & Fridell, L. (1984, June). Lethal force as a police response. *Criminal Justice Abstracts,* 250–280.

Locke, H. G. (1995). The color of law and the issue of color: Race and the abuse of police power. In W. A. Geller & H. Tock (Eds.), *And justice for all: Understanding and controlling police abuse of force,* pp. 133–149. Washington, D.C.: Police Executive Research Forum.

Meyer, M. W. (1980). Police shootings of minorities: The case of Los Angeles. *Annals of the American Academy of Political and Social Science, 452,* 98–110.

Porter, B., & Marvin, D. (1984). *The Miami Riot of 1980: Crossing the bounds.* Lexington, MA: Lexington Books.

Sykes, R. E., & Clark, J. P. (1975). A theory of deference exchange in police-citizen encounters. *American Journal of Sociology, 81,* 584–600.

Walker, S. (2001). *Police accountability.* Stamford, CT: Wadsworth.

Worden, R. E. (1995). The "causes" of police brutality: Theory and evidence on police use of force. In William A. Geller and Hans Tock (Eds.), *And justice for all: Understanding and controlling police abuse of force,* pp. 31–60. Washington, D.C.: Police Executive Research Forum.

9

Prosecuting Police Officers for Police Brutality

From a Minority Perspective

Christopher Cooper

Being a person of color I know the scars of police brutality personally. Having been a cop, I know all too well what I have written in this paper.

It is no secret in the United States that incidents of police brutality more often than not involve Black or non-White Latinos as victims and White police officers as the perpetrators (Weich and Angulo, 2000). More often than not police brutality is a general way of saying racist police actions. The epidemic problem of police brutality is not a "colorless" phenomenon. The American public knows the race of the officers and the race of the victims. This is not an epidemic of the police versus the citizens, as some would have us believe. Rather, the problem of police brutality is one unit or segment of the ongoing and growing racial dissention between Blacks and Whites in America. On other fronts, the prominent marks of the racial divide in America are the country's countless racially segregated neighborhoods, as evinced by Whites and Blacks not living side by side. Even more telling of the polarization of the races is the disagreement between Blacks and non-White Latinos as to the extent of White anti-Black and Brown racism in the United States. Poll after poll shows that Blacks and non-White Latinos experience racism from some Whites on a daily basis. Many Whites surveyed disagree. For them, racism was abolished with the end of the civil rights movement.

In a climate of so much racial hostility between White and minority people, there is an expectation by minorities (and some White people) that prosecutors prosecute police officers that brutalize citizens. Notice that I have used the words *some* White people rather

115

than *many* White people. For good reason, because research findings by Barkan and Cohn (1998) indicate that many Whites are supportive of police abuse of minorities. Via analysis of General Social Survey (GSS) data, the researchers found that racial prejudice contributes to Whites' support of police use of excessive force rather than the use of "reasonable force" against Black people (p. 749). If Barkan and Cohn's findings are not sufficiently convincing, an individual need only notice that antipolice brutality rallies such as those to protest the police killing of Tyisha Miller, Anthony Baez, and Malice Green, among so many others, are comprised almost entirely of minorities. This fact is compellingly indicative of either the support by many Whites for police brutality, the denial by many Whites of the existence of police brutality motivated by [police] racism, and/or the fear of Whites to attend such a rally.

With credible evidence showing that an incident of police brutality occurred, one would think that the police officers who engaged in it would be criminally prosecuted. Notwithstanding increased prosecution of police brutality cases in recent years, the reality is that police officers are seldom if ever prosecuted for having engaged in the crime of physically brutalizing a person. This author knows of no cases in which a White officer was criminally charged or convicted of anything—for harming or killing a minority. Why police officers are not prosecuted and, if they are prosecuted, why they are not convicted represents the focus of this chapter.

DEFINING POLICE BRUTALITY

Police officers have authority to use physical force primarily to restrain people, to defend themselves or others, and to arrest people. In addition to legislation and case law that mandate and guide police officers as to when they can use physical force (e.g., *Tennessee v. Garner*), there are police department directives as well. A typical police department directive instructs officers that they may use only the minimum amount of force necessary to achieve a legitimate purpose (e.g., to effect an arrest or prevent the commission of crime) when other options are not available or have been exhausted. Consider for example, the New York City Police Department's (NYPD) "Deadly Force Policy" reads in part: "Respect for human life requires that, in all cases, firearms be used as a last resort, and then only to protect life. Police officers shall not use deadly force against another person unless they have probable cause to believe they must protect themselves or another person present from imminent death or serious physical injury" (Patrol Guide, General Regulations, Procedure No: 203-12, 01/01/00: 1).

Police brutality can be a physical assault upon another (battery), as well as nonphysical as in verbal and psychological abuse. Battery (a physical assault) is a crime, and to be found guilty of battery a prosecutor must show that the perpetrator had criminal intent (*mens rea*). With this said, in this chapter the definition of police brutality includes a physical attack on another [person] or the physical manipulation of another [person] with criminal intent.

The terms *excessive force* and *police brutality* are virtually synonymous, with few exceptions. There are those, primarily some other social scientists, who take a contrary position. For example, Fyfe (1995) argues that excessive force is distinguishable from police brutality because excessive force, he says, is a mistake, as in misjudging the amount of force needed to restrain an individual. Using Fyfe's (1995) own words, excessive force is the result of "... ineptitude or carelessness and occurs when well meaning officers prove incapable of dealing with situations they encounter. ..." (p. 163).

While the author of this chapter agrees in small part that there are times when an officer's use of excessive force is in fact a misjudgment of the amount of force needed, therefore, not a crime (aka "police brutality"); he asserts that more often than not excessive force is seldom distinguishable from police brutality. Even if a misjudgment, the act could rise to the level of criminal recklessness. In this regard, a definition of excessive force as not criminal (ever), but a good faith *mistake* is a definition that fails to acknowledge that a mistake can in fact be reckless behavior and depraved indifference to human life, both of which can constitute a crime. To illustrate by using a definition of criminal recklessness that is common throughout the United States, reckless means "... foolishly heedless of danger; headlong; impetuously or rashly adventurous; indifferent to consequences; mindless; not caring or noting; not recking of consequences; rash; rashly, indifferently, or very negligent; regardless of consequences; utterly careless or heedless; wanton" (*Maude Stout v. A.T. Gallemore*). Criminal recklessness represents that the perpetrator was more than just "careless" and that his or her actions were sufficiently willful to satisfy a requirement for mens rea.

Verbal and psychological types of police brutality are of importance. Although the focus in this chapter is that form of police brutality that is physical, it is necessary to address other forms of police brutality. Take for instance the crime of threats to do bodily harm. If a citizen (nonpolice) could be prosecuted for threats to do bodily harm, so too should a police officer who threatens a person with physical harm when he [the officer] has no legal right to make such a threat. Similarly hate crime legislation should apply to police officers. Gifis in *Barrons Law Dictionary* (1996) defines a hate crime as the "commission of an offense where the person acted, or at least in part, with ill will, hatred, or bias toward, and with purpose to intimidate, an individual or group because of race, color, religion, sexual orientation, or ethnicity" (p. 50). In this regard, many reported cases of police verbal abuse of citizens involve an allegation that an officer used a racial epithet or made a racially insensitive remark (e.g., "Everybody knows niggers are too poor to live over here [Hyde Park]"; Annie Barnes, 2000). There are not many differences between this type of hateful verbal abuse by an officer and those words needed to constitute the elements of a "hate crime." There are situations when there are proven civilian complaints against police officers for which prosecutors could initiate a prosecution of an officer for a hate crime. But this is the real world and in it physical police brutality is seldom if ever prosecuted, hence verbal abuse by police is not likely to receive needed attention. Until things change, minorities must contend with prosecutors who are not likely to bring hate crime charges against a police officer.

When state prosecutors address bias, such as racial or gender, by an officer against a citizen, they could charge the officer with a statute that prohibits an officer from violating a person's civil rights, but this is very rare. On the federal level, prosecutors have at their disposal 18 U.S.C. Sections 241 and 242 (among others). These are the federal civil rights statutes used to charge a police officer accused of excessive force (police brutality). By illustration, the officers involved in beating Rodney King were criminally prosecuted by the federal government pursuant to 18 U.S.C. Section 242. Note the wording of Section 242:

> [Whoever], under color of any law ... willfully subjects any person ... to the deprivation of any rights, privileges, or immunities secured or protected by the Constitution or laws of the

United States, or to different punishments, pains, or penalties, on account of such person being an alien, or by reason of his color, or race, than are prescribed for the punishment of citizens, shall be fined under this title or imprisoned. (18 U.S.C. § 242)

Color of law means that the person "doing" the illegal act is using power given to him by a governmental agency. "The types of law enforcement misconduct covered by Sections 241 and 242 include excessive force, sexual assault, intentional false arrests, or the intentional fabrication of evidence resulting of loss of liberty of another" (U.S. Department of Justice, year not indicated). The fact the federal government more often than not declines to bring federal charges in a police brutality case shows that it is either difficult to show that an officer acted intentionally to deprive a person of his/her civil rights, or that some prosecutors perceive the wording of 241 and 242 as requiring a very overt verbal action, such as a police officer having used a racial epithet or an officer admitted that his actions were racially motivated.

A sensible definition of physical police brutality is that of a police officer intentionally and willfully doing something physical to a person in an attempt to cause harm to that person (injury is not required) and that the officer knows that he or she does not have a "legal" right to use such force. Examples include intentionally striking a person, placing a person in a headlock or chokehold, placing handcuffs too tight and stopping circulation, and shooting a person unnecessarily. The traditional crimes for which an officer should be criminally charged when he or she engages in one of these (use of force) actions without the sanction of the law include assault, battery, aggravated battery, mayhem, voluntary and involuntary manslaughter, and murder.

THE EXTENT OF POLICE BRUTALITY: REPORTING AND DOCUMENTATION

How often does police brutality occur in the United States? How a person answers this question is often directly related to his or her skin pigmentation. Although Blacks and non-White Latinos, specifically, assert that police brutality in the United States is a serious problem, many Whites feel otherwise (e.g., see 1999 poll by Quinnipiac College Polling Institute: New York Is Safer, but Police Brutality Is a Problem). In fact, differences of opinion on this subject between Blacks and Whites take even uglier turns. Recall the mention of Barkan and Cohn's (1998) findings that "racial prejudice contributes to whites' support of police use of force and that this relationship should be stronger for the use of excessive force than for the use of reasonable force against black people" (p. 749). This conclusion bodes well with findings by Niederhoffer (1969), Stark (1987), Goldstein, J. (1960), and Cole (1999) that many police officers are very oppressive in minority communities in some part because of efforts to satisfy demands by some Whites.

In an analysis of police-citizen encounters, Worden (1995) found that the use of force both reasonable and criminal (excessive, improper, or brutal) was more likely if the citizen was a Black male and over the age of 18 (pp. 32, 49, 59). Worden concluded that "race has significant effects on the use of force." He writes that since "officers are more likely to use reasonable force against blacks [the findings] might suggest that officers are, on average, more likely to adopt a penal or coercive approach to black suspects than they are to white suspects" (p. 50).

The position of this author is that police brutality is systemic in the United States. This is a position that cannot be easily proved through quantitative methods, for police brutality is not easily measured quantitatively. The horrid practice lends itself to measurement through qualitative analyses. Sadly, many scholars and politicians choose not to admit that police brutality is systematic unless there are quantitative (versus qualitative) statistical data to prove the position. With a shortage of quantitative data about the extent of police brutality it should come as no surprise then that there are many social scientists and politicians who vehemently argue that police brutality seldom occurs. For example, according to minorities, the torture of Abner Louima by New York City police officers in 1997 was just one more example of systemic police brutality in the United States; many Whites on the other hand, especially White social scientists, disagree. George Kelling, a well-known White criminologist, argues that there is no systemic problem of police brutality in the United States. Kelling (1997, p. 48) wrote of the sodomization of Louima with a broken broom stick: "The assault and torture of Abner Louima by New York City Police Officers. . . [is] not representative of the New York City Police Department, of policing generally or of good order-maintenance tactics."

Kelling's conclusion is reflective of his own socialization experience and the experiences that he has had as a White male in the United States. His experiences differ from those of minorities. Just as important, Kelling's conclusion that Louima's victimization was an anomaly is based on quantitative statistics; specifically, that there are few "reported" Louima-like incidents, or of police brutality in general. Official reports of the brutalization of citizens by police are not common. Kelling has interpreted the absence of police reports as meaning there is not an epidemic of police brutality against minorities by many White police officers in America. The author of this chapter takes an opposing position. He points to a wealth of reliable sources and information that show that official police reports are missing because, often, police and prosecutors ignore and discourage complaints of police brutality.

For example, it was not the New York City Police Department that encouraged Abner Louima to complain when it learned of his having been sodomized by New York City cops. In fact, the NYPD did nothing when it learned of the gruesome attack. It was a nurse at the hospital where Louima had been admitted who was adamant that a police report be taken (Kifner, 1997). NYPD Internal Affairs rebuffed the nurse, but because of her insistence that the NYPD take action, the media became involved. It certainly appears that it was only after the nurse's involvement and that of the media that the NYPD officially documented the horrific attack in its internal affairs files. Not surprising because, in general, when citizens attempt to file a report of police brutality they are rebuffed by station personnel and, in many instances, the complaint (although heard by an officer) is never officially documented. This is what happened with Louima's complaint. The NYPD Internal Affairs desk officer who received nurse Magalie Laurent's telephone call reporting Louima's sodomization at the hands of New York City police officers, failed to assign a log number to the call and complaint. The *New York Times* recounted Laurent's call to report the sodomization and abuse,

> . . . she [Laurent] called Mr. Louima's family, the police Internal Affairs Bureau and New York 1, the local all-news cable channel. Describing the reaction of the officer at Internal Affairs who answered the call, Mrs. Laurent said, 'It seemed like he didn't care.' 'I knew that they hadn't taken my call seriously,' she said. 'And it was proved to me. They could have gone to that precinct and secured the crime scene.' The police conceded on Friday that a call

to the Internal Affairs Bureau was bungled on the night after the beating. It was not until 3:55 P.M. Sunday, Aug. 10, about 36 hours after Mr. Louima says he was tortured in the station house bathroom, that the Action Desk, which receives Internal Affairs calls, logged in a complaint from the victim's family and began an investigation. (1997: B1)

In a 1998 report by Human Rights Watch, the organization found that police department complaint-filing processes (in general) were "unnecessarily difficult and often intimidating" (p. 50). In this regard, a former police chief with the Minneapolis Police Department affirmed, ". . . the police world has a hundred different ways of deflecting complaints" (p. 50).

This chapter takes the position that the less popular scientific methods enable for seeing that police brutality is a systemic problem in the United States, in particular, pursuant to racist policing. For example, measuring the sentiment of people on issues by analyzing what people are saying in public places and in the media would yield worthwhile information. Many minorities in the United States announce publicly that they have been the victims of police abuse (e.g., in a *New York Daily News* poll of 100 Black males, eighty-one report having been victimized by the police. See Casimir, Fenner, and O'Shaughnessy, 1999). Included in the cohorts of minorities who come forward are Black and Latino police officers, who also report having been physically or verbally abused by their colleagues (Chivers, 2001). So, the assertion by Kelling that Louima's victimization was an anomaly (and similar statements by Skolnick and Fyfe [1993]) is essentially saying that minorities are lying, imagining, embellishing, and exaggerating their (minorities) experiences with the police. Additionally, these scholars are saying that if you were really brutalized by the police you would have reported your victimization, and that if you did report it, it is not possible that the police failed to officially document your complaint.

The unwritten rule in minority communities is that you should not report your victimization because the police, politicians, or prosecutors to whom you will make the report will not take action. Weich and Angulo (2000, p. 47) write: ". . . the perception that the criminal justice system is not on their side leads many black and Hispanic Americans . . . [not] to report criminal activity." Worse, minorities know all too well that a trip to the police station to report police brutality often means that you may be wrongly arrested for disorderly conduct in the lobby of the police station—that is how you are punished for daring to question the police. In other cases, you are harmed physically, as in the following two examples.

Jamie Vales, who is Black, was charged with resisting arrest three days after his initial arrest and after his father had gone to the police department to protest his having been beaten by officers. Vale had suffered a shattered femur and broken leg among other injuries in the encounter with the police. The police testified that they did not know how the injuries occurred (Castaneda, 2001). The situation would be entirely different and not suspect had there been credible evidence that Vales had resisted arrest and that the officers had to defend themselves and, secondly, that Vales had been charged initially with resisting arrest. Another case is that of Kim Groves, a 32-year-old Black woman who observed Officer Len Davis physically brutalize a citizen in New Orleans. Groves reported the incident to the New Orleans Police Department Internal Affairs division. Internal Affairs promptly notified Officer Davis that he should try to scuttle the complaint. Davis in turn promptly telephoned a "hit man" and ordered Groves's murder. Within 90 minutes, the mother of two lay dead in a pool of her blood. The officer is now on death row (Nossiter, 1994).

So, although minorities are not inclined to talk with the police about abuse at the hands of other police, they are likely to talk publicly (e.g., at rallies, to media, among friends, and to community leaders). In this regard, is it possible for social scientists to compile data regarding how much abuse occurs, or how many newspaper and periodical articles present accounts of individuals' experiences with the police? This type of "content analysis" of written material enables for fruitful understanding of the extent of police brutality. Determining the actual number of incidents is not humanly possible—a scientific reality that every intellectual who denies the existence of systemic abuse can use to his or her advantage until the end of time.

Those who contend that Black and non-White Latinos are not being truthful when they assert that they have been the victims of a racist action by a police officer denounce the credibility of all media reports that say there is such a phenomenon as racially discriminatory policing. One such person, MacDonald (2001, p. 1), states: "There is no credible evidence that racial profiling exists, yet the crusade to abolish it threatens a decade's worth of crime-fighting success . . . the anti-profiling crusade thrives on an ignorance of policing and a willful blindness to the demographics of crime." MacDonald's outright denial that racially discriminatory policing exists is an affront to minorities who encounter the inequities of law enforcement and the administration of justice, particularly those inequities that lead to police brutality.

While a review of media reports can enable a determination of the extent of police brutality, minorities rightfully complain that the mainstream press presents much too little coverage of police abuse. For example, on May 2, 2001, a Black man was shot to death by a White Irvington, New Jersey, police officer (Patterson and Roberts, 2001). The officer claims that the victim attempted to run him down in the victim's car, despite the fact that the victim's fiancé and her two small children were in the car and the officer was actually *behind* the vehicle when he fired. The shooting rightfully enraged the Black and Latino communities (it should have enraged Whites as well). Additionally, there is overwhelming evidence that the officer stalked his victim. Witnesses say that the officer would pass by the victim "for over a year" and "pretend to shoot him with a cocked hand" (Jo Patterson and Roberts, 2001). This, just four years after the officer killed another Black man who he claims tried to run him over. The officer could even use the report that he filed in the previous shooting to explain the present shooting, changing only the name of the victim. This shooting is similar to the shooting death of another Black man, Deon Grimmitt, by a White Pittsburgh police officer in 1998. In that case, Officer Jeffrey Cooperstein became outraged when Grimmitt slowed to observe police activity ("rubbernecking") in which Cooperstein was involved. Cooperstein, who is allegedly involved with a White supremacist organization, went to his police car and subsequently performed a traffic stop on Grimmitt's automobile. Cooperstein states that Grimmitt tried to run him over and he shot him. The autopsy report revealed that Cooperstein fired his gun standing on one side of Grimmitt's vehicle, not in a place where he could have possibly been run over (McKinnon, 2000; Warnick, 1999).

It is not possible to determine the precise number of media reports, scholarly writings, and nonacademic writings that indicate that there is a systemic problem of racially discriminatory policing (especially in the form of police brutality) in the United States. If it were possible, those who argue that police brutality is systemic would have stronger ammunition to challenge the critics. Moreover, if proponents of the systemic position had financial resources to further investigate citizen accounts and publicly demonstrate the veracity of the experiences, the critics would likely still be critics but their counterarguments further weakened.

The sad reality is that most police brutality occurrences are not reported. Those reported are routinely deemed by prosecutors as failing the litmus test that would grant prosecutorial intervention; otherwise, there would be far more prosecutions of police officers. Minorities know the words "insufficient evidence" all too well, as they are often uttered following the shooting of minorities by White police officers. Victims and survivors are then left with the possibility of civil law remedies should they pursue the matter. Notwithstanding some justice received in the civil forum, the tragedy is that officers often go unpunished and many incidents of police brutality are solely addressed as torts. In their analysis of damages recovered by civil litigants, Sontag and Barry (1997) documented numerous cases of "gruesome" police brutality that were never given an appropriate criminal forum, yet the city of New York paid out 27.3 million dollars between 1995 and 1997. In one case, a man was beaten so badly by officers that he was blinded in his left eye, which was described as having dangled from the socket following the beating (Sontag and Barry, 1997). In this regard, it seems prudent to consider that one way of measuring police brutality is to add up the number of civil suits brought for police brutality and how much a jurisdiction pays out to settle them.

Reliance on police reports to determine the extent of police brutality is a method fraught with high potential for error. This is because a police officer can write a police report in any way he or she chooses (compare Cooper, 2001; Troutt, 1999; Prial, 1987). It is an authoritative version often molded to justify police brutality to say that illegal use of force was not brutality. Reports are written in such a way to mitigate the use of force and/or to deny its very occurrence. In spite of the obvious shortcoming of police reports, many of those (e.g., social scientists) tasked with informing the public about the extent of police brutality continue to champion the use of this methodology. Chevigny's (1969) findings that many officers will legitimize their actions in police reports by reporting falsely are still timely. He called attention to the practice of "catchall offenses" (e.g., resisting arrest and disorderly conduct) for which citizens are charged following having been brutalized— supported by what this author found to be true early on in his police tenure. The result is that many acts of police brutality are not accounted for in scholarly research projects.

For example, Fyfe (1982) used police reports to measure whether a police officer used the race (that the person was Black) of a person to decide whether or not to shoot the person. To use Fyfe's own words, he writes of the data collection method: "Our major source for these analyses consisted of New York City Police Department records of all incidents in which officers reported discharging weapons and/or being subjects of serious assault . . . for 1971–75" (p. 175). Fyfe continued in describing the findings of his research of police reports: "There is nothing in these analyses to support the contention that the disproportion of blacks among New York City police shooting opponents [black people killed or wounded by White New York City Police Officers] is reflective of police misconduct or racial discrimination" (p. 191). In other words, Fyfe is implying that between 1971 and 1975, not one Black person was killed or wounded by a New York City police officer because the officer held racial animus toward the Black person nor, Fyfe says, did the officer conduct himself in a manner unbecoming of a professional, objective-thinking police officer; or that the police officer in any way broke the law or departmental rules. Perhaps it was as if Fyfe expected to see written in a shooting report an admission by an officer that he (the officer) acted in a racially discriminatory manner.

POLICE SOLIDARITY AS AN IMPEDIMENT TO PROSECUTION

The police subculture, or what Reuss-Ianni (1982) defined as the "Cop Code" and what many people know as the "blue wall of silence," is worthy of discussion. The norms of the police subculture are somewhat different from those of other professions. Reuss-Ianni in her scholarly analysis of policing, documented the existence of a police subculture in which cops look out for cops, or said another way, that cops protect cops. This norm of the police subculture relates to prosecution of police officers for police brutality primarily in three ways. First, the norms or "Cop Code" require that all officers on a scene (police parlance for a *situation*) or having knowledge of the scene must, if called upon, regurgitate a police version of what happened on the scene. For example, officers who adhere to the Code are not always truthful about what they saw on a scene. Stoddard (1968, p. 203) defined this as "the sanction of the code which demands that fellow officers lie to provide an alibi for fellow officers apprehended in unlawful activity covered by the code." Crank (1998, p. 243) concisely asserts that support for perjury in police ranks is a "pervasive [police] cultural phenomenon."

Compare Barker's (1978) findings of the pervasiveness of police perjury based on self-reports of police officers. If the officer witnessed police brutality, he or she is expected to support the authoritative version of events that contends that no brutality occurred. For an officer to assert contrary to the authoritative report is to violate the norms of the police subculture, specifically the norm: "Don't give up another cop" (Reuss-Ianni, 1982, p. 14; Crank, 1998, p. 148). In the prosecution of White New York City police officer Michael Kelly for murdering a Latino man, which has been described as a racially motivated act, seven of Kelly's colleagues testified against him after being threatened with prosecution if they continued to hamper the prosecutorial effort. Kelly's fellow officers admitted that they had lied during the initial grand jury investigation to protect Kelly, explaining that it was accepted practice to commit perjury to help a fellow officer (see Reuss-Ianni, 1982, p. 48; for more recent perjury cases to uphold the Code, see the 1993 testimony by police officers before the Mollen Commission).

The second way the norm, "cops look out for cops," relates to prosecution of police officers for police brutality is evident in the role of internal investigations. The internal police department investigative body (i.e., Internal Affairs [division] or IA unit) is typically comprised of police officers. For prosecutors to make out a case against a police officer for brutality, the cooperation of IA unit officers is needed. Internal Affairs units are not only supposed to inform prosecutors of situations appearing to warrant prosecution, but IA units often conduct investigations for prosecutors as well. The problem is that IA-type units often adhere to the Code and will not, therefore, always address a report of an occurrence of police brutality. This is a phenomenon that demonstrates a need for neutral investigators to investigate police brutality. Recall the murder arranged by a New Orleans police officer. The New Orleans Police Department IA unit notified Officer Len Davis that Kim Groves filed a complaint against him, supposedly so that he could administer Code justice (though it is possible that IA did not realize that Davis would go so far as to have Groves killed).

If an investigation is commenced, it is likely to be done in such a way to protect the officer as in to not "give up another cop."[1] Kappeler, Sluder, and Alpert (1998) point out that "traditionally" citizen complaints are dismissed by IA units. By illustration, the IA units assert that a complaint is unsubstantiated (not sustained). For example, in an investigation of

---

[1] It is necessary to mention that there are many decent, honest internal affairs officers. One such person is Michael Dargan, a retired New York City Transit Police IAD officer. In 1986 when his office refused to take action, he went public with evidence showing how a group of White transit officers targeted, at random, Black and Hispanic males for false arrests. The unsuspecting victims were charged with ejaculating on White women on board New York City subway trains. Most victims pled guilty out of fear of embarrassment. The officers were prosecuted and convicted, in large part, because Dargan broke the blue wall of silence (Purdum, 1989; Glaberson, 1989).

the New York State Police, it was revealed that "more than one of every three complaints citizens made against troopers in 1994 were [held to be] unsubstantiated" (LaKamp, 1995, p. A8). The State Police held that it could not determine whether a misdeed occurred, although there was almost always overwhelming evidence that the misdeed in question did occur. The findings by LaKamp indicate complaints were unsubstantiated because it was the trooper's word against the citizen's. LaKamp found that when a complaint against a trooper hinges on the officer's word against the civilian's word, the investigating officer often accepts his colleague's version and closes the case without further inquiry.

The Christopher Commission's (1991) investigation of the Los Angeles Police Department (LAPD), formed in response to the rioting following the state trial acquittal of the officers who beat Rodney King, found that not only did the LAPD condone police brutality but also presented obstacles to people reporting it. Further, where reports were made, the Commission found that almost all were held to be "unsubstantiated." Like in Los Angeles, the workings of IA units in police departments throughout the United States are problematic. The Human Rights Watch 1998 publication, *Shielded from Justice,* exposed the ineffectiveness of police department internal affairs units when it reported that each of the 14 cities examined for its report, ". . . conducted substandard investigations, sustained few allegations of excessive force, and failed to identify or deal appropriately with problem officers against whom repeated complaints had been filed" (p. 63). The American Friends Service Committee (AFSC) writes of one IA-type unit, "Complaints appear to be routinely swept under the carpet . . . and the U.S. Attorney's Office does no better. Of the 63 AFSC-assisted complaints filed at different times over the 1995–97 period, all received back identical letters . . . " regarding the status of investigations (1999, p. 28).

The circumstances surrounding the gruesome shooting death of Kim Groves in New Orleans illustrate the dual role of many police department internal investigative offices entrusted with responsibility for investigating police criminal conduct (Cooper, 1995). The first of which is their function as seekers of police officers who violate the law. Contrast this with their second role of gatekeepers for the norms of the police subculture. It is the attention to the second role that impedes prosecutorial intervention in many cases of police brutality. Consider that New Orleans police officer Len Davis was not caught because of aggressive law enforcement by the New Orleans Police Department; rather, he was caught by federal law enforcement officers who were investigating him in connection with another matter (Perlstein, 1998). An accomplice who subsequently "turned state's evidence" testified that Davis was indeed a participant in a cocaine ring investigated by federal agents during the same time period. The witness's testimony further revealed that Davis was the police officer who ordered the execution of Groves, which was carried out within 48 hours of her complaint of police brutality to the New Orleans Police Department (Dvorak, 1997).

To whom does an honest cop report police brutality? Granted, police department policy instructs an officer to notify officials and/or an Internal Affairs unit. Typically, however, the vanguard for the norms of the police subculture—the Internal Affairs unit—labels the reporting officer as a "snitch" or "rat." Knowledge by officers that their police department IA unit punishes officers who violate the Code discourages officers from coming forward, which in turn makes it less likely that prosecutors will learn of police brutality incidents. Nashville police officer Reggie Miller, an African American, remembers what happened to him when he reported his racially motivated brutalization at the hands of fellow officers (all of whom were White) to the Nashville Metropolitan Police Department Internal Affairs division.

Miller was on duty in 1992, in plainclothes in an unmarked vehicle conducting surveillance, when he was assumed by White officers to be a criminal. They dragged him from his police department–issued vehicle and beat him savagely (Smothers, 1992). The beating stopped only after the officers realized that there were onlookers and that Miller's fellow officers, who had been sitting in other unmarked vehicles, were running to the beating scene shouting that Miller was a cop. Miller made it known to IA that he wanted the officers charged criminally. However, a grand jury failed to indict them despite the internal investigation that revealed two of the officers used excessive force (Harrison, 1992). For daring to "snitch" the Internal Affairs unit instead punished Miller, making him the target of a criminal investigation. The unit accused Miller of not identifying himself as a police officer and, worst of all, said that his account of what happened was not truthful. According to Miller, he was accused of lying under oath (Cooper, 1995). Miller's experience is indicative of how officers who come forward to report police corruption are accused of perjury or making a false statement. These accusations have replaced many of the physically gruesome methods once used by police to handle those labeled snitches and rats (e.g., there is ample evidence that Frank Serpico, the New York City police officer who spoke out about police corruption, was shot in the face at the request and by arrangement of some of his fellow New York City police officers). Perhaps the most tragic example of intimidation by threatening with a perjury charge was that used against New York City police officer Daisy Boria.

One writer referred to Daisy Boria's experiences as "prompting a fiery debate on police brutality and the role that the "Blue Wall" of silence plays in ensuring that officers are not held accountable for in-custody deaths or other actions" (Sounds of Silence, 1998, p. 7). Boria was on a scene in 1994 with fellow Officer Francis Livoti as well as other officers. Livoti became upset when Anthony Baez accidentally tossed a football onto his patrol car during a touch football game. Livoti responded by choking Baez to death. As he stood over the dead man, Livoti conspired with officers to say, among other falsities, that a fictitious Black man had killed Baez. Boria refused to partake in the conspiracy and reported the crime to Internal Affairs. Instead of being praised, she was not only accused of lying by the authorities but also received continuous death threats. Ultimately, Boria had to resign from the police force. Livoti was acquitted of criminally negligent homicide in a state trial but convicted of violating Baez's civil rights in a federal trial for which he was sentenced to federal prison.

Internal Affairs units, in complicity with prosecutors, may threaten officers who come forward to report corrupt behavior of other officers. They may accuse the officer of committing perjury and attempt to indict the officer. Another detrimental effect is that the complaining officer may be sent to a police department psychologist or psychiatrist. It is then that the officer's career is in jeopardy due to a naive notion by the examiner that the reports by the officer of police brutality, conspiracies, and frame-ups are products of a "wild imagination." Often, the result is the " black hole" or "Rubber Gun Squad," which is police parlance for reducing the job responsibilities of a police officer to non-law enforcement duties (e.g., duties similar to those of civilian clerical personnel). For illustrative purposes, consider Brookline, Massachusetts, Police Officer John Dirrane who reported police misconduct to the department chief. Dirrane refused to compromise his integrity by following orders of supervisors to commit perjury and to falsify and destroy official documents. Dirrane had achieved homicide detective status. But, immediately after he reported the lawless misconduct to the department chief, Dirrane was remanded to inside duties of call taker, computer operator, and dispatcher. In the civil lawsuit filed on

Dirrane's behalf, his attorney said, "the insults and ridicule from other officers began immediately. The remarks by other officers that Dirrane was assigned to 'the rubber gun squad' and 'bow and arrow squad' were said to have had an embarrassing impact on Dirrane" (*Dirrane v. Brookline,* Para. 258).

Another way that the norms of the police subculture relate to prosecution of police officers for police brutality is linked to investigations. The Code dictates that when an investigation is under way, whether by the Internal Affairs unit or prosecutor's office, officers who are perceived as witnesses should adhere to the Code by not saying anything that is contrary to the position taken by the officer or officers under investigation. Not surprisingly then, other officers proffer false testimony. For example, LaKamp (1995) shows how two former New York State troopers were forced to resign from their department for telling the truth in court about an improperly obtained search warrant. The testimony in such a case is usually that the officer (witness) knows nothing when he or she does have information. In this regard, the 1991 report of the Christopher Commission regarding the investigation into the Los Angeles Police Department states that "perhaps the greatest single barrier to the effective investigation and adjudication of complaints is the officers' unwritten code of silence, [which] consists of one simple rule: an officer does not provide adverse information against a fellow officer" (Christopher, 1991, p. 168).

In 1995, many New York City Police Department (NYPD) police officers traveled to Washington, D.C. for the annual Law Enforcement Memorial event. In a rampage that covered two D.C. hotels, New York City officers fired their service revolvers, slid down escalator railings naked, battered citizens, and engaged in thefts (Gearty, Siegel, and Marzulli, 1995). A criminal investigation by the NYPD ensued in New York City shortly thereafter, but most NYPD officers who were there would not assist the investigation in any manner. Within days after the incidents, then police commissioner William Bratton was asked by the press if any officers had come forward. He responded: "That has not occurred and being quite frank with you, I doubt very much it will occur . . . I am disappointed by that, but let's be realistic. The reality is that's not the way that it works" (p. 15). A newspaper editorial entitled, "They Saw No Evil" said of the situation, ". . . the Blue Wall of Silence stands firm. Impervious to threats, appeals, shame, or conscience, many in the NYPD rank and file take the conformity as a compliment" (*New York Daily News,* 1995, p. 28). After a series of threats by the New York City Police Department hierarchy that officers who were found to be withholding information could be terminated or prosecuted, some officers came forward. The Commissioner remarked of the slight turn in events: "The wall [Blue Wall of Silence or Code] is tumbling down" (Pierre-Pierre, 1995).

Investigations and a Weakening Subculture

The Blue Wall of Silence is tumbling down is another way of saying that the strength of the police subculture or Code has been dissipating, a contention supported by Reuss-Ianni (1982). Keeping the police subculture or Code intact relies on shared attitudes, values, and interests among other phenomena. It can be assumed that as the ethos "cops stick to together" loses support from police officers, prosecution of police officers accused of police brutality is much more likely because more officers are likely to testify against other officers.

The dissipation of the Code's strength is in part connected to a new influx of officers (Reuss-Ianni, 1982, pp. 6–7). Police ranks are losing their homogenous character. For example, they are becoming more integrated with visible minorities and women (Reuss-Ianni, 1982, p. 6).

The fact that the newcomers are not welcomed with open arms by the police subculture (and that many choose not to participate) means that many officers function outside of the police subculture (Dulaney, 1996, pp. 73–74). This has enabled the deterioration of adverse police subcultural norms such as those that impede a prosecution effort of another officer.

More recent findings show that in some police departments, more educated people are hired as police officers (e.g., more college-educated officers). It is plausible that a more educated officer, by virtue of his or her education, is less likely to participate in the norms of the police subculture or Code. Cohen and Chaiken (1972) and Cascio (1977) found that college-educated officers are not as likely as non-college-educated officers to receive citizen complaints. Perhaps this is because educated officers are more likely to ignore peer pressure and, unlike many of his or her predecessors, to build social relationships outside of the police subculture. This assumption may be contrary to a finding by Crank, Payne, and Jackson (1993) that officers with a more "professional outlook" were just as likely to support police violence mandated by the Code.

Reuss-Ianni (1982) found that there are actually two cultures of policing, one "management" and the other "line officers." Presently, this phenomenon has meant "infighting" and, as would be expected, infighting is contributing to the deterioration of the police subculture (1982, p. 11). Moreover, Reuss-Ianni found that large-scale investigations of the police (e.g., 1994 Mollen Commission in New York City; 1991 Christopher Commission in Los Angeles) disrupt the "organic relationships and allegiances" required by the Code. Relying on Reuss-Ianni's findings in part, the author of this chapter asserts that there really are more officers, than in the past, who are willing to testify against other police officers (compare Reuss-Ianni, 1982). This enables an inference that the increase of police officers testifying against fellow officers in the late 1990s and presently is indicative of a weakening of the Code of Silence.

Ethnic police associations appear to have contributed to a weakening of the Code. Dulaney (1996) in his scientific analysis of the history of Black police in the United States, writes of "the rise of black unionism": "A new breed of African-American police officer emerged . . . one who [speaks] out against racism in the police department, thus breaking the traditional code of silence. . . " (p. 74). The call for prosecutions of police officers by ethnic police organizations such as the National Black Police Association (NBPA) has given credence to the position that there is a problem of police brutality in the United States and that often police brutality is the result of White police anti-Black or Latino sentiment (NBPA, 2001). These organizations give the movement against police violence added legitimacy because it is the police criticizing the police. Who better to reveal the problem than the police themselves? Focusing on the NBPA for a moment, the association is comprised of active and inactive police officers. It is an advocacy group for Black police officers and Black communities with regard to policing phenomena. The NBPA rightfully and proudly violates a "Code" that adversely affects Black police officers and minority communities. Where in 1968, Stoddard, in his study, was able to find only one officer who would tell him of the inner workings of the police subculture, in the 21st century (notwithstanding former NYPD officer Frank Serpico's contribution of insider's knowledge) there is less hesitation by many police officers and ethnic police associations to air the dirty laundry of police work. This fact should contribute to increased prosecution of police officers for police brutality because it shows that there are police officers willing to violate the Code by assisting prosecutors.

It is safe to say that the chaos in the police subculture caused by Code violators helped enable the prosecution and conviction of Officer Kelly (mentioned earlier, see Reuss-Ianni, 1982, p. 47). One can infer that Code chaos, with similar causes, helped win the conviction of two of the officers who beat Rodney King; after all, a fellow officer testified that the force used on King was unauthorized, among other testimony (see *United States of America v. Stacey C. Koon, Laurence M. Powell, Timothy E. Wind and Theodore J. Briseno* [833 F.Supp. 769]). And there is more. The star witness in the trial of NYPD officer Justin Volpe for penetrating Abner Louima's rectum with a splintered, broken broomstick was another police officer. Officer Eric Turetzky's testimony, as well as that of a second officer, appears to have played a large part in why Volpe eventually admitted his guilt (Fried, 1999) and is now in prison. In the King and Louima criminal court cases, officers came forward and testified against other officers, even if begrudgingly. Granted, in many cases in which officers assist prosecutors, there are valid concerns that the testimony is not the result of an officer's moral conscience, but rather the officer's fear of being charged as an accomplice or charged with failing to perform a police duty. Notwithstanding, the protective shield of police solidarity appears to be damaged and the ensuing pandemonium that has resulted will surely encourage officers to give up other cops.

Addressing Why Officers Adhere to the Code

Many police officers opt not to assist prosecutors in prosecuting other cops out of allegiance to the police subculture. Other officers do not assist investigators or prosecutors although they do not adhere to the Code. They fear the Code punishment that could occur if they are branded a "snitch" in the police subculture (Cohen, 2000). The fear can be divided into two categories: that which is meted out by fellow rank-and-file officers, and that which is meted out by a police department administration (sometimes in collaboration with a prosecutor's office).

Beginning with the former, we can go back to Frank Serpico's experiences when he exposed rampant corruption in the New York City Police Department (Maas, 1973). He testified before the Knapp Commission about the resistance and retaliation that honest cops experience when they try to report police malfeasance (Knapp, 1973). Violating rules of the police subculture will mean social criticism and sanctions because "you're not behaving like one of us" (Reuss-Ianni, 1982, p. 13). The officer who is willing to buck the subcultural norms runs the risk of receiving limited backup because only the officers who are not adherents of the Code will assist the violating officer on calls-for-service. In other cases, the violating officer runs the risk of being "keyed out" [2] when calling for assistance on the

---

[2] I remember as a new patrolman witnessing the effects of an officer "keyed out." In this case, the many officers who were keying out the officer trying to make a radio transmission did not realize that she was trying to radio an ambulance. We were in the Southeast section of Washington, D.C. I was one of several foot patrol officers running after a suspect on foot. For a moment, the officer closest to the suspect lost sight of him. Officers in cars, on foot, and on motorcycles came to halt and stood in place waiting for another radio transmission. When the pursuing officer's voice was heard shouting into the radio we realized that the suspect had changed direction. One of the patrol cars was quickly thrown into reverse to make a U-turn and mistakenly ran over the motorcycle and its officer directly behind it. As the officer lay on the ground in excruciating pain with his mangled bike on top of him, the officer who tried to radio for an ambulance was prevented access to the "air." She had a bad reputation, not for being honest but for being perceived as an annoying supervisor.

radio—meaning, the violating officer is not allowed to call for backup—and to having drugs or weapons tossed into his or her unit car when on an assignment away from the vehicle.[3] One such incident occurred in Milwaukee, when, in January 2000, two police officers sued the Milwaukee police chief over a job transfer and won. In November 2000, the officers had to bring a new lawsuit because on six separate occasions drugs, drug paraphernalia, and a pistol were either planted or an attempt made to plant in one of the officers' police cars. The officers accused the police chief of ordering the planting and appear to have overwhelming evidence to show that the chief is responsible (Kertscher, 2000).

Times have changed—Serpico had to flee the country following his testimony before the Knapp Commission investigation. He had to go into hiding to avoid fellow police officers who vowed to kill him (Maas, 1973, p. 311). Renee Rodriguez—the Riverside, California, police officer who reported how White officers who killed Tyisha Miller in 1998 shouted racial epithets and "high-fived" each other after shooting her—and Daisy Boria—the officer who reported that Officer Francis Livoti murdered a man because the man's football struck a police car—did not have to flee the country (O'Connor, 1999). It appears that in the 21st century disgruntled cops are less likely to try to kill a fellow officer, but rather attempt to make the honest officer's day-to-day functioning miserable and, if possible, to place the officer either in danger or in a position in which he or she becomes a target of an Internal Affairs or prosecutorial investigation (see the earlier discussion on perjury as a punishment tool).

The experiences of Boria and Rodriguez demonstrate the conditional aspects of receiving benefits of the Code. While traditions of loyalty and silence are expected to extend to all officers, those who violate the Code by offering truthful information about police brutality are excluded from receiving Code benefits. Obtaining support by police officers in prosecuting police officers necessitates a police chief, Internal Affairs unit, and prosecutor's office committed to hearing about officers who engage in police brutality. An environment should exist in which an officer's safety or career is not jeopardized should he or she come forward and in which he or she is made to feel comfortable in coming forward.

THE DECISION TO PROSECUTE

In the United States, most allegations of police brutality are not investigated. Even in cases in which prosecutors know about an incident of police brutality many will not bring charges against officers. This chapter takes the position that most prosecutors (not all) are not interested in prosecuting police officers for police brutality because of the prosecutors' racial prejudice. Recall the GSS data and the conclusions by Barkan and Cohn (1998) that "racial prejudice contributes to whites' support of police use of force and that this relationship should be stronger for the use of excessive force than for the use of reasonable force against black people" (p. 749). If most prosecutors are White, and they are, then they are represented in the sample of people analyzed by Barkan and Cohn. Therefore, this chapter takes

---

[3] The intent is for the officer(s) relieving you to inspect the car after you have left for home, to find a gun, etc. stolen from the "property room" and/or that the property could be linked to a crime. The relieving officer(s) has a duty to turn in the property (e.g., to record in the property book). The targeted officer now must explain how a weapon used in a crime ended up in his or her auto or why glassine packages of "crack cocaine" are inbetween the seats of the patrol car.

the position that racial prejudice by Whites against Blacks and non-White Latinos is the number one driving force behind prosecutor unwillingness to pursue prosecutions against brutal police officers where the victims are Black or non-White Latino (see Wright, 1993). "Without a doubt, prosecutors and judges treat police differently and use double standards of justice," said state Rep. Harold James, a former Philadelphia police officer and a leader in efforts to eliminate misconduct by police and prosecutors (Washington, 1999). One way to support the contention that many prosecutors are racists and that they use race in decision making is to look to Weich and Angulo's (2000) research. They found that "racially skewed" charging and plea bargain decisions by prosecutors unfairly victimize Blacks and Hispanics. Then there are the data that show that prosecutors are more likely to seek the death penalty where the defendant is Black and the victim is White (Baldus, Woodworth, and Pulaski, 1990; Death Penalty Information Center, 2000). Since 1976, only 11 White people have been executed for murdering a Black person, while 145 Black people have been executed for murdering a White person (Death Penalty Information Center, 2000). Moreover, the prosecutor who prosecuted the officers who killed Amadou Diallo was Black. Ask yourself this question: Based on the history of Black-White relations in this country, current Black-White dissention, and the thousands of shooting deaths of Black men by White police officers, how likely is it that a White prosecutor would have prosecuted the Diallo case?

So, when is it that prosecutors take action? The findings of the research done pursuant to writing this chapter show that prosecutors take action when they feel compelled to investigate an allegation of police brutality. Often, the compulsion is community or public outrage and protest, specifically vocalness on the part of Blacks, Latinos, and some Whites (see Cooper, 2001b, for a discussion on liberal and conservative Whites). The conclusion makes sense when an individual considers that a massive outpouring of anger directed at the police preceded the prosecutions of White police officers involved in beating Rodney King, the killing of Tyisha Miller, and the shot-gunning death of Eleanor Bumpurs—the 66-year-old Black grandmother confined to a wheelchair (New York City, 1984). In this case, the police were called to evict the grandmother from her apartment. When she refused to leave, officer Sullivan, a White male, confronted her with a shotgun. She retrieved a kitchen knife so he shot off one of her hands, then waited for what many believe was a full minute before shooting the crying, wheelchair-confined grandmother to death (Raab, 1987). The city of New York defended the officer's actions. Additionally, it did not appear that a prosecution of Sullivan was on the horizon until there were massive and continuous demonstrations throughout the city of New York. Only then was Sullivan indicted, though he was later acquitted at a bench trial for the killing of this wheelchair-bound elderly Black woman. Based on a lack of trust in the justice system, minorities were not surprised.

The Use of Grand Juries

When prosecutors actually do prosecute police brutality, they [prosecutors] intentionally perform in a lackluster manner as in "throwing the fight." For example, the prosecutor puts on a lackluster performance before a grand jury in order that the jurors will not vote for an indictment. The contention of this author is that this happens because the prosecutor does not desire that a police officer be indicted. The reader should consider how many times he or she has read or heard that a grand jury opted not to indict a police officer for battering or killing a citizen, then compare that number to the number of times they have heard that a grand jury returned a "true bill." When one considers the old saying that a prosecutor "can get a grand jury to indict a ham sandwich," the reader should accept that a prosecutor is capable of taking a grand jury nearly anywhere that the prosecutor wants. The following examples will prove the points presented.

In July 2000, a White Omaha police officer shot and killed George Bibbins, an unarmed Black man who took police on an eight-minute car chase. Bibbins was shot as he sat inside his vehicle after it crashed into a telephone pole. In this case, the police chief, who is White, stated publicly that he couldn't pinpoint a reason why the officer shot George Bibbins. The chief stated, "As we indicated, there are concerns about what happened. We can't put our finger on the justification. . . " (Gonzalez and Spencer, 2000, p. 1). The local district attorney charged the officer with manslaughter, but did not use a grand jury process.

In the same time period, a "Special Prosecutor" was appointed to the Bibbins matter. The special prosecutor requested a dismissal of the local prosecutor's charges against the officer arguing that a police shooting incident is not under the purview of local prosecutor, but a special prosecutor. In the opinion of this author, the special prosecutor had other motives; specifically, that he was unhappy that charges were filed against a police officer. Perhaps the prosecutor had marginalized Bibbins's life because Bibbins was Black. A judge sided with the special prosecutor and dismissed the charges against the officer. The special prosecutor presented the case to a grand jury. It was no shock to minorities that the grand jury would not indict the officer. What did shock, offend, and incite minorities was a statement by the special prosecutor to the daily Omaha newspaper (see Brunknow and Spencer, 2000) that he did not know why jurors came to a conclusion not to indict the officer. The statement represented arrogance on the part of the prosecutor—how could he not know? After all, he convened and facilitated the grand jury process.

In addition to being an example of what appears to be a lackluster performance by a prosecutor, the Omaha case is one of many cases where officers appear to shoot not because they are justified, but because they know that they can most likely get away with it. This is similar to officers shooting the driver of an automobile then lying by saying that the driver tried to run them over (Cooper, 2001). The fact that the justification of "he tried to run me over" by police officers sometimes makes it to grand juries is not much solace to minorities because many prosecutors act as gatekeepers to protect officers from prosecution for police brutality. They (prosecutors) intentionally present facts to grand juries in such a way that they (grand jurors) will find that the officer(s) acted properly. In other words, the rash of grand jury declinations to indict in police brutality cases in the United States, where the officers are White and the victims Black or Latino, are indicative of many prosecutors who "throw the fight." Certainly, the prosecutor does not always intentionally or willingly throw the fight, but rather that based on his or her socialization process—which for many includes a notion that the police are benevolent and that in the post–civil rights era, racism no longer exists—the prosecutor does an impassionate and inarticulate job of convincing grand jurors that they should indict.

Omaha is not alone in experiencing the lack of indictment for wrongful conduct by police officers through the grand jury process. In August 2000, Black residents in the St. Louis area learned that a grand jury declined to indict two White police officers who killed two unarmed Black men (Lhotka, Hollinshed, Jonsson, and O'Connor, 2000). The police officers killed Earl Murray and Ronald Beasley in what they claimed was self-defense. Interestingly, in a city where public officials admit race relations is a persistent problem, police officials in this matter refused to disclose the race of the police officers. Of the two suspects, Murray was deemed a drug suspect by police officers while police did not want Beasley for any reason. In that case, "undercover officers said the driver caught his back bumper on the undercover police vehicle behind [it]." The officers claim that they feared that the "car would break free and hit them" so two officers opened fire. The grand jurors were told to consider manslaughter charges against the two officers rather than murder charges. The prosecuting attorney, Robert McCulloch, said of the grand jury's decision not to indict: "We [the prosecutor's office] reviewed the same evidence they did. I don't disagree with the outcome of the grand jury." Yet, experienced Black and Latino police officers know better. They know that many White officers fire when they do not have to, but fire anyway because they have marginalized the victim's self-worth because the victim is a minority. And as is common, many Whites describe police brutality as a mistake or tragedy. Note McCulloch's words: "It was a horrible tragedy," McCulloch added, ". . . but it was not criminal conduct" (p. A1). (Patronizing Black and Latino people with the word *tragedy* in police brutality cases has become a fad for racially and ethnically insensitive prosecutors. One of the countless examples involved the California prosecutor who refused to charge the four White police officers in Riverside, California, who killed Tyisha Miller, a 19-year-old woman who was sleeping in her car. The prosecutor termed Miller's death a "terrible, terrible tragedy" (Washington, 2000). He stated that the tactics used by the officers represented a "mistake in judgment." The California Attorney General agreed, he said that the officers' actions were "unwise and ill-conceived" (Washington, 1999).

In July 2000, a New York City grand jury declined to indict an officer who shot Patrick Dorismond, a man who was not breaking the law and was not wanted, but was only hailing a taxi. The officer who killed Dorismond said that it was an accident, although from a minorities perspective it was a willful and intentional killing (Chivers, 2000). A similar outcome happened in May 2000 in Providence, Rhode Island, when in spite of overwhelming evidence showing criminal conduct, two White officers were cleared by a grand jury after they killed their Black colleague, Cornel Young, a fellow police officer in plainclothes trying to help them make an apprehension. The death of Young shows that even those of us—Black men who wear a badge—fear abuse of use of force policy from many fellow White officers.

In 1994, New York City's Black community loudly expressed its disapproval of what appeared to have been a racially motivated shooting by a White New York City police officer of a Black plainclothes New York City police officer. The White officer shot the officer in the back four times as the Black officer lay on a subway platform after being downed by the White officer's earlier gunfire. As the Manhattan District Attorney (DA) announced the indictment of the officer, he called the indicted officer "a sympathetic figure who had acted after finding himself in a frightening and very difficult situation" (Sexton, 1995, p. A1). That a prosecutor would make such a statement is inappropriate. The statement implies that there was prosecutorial reluctance to even present the matter to a grand jury. It appears that it was the vocalness of Blacks and Latinos in New York about the shooting that prompted the prosecutor to seek an indictment. The prosecutor knew that he had to "work hard" in the grand jury room, but obviously not work hard enough, as evidenced by the fact that the grand jury did not indict the officer on the more serious charge of attempted murder.

Grand jury processes are unfair because they are one-sided—the conspicuous and controlling performance is that put on by the prosecutor. Judges, defense attorneys, and strong rules of evidence do not have a part in grand jury processes. The decision not to indict in Omaha and in other cases in other venues throughout the United States experiencing abuse of use of force policy by police is less indicative of a shortage of evidence (i.e., an assertion by prosecutors that there was insufficient evidence to indict) than of prosecutors who presented facts to grand jurors in a way that was advantageous to getting grand jurors to find that officers acted properly. Then, as a way to deflect criticism by Blacks and Latinos of how prosecutors convened the grand jury process in police brutality cases, prosecutors assert "ignorance" and that the critics are out of line because grand jury proceedings are secret (as a general rule, what was said in a grand jury room is never to be made public). If the processes are secret, many prosecutors contend "you" have some nerve asserting that they (prosecutors) did not do their duty. In a police brutality case in Philadelphia, in which the DA was asked to show a reason for not charging two law enforcement officers with murder, a Philadelphia municipal court judge responded to this all-too-common secrecy assertion and strategy when the elected Philadelphia district attorney used it. The judge said ". . . the district attorney cannot cloak its reasoning behind the secrecy of the grand jury process" (Racher, June 18, 1999). I add, one does not need to be in the grand jury room or privy to the dialogue in the grand jury room in order to infer that a prosecutor was less than zealous. Especially, when one considers the manner in which the grand jury process is carried out, specifically that the prosecutor determines what the grand jury is told and not told, as well as that he or she can express an opinion as to whether or not he or she believes that the officer should or should not be indicted.

The fact that it is mandated in some jurisdictions that "all" (police) shooting incidents are presented to a grand jury does not mean that justice is meted out. Grand juries used this way serve a purpose because they play an investigatory role. However, in far too many cases grand juries are used inappropriately, such as where prosecutors use the process to persuade grand jurors that the police (authoritative) version of a shooting should be believed. The fact that a grand jury process is one-sided and, hence, essentially does what a prosecutor wants it to do, is indicative of a legal process that is outdated, draconian, and perpetuates police brutality. In the name of improving police-minority relations, it seems prudent that community and civil rights leaders work diligently to abolish the grand jury process (as England abolished theirs in 1933).

Incommensurate Charges

Often, when criminal charges are filed against an officer for police brutality, the charges are not commensurate with the offense. To illustrate, for cases in which the officer's actions would constitute murder if committed by a civilian, these same actions produce a manslaughter charge (or something similar) when committed by an officer.

In Cincinnati, on April 7, 2001, Officer Stephen Roach shot and killed Timothy Thomas as he ran away. Thomas was wanted for minor violations, specifically traffic. On May 7, 2001, Roach was indicted for "negligent homicide," which is a misdemeanor in Ohio (Wilkinson and McCain, 2001). Additionally, he was indicted on another misdemeanor, "obstructing justice," because he gave conflicting statements of what happened. The shooting sparked three days of race riots in Cincinnati. Although the shooting was in violation of the United States Supreme Court holding in *Tennessee v. Garner* (1985) and, although Roach intended to shoot and kill Thomas, it appears to this author and minorities in Cincinnati that the prosecutor worked diligently to make sure that Roach was not charged with murder or manslaughter. The Cincinnati Black community responded with outrage to the lenient charges. The prosecutor shot back: "They [grand jurors] made the right decisions" (Wilkinson and McCain, 2001). To no one's surprise in the Black community, Officer Roach was acquitted of the two lenient charges in September of 2000.

Another case demonstrating incommensurate charges is that of Carlton Brown, a Black man who was beaten so badly in 1992 by two White New York City police officers that today he is a quadriplegic. Rather than charging the officers with attempted murder, the officers were charged and acquitted of assault (Fried, 1999).

This again illustrates how it was unusual that the officers who killed Amadou Diallo were charged with second-degree murder, a crime commensurate with the actions of the officers. The reality in America is that prosecutors seldom charge police officers with murder in cases of police brutality. Manslaughter is a common charge, even when the victim died under circumstances in which it can be shown that the officer demonstrated a depraved indifference to human life (the definition of second-degree murder, not manslaughter). This chapter takes the position that (1) racial and ethnic prejudice on the part of prosecutors, and (2) the mythical notion held by many prosecutors that "all" police officers are benevolent and could never commit murder account in large part for why manslaughter and not murder is charged.

LESS THAN ENTHUSIASTIC PROSECUTORIAL ACTION

A glaring example of the actions described previously, including (1) blatant disregard by prosecutors of the role of prosecutors in this country, (2) blatant disregard for police brutality in America, and (3) racially discriminatory prosecutorial actions is demonstrated by the words of Maryland Assistant State's Attorney Michael Pearson. At a June 2001 criminal trial of a Black man charged with resisting arrest, the defense showed evidence that their client should not be convicted for resisting arrest because their client's broken femur and broken leg, among other injuries, were not the result of the suspect resisting arrest but rather a brazen act of brutality. In turn, Pearson, the prosecutor, told jurors: "I don't know whether excessive force was used. But it's not my job to determine that, and it's not your job to address that" (Castaneda, 2001, p. B5). He then went further, telling jurors that "if [the] officers brutalized" the suspect—the suspect "could seek redress through the civil lawsuit he intends to file." Fortunately, the jury disregarded Pearson's contentions and found the defendant not guilty because they didn't believe the officers' account of the arrest (Castaneda, 2001, p. B5). Additionally, it appears that the FBI had launched an investigation into the behavior of the police prior to the trial and that Maryland prosecutors only launched an investigation of their own on the heels of possible public outrage at the position Pearson took at the trial.

Valid concerns about whether prosecutors shirk their responsibility are not limited to prosecutors who do not prosecute when they should, but also include the many prosecutors who are willing to accept, unquestionably, police explanations and to disbelieve a victim or witness account of a situation (Troutt, 1999). Just as serious is the problem of a prosecutor who "drags out a case" by not dropping charges against a victim of police brutality where there is ample evidence that a crime was not committed and that the accused was arrested as a guise to justify police brutality. The prosecutor only dismisses the charges in such cases after many court appearances. It is well known in minority communities that this practice occurs. Not so fortunate are the many victims of police brutality who are left with no choice

RACE, PROSECUTORS, & PHILADELPHIA

Perhaps nowhere in the United States are the allegations of racist prosecutorial decisions louder than in Philadelphia. At a minimum, the city has been polarized by a widening rift between Philadelphia's White District Attorney, Lynne Abraham, and the city's Black and Latino community (see Taylor & Mullen, 2001). No wonder that a *Philadelphia Daily News* article was entitled "Race in the DA's Race" (Id.) and that a July 24, 2000, rally against police brutality had as a focal point, the district attorney's failure to prosecute police brutality cases (Medina and Lucey, 2000, p.7). In an April 2001 *Philadelphia Daily News* article, Abraham was described as having been for some time "dogged by charges that she treats minority suspects and minority police officers differently from how she treats white suspects and [white] police officers" (Taylor & Mullen, 2001, p.7). The writers of the article went on to describe nine incidents in which race was an issue and how Abraham handled each matter. They wrote about cases in which there was overwhelming evidence that a law enforcement officer used unjustified force, but Abraham either declined to prosecute or, as some would argue, put forth a lackluster effort when she did prosecute. In at least two of the cases, officers were deemed by the Philadelphia Police Department to have used unauthorized deadly force, yet Abraham still declined to prosecute.

In another incident, Abraham criticized and blocked the nomination of a Black woman who would have become the city's first African American woman on the U.S. District Court. Abraham has denied that her action was racist rather that, in her opinion, the Black judicial nominee was not supportive of the police (Id.). In yet another racial incident, Abraham asserted that racism is not a problem in the criminal justice system rather African American crime rates are. So it was no surprise when her office prosecuted a mutual racial confrontation between Blacks and Whites, but Abraham charged only Blacks (Id.). In those rare cases in which Abraham has charged police officers for wounding or killing Black or Latino people, the charges are typically dismissed by a judge, or the grand jury convened by her office fails to return an indictment. The city's Black leaders explain these outcomes as the result of deliberate, less than zealous prosecution attempts by Abraham (p.7). Abraham has been described by Philadelphians as sharing the likes of [exposed] racist, former Los Angeles Police officer Mark Fuhrman and Bull Conner, the southern police chief known for his brutality against Blacks in Birmingham, Alabama (Brennan, 2001, p.5).

From a people-of-color perspective, prosecutorial inaction by the Philadelphia district attorney's office offers a stinging, vivid illustration of a lack of prosecutorial enthusiasm to address police brutality. Weich and Angulo's (2000) finding "that prosecutorial discretion is exercised to the disadvantage of black and Hispanic Americans" is perhaps nowhere more evident than in Philadelphia (p.12). Consider three separate police brutality cases in which the Philadelphia DA's office was involved. The first involves the actions of White Philadelphia police officer Christopher DiPasquale. On October 1, 1998, Donta Dawson, a Black male, sat in his automobile and would not respond to questions from DiPasquale and his partner; he ignored the officers. The agitated DiPasquale aimed his service weapon (gun) at Dawson's head and fired two rounds.[i] One of the bullets entered Dawson's right eye and pierced his skull, causing his death.[ii] In his eight years as a police officer, this was the third time that DiPasquale had killed a person of color (Taylor & Mullen, 2001, p. 7). Yet, the district attorney, Lynne Abraham would not bring murder charges against DiPasquale, although, many a lawyer would find that the facts of the case satisfied the elements for either first-degree or third-degree murder under Pennsylvania law.

"Civilian eyewitnesses say Dawson never moved before the fatal shot by DiPasquale, an officer with a record of 11 civilian complaints alleging abuse. In 1996, DiPasquale received a ten-day suspension for participating in a police cover-up of the fatal beating of a Hispanic man two years earlier" (Washington, 2000; Boyer & Gibbons, 2000). A Police Department Internal Affairs investigation ruled the Dawson shooting unjustified, hence subsequently fired DiPasquale (Boyer

(continued)

and Gibbons, 2000; Smith, J., 2000, p.6). The arbitrator who heard DiPasquale's appeal held that "DiPasquale improperly put himself in danger and fired his weapon after he ordered Donta Dawson to show his hands during a traffic stop . . . he was shot before he had an opportunity to comply . . . " and Officer DiPasquale's "actions were inconsistent with police directives to preserve human life' "(Boyer and Gibbons, 2000).

Instead of filing murder charges against Officer DiPasquale, the district attorney brought [less serious] manslaughter charges against DiPasquale. The charge was twice dismissed by two magistrates who ruled that the DA had not established a *prima facie* case for manslaughter.[iii] Washington (2000) writing for the *Philadelphia Tribune* noted that Abraham "decided" not to mention the police internal affairs investigation and its conclusion of the shooting at the magistrate's hearing. The newspaper held this was "another curious element in the DiPasquale [probable cause] hearings" (online edition). So many mysteries from the office of the DA led Philadelphia's Black leadership to hold that Abraham did not make a zealous effort to have a judge find that there was probable cause to bring DiPasquale to trial. Most convincing and revealing as to Abraham's motivation and (lack of) enthusiasm for prosecuting DiPasquale is that she filed charges against DiPasquale only after mass protests by Blacks, Latinos, and civil rights groups (Id.).

In the same time period there was another case involving a Philadelphia police officer who people of color believe should have been charged with murder. Officer Thomas Hood, a White male, and his partner were in plainclothes and in an unmarked police car on October 3, 1997. Hood says that he noticed an automobile pull off quickly from a stoplight when the light turned green. Hood added that he thought that the victim's license plates had expired. Hood drove ahead of the car and pulled in front of it as it was stopped at a subsequent light. Eyewitnesses describe an understandably terrified victim, a Black male, who was approached by two men, with guns drawn, who did not identify themselves as police officers. In an effort to get away from the fast approaching armed men, the victim backed his car up, striking the car behind him, then out into incoming traffic. Hood then fired his gun four times, striking the victim, as well as shattering glass over the victim's nine-year-old niece who was in the back seat. The bleeding victim, in an incapacitated state, began to blink his lights to get the attention of a marked police car a few blocks away. He was transported to a hospital and arrested for aggravated assault, simple assault and reckless endangerment of another person. Hood said in his report, the victim drove "directly at me." In "Code" or, in police subculture parlance, Hood was saying "he tried to run me over." Eyewitnesses and a police department ballistics expert asserted that the victim could not possibly have been trying to run down Hood (McGriff, 1999, p. 3A).

"A Philadelphia Police Department internal investigation concluded that virtually every action Hood undertook, up to and including the shooting of the victim and almost shooting the man's nine year-old niece, was in violation of police policy" (McGriff, 1999, p. 3A). The report labeled the gunfire an inappropriate shooting. It went on to say that Hood's ". . . actions were overly aggressive, placing" himself "in jeopardy of being struck by Campbell's [the victim] vehicle and would have placed a reasonable [victim] person in fear for their safety" (Id.). In spite of this report, the district attorney's office cleared the officer of criminal wrongdoing. *Philadelphia Tribune* staff writer Milton McGriff wrote of the refusal to prosecute: "Serious questions . . . arise about the decision of the district attorney's office not to prosecute Hood, exactly when they made that decision, and precisely what criteria went into that conclusion" (Id.). McGriff suggested that this instance of obvious police brutality was not prosecuted since it received little media attention.

Finally, two parole officers fatally shot unarmed Kenneth Griffin in front of his girlfriend and two small children as they all lay in bed (Racher, 2000). Abraham presented the case to a grand jury and the grand jury declined to indict in spite of damning witness accounts that Griffin had done nothing to provoke the officers. It was this case in which outrage in the Black community manifested itself through an effort by Attorney Leon Williams to bring the officers to trial for murder when the DA would not.

In what appears to be unprecedented action in modern times, realizing that an infrequently used Pennsylvania statute[1] enabled a private citizen to initiate a criminal prosecution through the district attorney's office (see PA Rule of Criminal Procedure # 106), Williams drafted murder charges against the officers who killed Kenneth Griffin. Williams presented his criminal complaint to the DA's office and waited for Abraham to execute the complaint by arresting the officers and charging them with murder as the complaint charged. That did not happen, rather Williams was rebuffed by Abraham's office, she refused to act on the complaint. Williams then brought the matter before a municipal judge. The judge in turn ordered that the DA have the officers arrested immediately and that they be charged with murder (Racher, June 18, 1999, p.6). The judge didn't stop there; she issued "a scathing denunciation of Abraham's behavior in the case. The judge accused the DA of an abuse of discretion in failing to explain why her office rejected William's complaint" (Racher, December 23, 2000, p. 6). The judge added: "The public interest is the only interest in which the district attorney owes a fidelity, and that duty is not met when no clear statement is provided stating why declining to prosecute" the officers "was in the public interest . . . The district attorney cannot cloak its reasoning behind the secrecy of the grand jury process" (Racher, June 18, 1999). Abraham's response to the court order can best be described as cocky, and vehement about protecting officers from being prosecuted for brutality. She verbally attacked the justice (Racher, June 18, 1999, p.6) and refused to follow the court's order vowing to appeal the decision to the Pennsylvania State Superior Court.

Not long after, in January 1999, a group of Black elected officials used the same law that had been dormant for so many years to file first- and third-degree murder charges against Officer DiPasquale for his having killed Donta Dawson. The elected officials and their attorney, Michael Coard [hereinafter referred to as the petitioners], sent the private criminal complaint to Abraham with correspondence which read in part: ". . . it is respectfully requested that your office re-arrest Officer DiPasquale on all appropriate charges and direct that another preliminary hearing be scheduled or that a grand jury be summoned to completely inquire into all appropriate charges and, in addition, that your office petition the United States Attorney to prosecute Officer DiPasquale on all appropriate federal charges."[2] A response from Abraham reads in part, "Please be advised that your request for a private criminal complaint charging murder of the first degree . . . is respectfully disapproved."[3] In response, Attorney Michael Coard, representing the alliance, petitioned the municipal court (Court of Common Pleas) to compel Abraham to bring murder charges pursuant to the private criminal complaint against Officer DiPasquale. The court agreed that the petitioners had established a prima facie case for charging DiPasquale with murder. The judge ordered Abraham's office to arrest and charge DiPasquale with third-degree murder (Washington, 2000, online).

As she did in response to the court's order with regard to private criminal complaint filed by Williams, Abraham refused to follow the court's order and appealed the decision to the Pennsylvania State Superior Court. Once again, Abraham's tone was so vehement against prosecuting DiPasquale that one cannot help (knowing the circumstances of Dawson's death) but wonder if her actions were racially motivated. One must ask, why would a prosecutor fight "tooth and nail" to prevent the prosecution of a police officer who was involved in three deaths, all of which aroused overwhelming suspicion, and that two of his victims were Black and the other a non-White Latino? Moreover, DiPasquale was fired by his police department for killing Donta Dawson. Just as alarming as to the zeal with which Abraham fought the private criminal complaints brought on behalf of Dawson and Griffin, Abraham not only appealed all the way to the state's highest court, but also refused to follow the instructions of the respective courts. Then she hired a highly influential former prosecutor to fight the orders of the judges to arrest DiPasquale and

(continued)

the officers who killed Kenneth Griffin (Caparella, May 10, 2000, p. 31). Perhaps, a vivid, compelling illustration of Abraham's actions is found in the title of a news article that was highlighted and in uppercase: "**DA HIRES TOP-GUN SPRAGUE HE'LL HANDLE FIGHT OVER COP RULINGS**" (Id).

Abraham got her wish and argued before the Pennsylvania State Superior Court that she should not have to prosecute the officers who killed Dawson or Griffin. The court agreed, although it did not rule on the merits of the facts in the private criminal complaints. Rather, the court held that the attorneys and other parties representing the interests of the deceased Dawson and Griffin lacked legal standing to bring private criminal complaints. Certainly, this interpretation of the private prosecution law is in opposition to the interpretation of the law held by many others.[iv]

As a sidebar, even if a court should compel a prosecutor to charge a police officer as the result of a private criminal complaint, there are valid concerns that a prosecutorial effort will prove to be lackluster, to the say the least. Perhaps, fortunately, legislation provides for the appointment of a special prosecutor. Additionally, the petitioners may request that the office of the Pennsylvania Attorney General prosecute the cases.

The strategy in Pennsylvania calls attention to how in other parts of the country, there is likely legislation available that may need to be tapped to address police brutality. An unfortunate task, since there should be an expectation that prosecutors will diligently pursue claims of police brutality. Attorney Michael Coard writes (May 5, 2000): "Pennsylvania's private criminal complaint law, as found in Rule of Criminal Procedure 106, is an essential weapon for private citizens in the battle against politically protected and pervasive police brutality. I therefore urge private citizens and lawyers throughout the country to research the law of their states to locate and use 'private criminal complaint' or similar legislation. And if there is none, then petition, demand, and agitate until such legislation is introduced and passed" (interview of Michael Coard, Attorney, May 5, 2000).

---

[1]Rule 106, Pennsylvania Rules of Criminal Procedure.

[2]Memorandum. Letter to District Attorney from State Representatives LeAnna M. Washington and James R. Roebuck Jr. (January 20, 1999).

[3]Memorandum. Letter from District Attorney to State Representatives LeAnna M. Washington and James R. Roebuck Jr. (July 1, 1999).

[i]DiPasquale claimed that the unarmed Dawson made a furtive gesture.

[ii]*Commonwealth of Pennsylvania v. Christopher DiPasquale*, Private Criminal Complaint, April 7, 1999, Court of Common Pleas, Philadelphia.

[iii]Michael Coard, a Philadelphia attorney, argues that the magistrates dismissed the charges because the DA filed manslaughter instead of murder charges (Ousley, 1999, p.4).

[iv]On May 3, 2000, the *Philadelphia Daily News* reported that federal prosecutors held that there was insufficient evidence to prosecute DiPasquale or the officers who killed Griffin. An attorney described by the *News* as one of the attorneys representing one of the officers said of the federal government's decision not to prosecute: "It completely vindicates these officers . . . Had the victims obeyed the officers instead of acting hostile and in an aggressive manner, they'd be alive today" (Smith, 2000, p. 6).

but to accept convictions via a plea bargain for a crime (e.g., disorderly conduct) that they did not commit.

What can be said about prosecutor conduct in the following four contemporary scandals?

Miami In September 2001, thirteen Miami police officers were charged with shooting and killing unarmed minority men, then planting weapons on them and concocting lies to cover up the behavior (Kidwell and Tanfani, 2001). The indictments describe a well-orchestrated conspiracy in which a band of officers was "quick to shoot unarmed suspects, ready with a stash of 'throw-aways' and steadfast when it came to lying for each other." In exchange for leniency, two of the officers, now retired, admitted to prosecutors that they were among five officers who murdered two "smash-and-grab" robbers then planted guns on the bodies (Kidwell and Tanfani, 2001). The first of these shootings occurred in 1995, with the most recent in 1997. All had been ruled justified and legal by the Miami Police Department and the local prosecutor's office, in spite of dozens of signs and persuasive evidence that showed the shootings were unjustified. Incredibly, the prosecutor's office likely wants us to believe that it did everything that it was supposed to do after each shooting and that it did not notice the pattern (the same officers involved in multiple shootings in a 19-month period) of behavior by the officers. I suggest that this inquiry in Miami realize the culpability of the prosecutors involved. The inquiry should be widened to include investigation of the prosecutors who rubber-stamped these shootings as justified and unworthy of prosecution.

California The Rampart Division of the Los Angeles Police Department was involved in several acts of brutality and misconduct in the late 1990s (discussed in greater detail later in the chapter). Police officers who were in charge of cleaning up gang violence from the streets of Los Angeles filed countless false reports, some of which covered their actions in committing attempted murder and murder. The prosecutors involved in the cases accepted at face value the police reports that stated that the gang members had pointed guns at cops (Cohen, 2000).

Pennsylvania In 1995, six officers from the Philadelphia Police Department admitted to targeting Black citizens at random. The officers pleaded guilty to making false arrests, planting drugs, violating citizens' rights, and filing false reports to cover their actions. One of the victims was a grandmother, Betty Patterson. She was charged with selling crack and spent three years in prison until the officers admitted that she was not a drug dealer and that they had planted narcotics in her row house (Terry, 1995; Cooper, 1995).

New York In 1986, the New York City Transit Police falsely charged more than 200 Black and Latino men with ejaculating on White women while on board the subway trains (Levine and Neuffer, 1987; Glaberson, 1989a, 1989b). One of the accused happened to be an off-duty New York City police officer (Levine and Neuffer, 1987). In another case, the woman identified as having been the victim of sexual abuse by a Black man was later subject to marital strain from the publicity of the false arrests and the arresting officer's insistence that she corroborate his false accusations (Glaberson, 1989b). Many of the those accused were so embarrassed by the charges that they plea-bargained to a lesser offense.

Prosecutors had to know who was entering into plea bargain arrangements accompanied by the vocal complaints by arrestees that they had not ejaculated on anyone. The officers involved were caught, thanks to a courageous IAD officer who took the scandal public when his IAD office would do nothing. Two of the officers were found guilty in federal court (Glaberson, 1989a).

It is unlikely that the prosecutors in the four above-cited cities did not know of the police corruption. For example, they surely saw the strenuous efforts of defendants—personal heartrending pleas—to make it known that they were the victims of police corruption. We should not accept that the involved prosecutors did not know anything. In Miami, Los Angeles, Philadelphia, and New York City the involved prosecutors had all of the warning signs, but chose to ignore them.

The vast majority of cases involving police brutality of which a prosecutor's office learns are never prosecuted. Many would argue that prosecutors are not interested in prosecuting the police because they (prosecutors) rely on police to help them establish cases against others. This ties into the shared ethos between many police officers and many prosecutors that achieving a safe and crime-free society necessitates breaking the law sometimes (Stoddard, 1968). This is indicative of complicity in police malfeasance of public officials such as prosecutors. Moreover, the numerous real-life cases presented thus far show that some prosecutors, like some cops, look the other way when called on to address police brutality. This is likely due to the fact that the victims are minorities or those considered unpopular: drug dealers, drug abusers, people with criminal records, and the poor.

Speaking, perhaps, to the lack of enthusiasm on the part of many prosecutors and the inaction of IA units, John Dunne, assistant attorney general for the Civil Rights Division of the U.S. Department of Justice said in 1991 while testifying before Congress, "We [the Civil Rights Division] are not the front line troops in combating instances of police abuse. That role properly lies with the internal affairs bureaus of law enforcement agencies and with state and local prosecutors. The federal government program is more of a backstop, if you will, to these other resources" (Dunne, 1991, p. 348).

RACE

It appears that most victims of police brutality are visible minorities (see Chevigny, 1995, for a discussion of the Los Angeles riots after the Rodney King beating). In this regard, there are credible arguments by minorities that some prosecutors foster racial and ethnic animus for minorities and as a result, in police brutality cases, prosecutors will seldom initiate prosecutions where the victim is a Black, for example, and the officer is White. Nugent (1994, p. 47) rightly points out the existence of data that allow inferences that racial and ethnic biases "consistently impact the charging decisions of prosecutors, particularly when the victim is Caucasian and the defendant is a minority" (see Schmitt, 1991, for an analysis of 700,000 criminal cases in which Blacks and Latinos were disproportionately charged). While concerns about racist policing in the United States are omnipresent for minorities, many prosecutors, most of whom are White, readily admit that they do not believe that racist policing exists. In such a climate it seems reasonable that minorities are suspicious of the justice system. It is not difficult to see why in minority communities there is always an expectation that (1) officers who engage in police brutality will not be prosecuted, (2) if prosecuted they will be charged with an offense that is lenient relative to the offense actually committed, and (3) if prosecuted, the officer will likely be acquitted.

Rudolph Guliani, the mayor of New York City, was a career prosecutor prior to becoming the city's mayor. It is no secret that Guliani believes that racial profiling does not exist. He has nothing but harsh words for the United States Civil Rights Division and Black leaders who suggest that there are New York City police officers who engage in racial profiling (see Colangelo and Marzulli, 2000, p. 43). The mayor and his police commissioner (Howard Safir at the time) dismissed a Civil Rights Commission report, finding racial profiling by New York City Police, as flawed and described the commission as "lazy and not skilled" (Colangelo and McPhee, 2000, p. 2). In this regard, one should try to imagine how Guliani made decisions as a prosecutor, specifically with regard to decisions to prosecute when a citizen claimed that a police officer treated him or her in a degrading manner, or that the officer brutalized him or her and that the officer's motivation was racism. Guliani did not believe then, when he was a prosecutor, that there were racist cops and he does not believe now that there are racist cops. There is little doubt, then, that Guliani would not have prosecuted behavior (e.g., holding that no crime had been committed) that would likely have been prosecuted by a person who believes that there are police officers who act out of racism. We know from national polls and day-to-day conversation that many Whites, not just prosecutors, share Guliani's opinion that racist policing does not occur. Note the words of a prominent, well-respected New York City White journalist, Mike Barnicle: "Too many among the black clergy can't stop screaming about the bogus threat supposedly posed by the police . . ." (Barnicle, 2001, p. 40).

What would be different about the prosecutorial landscape if the majority of prosecutors were Black and non-White Latinos? Better yet, if the majority of prosecutors were not only racial minorities but also women? In this regard, consider what we as human beings bring to the decision-making table based on our most significant socialization processes: our upbringing, the subcultures in which we were raised, our experiences in life, and the influences of social circles in which we function daily. "The habits you are trained in, the people with whom you mix, lead to your having a certain class of ideas of such a nature that, when you have to deal with other ideas, you do not give as sound as accurate judgments as you would wish" (Lord Justice Scrutton, 1921). So, we live in a world in which some people make judgments out of racial animus while others have no malicious intent yet still behave in a racially discriminatory manner. Both types of individuals are overly represented on the existing prosecutorial landscape.

Let us now talk about racism and the actions of some prosecutors. Racist behavior or racially discriminatory behavior by a prosecutor includes a prosecutorial decision not to charge a police officer for battering or killing a citizen because the victim or suspect was Black or Puerto Rican, for example. This would be the prosecutor marginalizing the self-worth of the victim because of the victim's race or ethnicity. This brings up the issue of White prosecutors who suggest that there is no such thing as a "legitimate victim" in minority communities. A prosecutor who is always suspicious of the minority crime victim's account of the crime characterizes this. Consider, for example, that one of the victims in the ongoing Los Angeles Police Department Rampart Division scandal, Javier Ovando, was unable to get the prosecutor to believe that Officer Rafael Perez shot him as he lay handcuffed. Perez would later admit his actions, including that he shot Ovando and then that he planted a rifle on him, saying the shooting was necessary because Ovando stood upright and pointed a gun at him (Cohen, 2000). Today, Ovando is a paraplegic as a result of Perez's gunfire. In exchange for prosecutorial and judicial leniency, Perez has exposed some incidents of gruesome police brutality in Los Angeles. Known as the Rampart scandal, it includes many officers who shot civilians and then lied on police reports in saying that the victims had pointed guns at them (Cohen, 2000).

Ovando is a good example of the powerlessness of many victims of police brutality. He is a non-White Latino and was singled out because of his ethnicity and lower socioeconomic status. Birkbeck and Gabaldon (1996) found in their research of police brutality in Venezuela a phenomenon that holds true in the United States: "The use of force is more likely when citizens are perceived to be powerless to register a successful complaint" (Birkbeck and Gabaldon, 1996, p. 113). Closer to home, Crank (1997, p. 76) writes, "victims of excessive force understand that they have little recourse, that they will confront difficulties in filing a complaint, that they invite further problems, and that the courts will likely look the other way." In this regard, it is not so far-fetched to assume that the some prosecutors marginalize the victim's self-worth because of the victim's social or socioeconomic status, race, or ethnicity.

Nugent (1994, p. 17) writes of his experiences as a judge: "Judges do not come to the bench 'tabula rasa,' that is with a blank slate. Rather, their beliefs and attitudes, formed by their previous experiences, both on and off the bench, are well entrenched, and everything that is seen and heard by the judge will be filtered through these." Analogously, prosecutors do not start their tenure as prosecutors with a blank slate. Using what we know about prosecutors in the United States, many initiate their tenure following a lengthy socialization process as a Caucasian in a country where skin pigmentation determines the nature and quality of daily social interactions. For example, the Black and Brown American learns all too quickly that he or she will be followed around retail stores because he or she is assumed to be a thief. With regard to policing, the interaction that most law-abiding White Americans will ever have with an on-duty police officer will be pursuant to a traffic stop, and that the interaction will be characterized by brief dialogue between the officer and citizen regarding grounds for the issuance of a traffic citation. The experiences for minorities are distinguishable. Although law abiding, they will experience being thrown up against walls, having guns drawn on them, and suffering verbal abuse by police officers who assume (1) that the minority person is in a White neighborhood to perform a burglary, (2) that the minority person is a drug dealer because of the expensive car that he or she drives, or (3) that the minority person is a criminal because that person wears his or her hair in braids.

Nugent (1994, p. 3) distinguishes between bias and prejudice. Prejudice he says is "overt and forceful" while bias he says is "usually less overt or sublime." Perhaps this is one way of distinguishing between the admitted aversive racist versus the well-intentioned individual who behaves in a racially discriminatory manner. Although this paper takes the position that many White prosecutors operate with an aversion for Blacks and non-White Latinos, there are other White prosecutors who want to be impartial and not racist but their "sociological baggage" (all of the phenomena that contributed to their socialization process) cause a manifestation of biases (e.g., preconceived notions). Whether it is unintended racism or willful racist aversion, both contribute to prosecutorial decision making with regard to police brutality (i.e., whether to investigate, whether to present the case to a grand jury for indictment, what information will be given to the grand jury, what charges to file, etc.).

The prosecutor who is a purposeful racist and uses his or her position to further antiminority sentiment in America should be relieved of his or her duties. Easier said than done, because discovering him or her in the post–civil rights era is difficult. He or she knows not to use racial epithets or ethnic slurs, as this is not "politically correct." He or she knows to do everything not to be discovered. He or she knows that others cannot easily probe his or her subjective mind. For example, Weich and Angulo (2000) found that not one White person was prosecuted on crack cocaine charges by the U.S. Attorney's office in Los Angeles between 1988 and 1994, even though surveys found that Whites made up approximately one-third of "frequent" crack users in Los Angeles. Because the Los Angeles prosecutors did not openly use racial epithets or announce publicly that they were behaving in a racist manner, they can comfortably rebut, to the satisfaction of many in the White populace, that any accusation claiming they behaved in a racial manner is false. We have yet to reach a point in this country in which many Whites understand that racism can occur without epithets or admissions.

Some prosecutors mean well and do not realize how they operate with preconceived problematic images and negative notions about minorities. Consider Nugent's suggestion for those in judicial service (remember that Nugent is a judge and was once a prosecutor): When judges educate themselves "about the various areas where bias commonly occurs, we [judges] take great strides toward eliminating the harmful impact that bias may have on an otherwise fair and just system. . . it is a disservice to judges and the system if they [judges] presume that bias and prejudice do not enter the decision making process . . . " (Nugent, 1994, pp. 3–4). So, too, should White prosecutors acknowledge that they are operating from a position of "privilege": that of being a White person in America. For good reason, minorities charge that many White prosecutors have difficulty being objective when addressing situations in which Blacks or Latinos are involved. For example, the prosecutor marginalizes the victim's worth because of the victim's skin pigmentation as in filing lenient charges against an officer for a horrific act of police brutality (e.g., the shooting death of Black Timothy Thomas by White Cincinnati police officer Stephen Roach). Yet, in some cases, the prosecutor is unable to see how he or she marginalized the victim because of the victim's skin pigmentation. The prosecutor never considers for a moment that his or her socialization process in the world from the day that he or she was born suggested that minorities are dangerous, unclean, unkempt, unmotivated, uncivilized, or to be pitied. As Nugent tells judges: "there is [an] absolute necessity . . . to recognize the possibility that gender, race, or ethnicity may influence . . . judicial decision-making" (Nugent, 1994, p. 48). Analogously, it should not be ignored that a White prosecutor's outlook is likely clouded by racial and socioeconomic privilege and, in many cases, racial animus, all of which influence decisions to charge police officers who engage in police brutality. By acknowledging what is in one's sociological baggage, the White prosecutor can do things to ensure that he or she behaves in a fair and impartial manner.

PROSECUTOR CULTURE

The ethos of prosecutor culture is a most prominent impediment to (1) getting prosecutors to charge police officers who engage in police brutality, and (2) getting prosecutors to charge an officer commensurate with the offense that the officer committed. The literature, scholarly and non-scholarly, documents a culture of men and women, many of whom have little regard for the truth or justice but who are just concerned about winning (Armstrong and Possley, 1999). The public is learning about one case after another in which prosecutors knew that confessions were beat out of people and that innocent people were being sent to death row. One of the best examples of this phenomenon involved Anthony Cruz, a Chicago man who spent 12 years on death row for a crime he did not commit. DuPage County Judge Ronald Mehling overturned the conviction, not because of legal technicalities, but because he said the initial murder investigation was "very sloppy" and the government's case against Cruz was riddled with lies and mistakes (p. 25). Following public pressure, both prosecutors and police officers were prosecuted for conspiring to send the innocent man to prison. In spite of their acquittals, there is credible evidence that someone in law enforcement and the prosecutor's office doctored evidence against Cruz. In Los Angeles, the number of people freed from jail and prison pursuant to the Rampart scandal is staggering. The police version of events involving many of those freed was accepted at face value by prosecutors who disregarded the obvious signs that the authoritative narratives and testimony of police officers needed to be treated as suspect (see Troutt, 1998).

Prosecutors' Knowledge Base as an Impediment

Prosecuting police officers for police brutality presents formidable challenges. For example, getting around what the officer says was his or her state of mind at the time of the use of force could require time-consuming investigation. In many cases, the prosecutor is faced with false statements and perjury not only by police but also reluctant witnesses. These witnesses are fearful because of vengeful criminals as well as vengeful police officers. These phenomena contribute to a position or, rather, a prosecutorial interpretation of the brutality allegation as "unmakeable," as if to say that it is an allegation plagued by insufficient evidence and hence lacking in prosecutorial merit. To put this in perspective, it is questionable whether the police officers who battered Rodney King would have been prosecuted had the beating not been videotaped. King's beating could have been described as "unmakeable" but for the videotape. After all, as discussed earlier, police officers are not known for assisting prosecutors in the investigation or prosecution of a fellow officer. Hence in a trial, prosecution witness and victim testimony is likely to be doubted by the fact finder due to an entourage of police officers who present identical, supportive testimony for the officer(s) involved. In communities where the common ethos is that "all" police officers are benevolent and incapable of racism or police brutality (e.g., Simi Valley, the venue of the state criminal trial where the officers who battered Rodney King were acquitted) and in communities in which police officers are held in high esteem, prosecutors will no doubt have difficulty getting convictions of rogue police officers. Because many police brutality victims are socially powerless because of their economic status or that they are visible minorities, their testimony is not likely to be taken seriously by status quo juries.

Conversely, there is credible proof that juries comprised of Blacks and Latinos are not likely to believe the testimony of police officers (see Coke, 1994, pp. 356–7). This is the direct result of so many minorities having had negative experiences with police officers. In response, many police officers charged with police brutality in venues where Blacks may sit on the jury request a bench trial (although there is no evidence that minority officers accused of police brutality request bench trials more frequently). It is the officer's hope, and he or she is usually right, that the judge will acquit because he (the judge) is unwilling to accept that police brutality is widespread and that it occurred in the situation at issue. Nugent (1994, p. 52) writes of a criminal defendant's desire for a bench trial: "It is because the defendant feels the judge will be more favorable or biased in their favor than a jury . . . thus, the defendant in a criminal case would seek to exploit the justice system by utilizing potential biases a judge may unconsciously possess to the defendant's advantage. . . . Exploiting the justice system, by taking advantage of judge's personal bias." Just as problematic is the fact that in most states, a prosecutor's permission is needed for an officer to receive a bench trial. In this regard, many times prosecutors assist police officers in exploiting the system by never denying a request from a police officer for a bench trial.

In opposition, White NYPD officer Mark Conway was charged with assault for shooting a Black teenager in the Bronx. (Note that the Bronx, unlike the other boroughs, has a Black district attorney; the same prosecutor who charged the officers who killed Amadou Diallo with second-degree murder.) Like most of Conway's colleagues before him who were charged with shooting Black or Latino people, Conway requested a bench trial. I am sure that it was to his "shock" when he learned that the trial judge was a Black woman. This is not to imply that she would give up her impartiality to favor a Black victim. Rather, that this judge would operate from a mind-set of being a Black woman in the United States and that she would bring to her cognitive decision-making process her experiences and socialization in a country fraught with racism and sexism (compare Nugent, 1994). Conway was convicted on June 5, 2001 (Waldman, 2001, p. B1); indeed, an out of the ordinary occurrence. A *New York Times* writer wrote: "The verdict seemed to catch Officer Conway's family and supporters by surprise. Like most police officers who go on trial in the city, and especially in the Bronx, Officer Conway had waived his right to a jury trial, hoping he would fare better before a judge" (p. B1). Conway's conviction may cause a rethinking of the bench trial strategy of police officers who illegally harm Black and Latino people.

Having named many of the obstacles that prosecutors either encounter or claim they encounter in investigating and prosecuting police brutality, let us consider how prosecutors can navigate their way around real or perceived roadblocks. I begin by posing the question: Is there something other than the "Black letter law" that a prosecutor must know in order to achieve a successful police brutality prosecution? I answer "yes." Prosecuting police officers for police brutality requires a conceptual understanding of police work's nuances and protective subculture.

The Practising [sic] Law Institute publishes a book entitled *How to Handle Unreasonable Force Litigation: Prosecution and Defense Strategies in Police Misconduct Cases,* which is updated annually and is described by the publishers as an educational supplement and a lawyer's "handbook." One can effectively argue that the book's emphasis on procedural strategy is helpful to the prosecutor who prosecutes police brutality cases, but that it is not enough. The book does not address the phenomenon of the dynamics of police actions and police subculture, or suggest gleaning from the police literature (e.g., scientific research). I take the position that a firm conceptual understanding of police dynamics, the police literature, and police subculture can offer a great deal of insight as to what happened on a *scene*. All three enable a prosecutor to ask the right questions and know when to be suspicious. Otherwise, prosecutors left with being told, by police, that an officer's action was a "split second decision" that can't be judged unless "you were there" (police parlance) in that officer's body. Knowing how a foot chase transpires, for instance, or what it is like to run after a man believed to have a gun is absolutely necessary if you are to prosecute police officers for police brutality. Moreover, getting some semblance of an understanding of the nuances and dynamics of the actions by police officers necessitates that prosecutors spend time on "ride-alongs" and listen to radio transmissions that occur when a "priority" or "1013" or "1033" are called by an officer. Otherwise, prosecutors will be dogged by the following explanations given by officers and defense attorneys: (1) "you (the prosecutor or fact finder) weren't there," (2) "there was still a threat—if there is a videotape, you can't see it, but he (suspect) was still resisting," (3) "I feared for my life," (4) "you aren't a police officer, hence you don't know what I experienced," and (5) "police work is dangerous and you (prosecutor) should not second-guess an officer's split-second decisions."

A prosecutor who takes on prosecuting police brutality must have more than a passing or general interest in police subculture if he or she is to adequately handle and rebut this type of testimony. Simply knowing that cops stand up for cops is not enough. Rather, prosecutors must become knowledgeable of the police subculture via the scholarly policing literature as well as by reading reports documented in the media among other sources. Although the literature has its biases and problems as noted earlier, the policing literature has documented a great deal about the way that day-to-day police duties are performed and actions occur (e.g., Reuss-Ianni, 1982). Specifically, the literature has documented the inner workings of the police subculture. Take for instance the subcultural norm that "If you run from the 'poe-lice' [sic] you get fucked-up." When a prosecutor is faced with a case in which the victim or defendant says that he or she was kicked in the face by a police officer while lying prone on the ground after the victim saw a police car and ran, out of fear of having interaction with the officer, the prosecutor should possess a willingness to investigate further (see Kriegel, 1998; Halbfinger, 1998). The reason is that a police officer learns early in his tenure that people who run from the police are to be abused—says the "Code" (Cooper, 2000). For a prosecutor to accept at face value the officer's account that the victim is lying, in the face of overwhelming documentation that there is a subcultural norm that calls for street justice when you run from the police, is to commit a more serious injustice and to demonstrate utter indifference coupled with ignorance.

Other subcultural norms include that "dead men tell no tales," hence, once you have shot a man who lies wounded you are supposed to "put a cap in him" or he will sue you (the officer) in a complaint littered with falsities. This norm is relevant to a prosecutor's toolbox because a common problem with prosecuting police officers for "bad shootings" is effectively rebutting the officer's explanation as to why the officer shot a person. In this regard, the police subculture has scripts, already prepared, to handle bad shootings. It includes, first and foremost, asserting that you feared for your life or something to that effect. It is followed by one of these three primary assertions: (1) he tried to run me over (with his car), (2) he pointed a gun at me, and (3) he lunged at me (e.g., with a knife). There is even a cartoon that is passed out in police locker rooms that is referred to as the "Police Shooting Report Checklist," which includes the aforementioned choices.

It is not by accident or simply rehearsal for trial that the testimony of the officers in the Amadou Diallo trial was virtually identical (whether you believe that the officers acted properly or improperly in the shooting). *New York Times* writers Dan Barry and Amy Waldman (2000, p. B1) said of the identical trial testimony: ". . . prosecutors have . . . encountered a blue wall. . . [in] which officers used almost identical language to defend their actions." In this regard, the Code information transferred to a new police officer in the subculture socialization process should alert the prosecutor not just to what the defendant officer is going to say at trial but what may have really happened at the scene.

Police officers realize that most of the public, including most prosecutors, are ignorant as to the dynamics of police shooting situations and other use of force situations. They know from information passed down from old cop to young cop that most prosecutors will not ask further questions—many don't know what to ask. Rather, many civilians and prosecutors accept police versions of events such as "we fired upon individuals who pointed guns at us." Yet, in reality, there are far more situations in which a person is holding a gun and does not know of an officer's presence, and hence would not point a weapon at the officer. In almost all cases, the individual with a gun who is chased by a police officer is running away from the officer and "tosses it." Although it happens, it is rare to be fired upon by suspects who are running away from the officer. Officers spend more time searching "dumpsters" for example, among other places, looking for the gun that the suspect tossed in the foot chase. I know this personally from (1) being in a police uniform and having guns fired at me, (2) having guns pointed at me, and (3) in other cases, the suspect not knowing I was watching him or her. As an example in the latter case, in October 1996, the wife of Larry Harper sought help from Albuquerque, New Mexico, police when her husband threatened suicide. He committed no crime, but the distraught man ran from police and "cowered behind a juniper tree." When nine officers of the department's paramilitary unit found Harper (unbeknownst to him), they shot and killed him (Egan, 1999).

It is taught in the police subculture that when dealing with minorities or anyone marginalized in society: "shoot first and ask questions later." Note the following radio transmission taped by the Christopher Commission (1991) investigating police brutality in Los Angeles following the Rodney King riots: "If you encounter these Negroes shoot first and ask questions later." The Commission goes on to say that ". . . Officers also used the communications system to express eagerness to be involved in a shooting incident" (pp. 4–5).

It should come as no surprise to prosecutors when they take some time to become knowledgeable of the police subculture that many officers shoot people who do not pose a threat, but that the officers write an authoritative narrative of the shooting incident that indicates that the suspect pointed a weapon at the officer (compare Troutt, 1999). That is, the officer knows that his or her life is not in danger, but fires anyway because he or she knows that most prosecutors, among others, will not second-guess the officer's decision or look with suspicion upon the situation. In the 2000 Providence case in which a Black Providence police officer (Cornel Young) in plainclothes was shot and killed by two White Providence police officers, the White officers stated that they had repeatedly warned their fellow officer to drop his gun and—saying that he refused—they described a standoff between the police and the police. For minority officers, this version of what happened is preposterous and offensive. So, the issues in the Young case and many cases where Black police officers are shot by White officers are (1) officers dispense with protocol as in not shouting commands (e.g., "Police, Don't Move"), then they lie and say that they did make their presence known to the victim, or (2) officers shouted commands contemporaneous with initiating gunfire.

The officers who killed Officer Cornel Young asserted the same things that other White police officers who have killed Black police officers (and people in general) have asserted (i.e., "I told him to drop the gun and he disobeyed my command") (i.e., see Duggan, 1995, p. E1; Boyer and Gibbons, 2000). All of the authoritative (police) reports read almost identically regardless of the venue. These practically identical reports, coupled with overwhelming evidence from what constitutes the norms of the police subculture, generate reasonable suspicion for which prosecutors should be concerned (see Mozingo, 2000; Zamora and Hendricks, 1998). This is to say that in presenting a case to a grand jury for indictment, prosecutors would need to inform grand jurors about the norms of the police subculture—in particular, the norm (Code rule) that holds that a police officer should dispense with protocol (e.g., drop the gun) by shooting first and then asking questions later when confronting the socially powerless (minorities) perceived to be suspects. Granted, grand jury proceedings are secret, but one can be almost certain that few, if any, grand juries investigating police brutality are educated by prosecutors about how the norms of the police subculture may have influenced the events for which the grand jury is investigating. For this reason, one can understand how Blacks and Latinos who sit on grand juries and trial juries will vote not to indict or not to convict. These individuals are working with the information provided to them. For example, in the criminal trial of the officers who killed Amadou Diallo, you cannot say that the Black jurors concluded that the officers acted in a racially discriminatory manner or that they did not act in a racially discriminatory manner because race was never made an issue in that case by either the defense or prosecution. Additionally, in that trial as in many, stringent, limiting instructions (e.g., don't add race to the equation) to a jury as to how they are to determine if an officer is to be convicted account for the manner in which many non-White jurors sometimes vote in police brutality cases.

The Code provides trial preparation long before the officer acts. Because many prosecutors know little or nothing about the premeditation for police brutality that the police subculture provides, the prosecutor will not understand the need to be suspicious. There are those prosecutors who know about and accept the premeditation perversion, yet do nothing, while others refuse to believe that it exists. The result of which, in either situation, is that egregious human rights violations remain unchecked.

Many cops talk with each other about how they take the legal use of force right to the edge. As a cop you learn how to create situations that are legally indecipherable (Crank, 1998), such as by intentionally placing yourself in front of an automobile to enable a fear of life claim. For example, in the case of Desmond Rudolph in Louisville, Kentucky, the nine-page police investigation noted numerous instances in which the officers who killed Rudolph committed tactical errors. When asked if the shooting could have been avoided, the lead investigator said, "One could come to that conclusion." A grand jury was convened and voted along racial lines. Because there were fewer Blacks than Whites, the grand jury voted not to indict. Even with the incriminating report, the officers were given medals of valor for shooting and killing Rudolph (Zambroski, Shafer, and Tangonan, 2000, p. A1). For prosecutors to get a sense of what happened at the scene where an officer said that the victim tried to run him over, they would need to know about how some officers will place themselves in front of an automobile. A prosecutor will be able to see a pattern if he or she looks at other cases along with examining police subcultural norms. Once having discovered the pattern, he or she can see if the Code dictated when and in what manner force was likely employed in the situation under investigation. No doubt, no two scenes are alike; however, pattern and practice (based on what the officer did on previous scenes and what is a common practice by officers in the department) enable knowing what questions to ask and what suspicions to maintain. Only then can a decision to prosecute be solidly made.

One of the Los Angeles officers convicted and sent to prison for violating Rodney King's rights, Sergeant Stacey Koon, remarked of his upcoming federal trial prior to its start, "Piece of cake, . . . It's just a matter of educating the jury" (Stewart, 1993c, p. 2A). Fortunately, in that case prosecutors knew what they were up against—a daunting subculture of norms that can kill a prosecution effort.

THE SUBJECTIVE STATE OF MIND AS AN IMPEDIMENT

> Of course, in assessing the credibility of an officer's account of the circumstances that prompted the use of force, a fact finder may consider, along with other factors, evidence that the officer may have harbored ill-will toward the citizen. (*Scott v. United States*, 1978)

In a February 10, 1999, *New York Times* article, writer Benjamin Weiser wrote "in several cases where officers' perceptions of danger have been an issue, state prosecutors have failed to bring charges against officers involved in shootings of unarmed civilians" (p. A1). This phenomenon calls attention to the issue of the subjective state of mind of the officer at the time of the use of force.

In determining the legality of use of force by police, a legal standard by which an officer's actions are to be judged is that of a reasonable police officer. This can be asked in two ways: (1) Was the officer's action (force) reasonable? (2) Did the officer act in a manner in which a reasonable officer (similarly situated) would have acted under the circumstances? Determining reasonableness has its challenges, the first of which is a defense strategy that seeks to control the fact finder's definition of reasonableness. For example, the defense influence on the jury in the Amadou Diallo trial as well as on the judge was shown by the judge's charging instructions to the jury. Though I don't believe that the prosecution intended to blunder the case, the prosecutors did not educate themselves on the norms of the police subculture (the Code). One critic of the prosecutors stated that he thought " . . . the prosecutors should have asked that the judge say in his instructions to the jury that, even if the use of deadly force is necessary at first, it can become unjustified later" (Waldman, 2000, p. B5). The defense intentionally tries to show the fact finder (in particular, juries) that police work is so unique that only people with police experience can evaluate police actions. For example, the defense argues: "that you [the jury] don't know what it's like to be a cop and having to make a 'split second decision' as a cop." Such defense arguments make it very difficult for jurors, for example, to measure reasonableness. The fact finder's (judge or jury) automatic acceptance of the defense interpretation of reasonableness, coupled with fact finder naiveté, sometimes awe, or even feeling intimidated by the "you're not a cop argument," means that it is highly unlikely that the officer could possibly be found to have acted in an unreasonable (brutal) fashion.

Officers learn very early on in their police tenure that they will likely be exonerated when they state that their subjective state of mind was that they feared for their lives (or something to that effect). Officers are just as aware as civilians that police officers are seldom if ever prosecuted for police brutality and if prosecuted, seldom convicted. Officers know that prosecutors' investigations into use of deadly force rarely second-guess what the officer says was his or her state of mind at the time.

There is strong likelihood that a prosecutor's decision not to pursue a matter (e.g., not to present the case to a grand jury "for indictment"), a grand jury's decision not to indict a police officer accused of police brutality, or a fact finder decision not to assign guilt is the result of acceptance of the officer's version of what his or her subjective state of mind was at the time of the brutality occurrence. Such automatic acceptance by prosecutors is to ignore abuse of the use of deadly force policy. This avoidance reduces the number of cases presented to grand juries and/or successfully prosecuted.

Police officers are in numerous situations in which they do not shoot, although the rules of deadly force allow them to shoot. The countless cases in the United States of minorities shot by White police officers unjustifiably are evidence that many officers do not use the discretion that is expected of a police officer. Instead, they shoot according to the lowest—the minimum—criteria allowed for use of deadly force. The problematic officer shoots when he or she knows that he or she does not have to shoot, but does so anyway because he or she knows that the shooting will be ruled justified. By illustration, consider some calls-for-service that involve domestic violence. A cop with more than a month on the street knows that a woman who is abused by her partner may grab a knife to defend herself from her attacker. When the police arrive, sometimes she is holding the knife (or other weapon)—she will drop it if you give her a chance, you don't shoot her! But many officers do. Decisions to prosecute usually fail to consider that the officer did not have to shoot. Rather, decisions to prosecute more often than not are based on ballistics tests, photographs, and a volley of other scientific evidence. A former homicide detective from a major city, speaking at a conference in 2000, explained that there were police shootings that he investigated that he had to find "legally justified," although he exclaimed that he could not find them "morally justified." Here lies the problem. It seems prudent that changes occur in use of deadly force policy that enable morally unjustified shootings to bring the wrath of the criminal system down on a rogue police officer.

Officers who are prone to abuse the discretionary latitude inherent in use of deadly force policies know that the norms of the police subculture mean that their fellow police officers are not supposed to "sell them out." So some officers shoot at the slightest indication that deadly force may be justified even if other non-deadly alternatives are available to control the situation. In many cases, this is abuse of the furtive gesture rule—a slight, harmless movement by a citizen is known to be harmless by the officer, but the officer shoots because he or she knows that the movement can be described as threatening. Prosecutors should remember that officers are trained to say that they feared for their lives.

There are legitimate concerns that some officers use force, and especially deadly force, on citizens as a result of the officers' racial bias. In the 21st century, it is less likely that the closed-minded police officer will accompany blows or shots with racial epithets. His or her caution is the result of knowing the consequences. These include discovery of having committed a hate crime as well as coming under the purview of federal prosecutors for having violated a citizen's rights under color of law. Prosecutorial investigations must not leave out a much-needed analysis of the sociological and psychological phenomena, which explain why, in some cases, the officer shot in line with the minimum threshold requirement for engaging deadly force. To not ask questions about what was in the officer's sociological baggage at the time of the use of force means that many police brutality victims will never receive justice.

Police officers have discretion. They are tasked with using their common sense and good judgment in determining how much force is necessary. Prosecutors must contend with a situation in which the officer's subjective state of mind told him or her to use the amount of force employed. Because no two physical encounters are alike and because we are not mind readers it can be difficult to investigate the officer's actions; however, there are ways (techniques) available to help prosecutors determine if the officer is not being truthful about having feared for his or her life. Eventually (and hopefully) many police agencies will add more restrictions to use of deadly force policies. Such restrictions will contribute to a reduction in acts of police brutality.

Diallo Defense Team Used Norms

One spectrum of the Code demands that civilians must have sympathy for police officers and be in awe of the police profession. This is an arrogance that engenders the notion that police officers have a sole right to claim masculinity. Firefighters, football players, and soldiers who go to war, among others, are excluded by police officers as having an entitlement to claim dangerous and difficult duties. I call this use of "The Danger Card," an effective and often successful strategy for beating prosecutors in police brutality cases.

The idea behind the Danger Card is to have civilians assume that police work is a thankless job and that officers put their lives on the line each day and that Mr. or Ms. Civilian lacks the courage to do what police officers do. I argue that in reality, policing is a very rewarding profession. Many would not give it up even with an opportunity to participate in another profession. Moreover, driving a taxi can be far more dangerous than police work. Let us not forget that many police officers work in administrative capacities such as preparing the payroll. In fact, most police officers work in jurisdictions in which violent crime is not rampant (U.S. Department of Justice, Bureau of Justice Statistics LEMAS, 1999). It is not that many civilians couldn't do what some police officers do; it is that many have chosen other occupations. One does not lack the courage expected of a police officer because one chooses to become a medical doctor, for instance. Tying this into the prosecution of police officers for police brutality, the defense team in the prosecution of the officers who killed Amadou Diallo built its case around the dangers of police work (see numerous media accounts of the trial, including references to testimony by Dr. James Fyfe and the trial transcript: *The People of the State of New York v. Kenneth Boss, Sean Carroll, Edward McMellon and Richard Murphy*). The defense team conveyed to jurors and laypeople (in the general populace) that if you were not a cop, you could not conceptualize danger; hence, you would be unable to understand why the officers killed Amadou Diallo. Rather, you should have sympathy for police officers because of dangerous situations that police officers sometimes encounter.

To make a point that a police officer encounters danger like no other person, the defense team in the Diallo case put a well-known police scholar, Dr. James Fyfe, on the witness stand. In his testimony, Fyfe, a former cop turned academician, spoke to the dangers of police work and how laypeople would not be able to understand. In other words, the defense endowed itself with knowledge of policing, then, with Fyfe's help, it used the information in a manner that was helpful to it (defense). One would expect that the prosecution would have endowed itself with knowledge of policing as I called for in a previous section of this chapter—but it did not. Fyfe's testimony was never rebutted nor did the prosecution present its own policing expert. From media reports we know that Fyfe's testimony had a powerful impact on the jurors. Jurors walked away believing what the defense expert had told them (Waldman, 2000, p. B5). The jurors accepted that since they were not and had never been police officers, they were not qualified to second-guess a police officer's split-second actions. Additionally, media reports also revealed that some jurors expressed dismay at Dr. Fyfe's testimony not being rebutted (Waldman, 2000, p. B5). Obviously, many jurors are reluctant to second-guess police officers. This is an impediment to the prosecution of police officers for police brutality. But it is a problem that prosecutors can get around by presenting experts to rebut defense testimony.

What Makes a Police Brutality Case Prosecutable?

In February 2000, a White New Milford, Connecticut, police officer, Scott Smith, was found guilty by a jury of first-degree manslaughter for shooting and killing Franklyn Reid, a Black man, by shooting him in the back (Gottlieb, 2000). It was the first time in Connecticut's history that a police officer was found guilty for an on-duty shooting. In 1997, in New York City, Kevin Cedeno, a Black man, was shot in the back by a New York City police officer as he fled from a nightclub. Though the coroner's report clearly showed that Kevin Cedeno was running away from a police officer when he was shot and killed, the officer told investigators that Cedeno was about to strike him with a machete. (Mcquillan & Garcilazo, 1997). Reid's death and Cedeno's death were very similar (both men were shot in the back, although they did not pose a threat to anyone), yet the Connecticut officer was charged and the New York City officer was not charged.

In another New York City case, on Christmas Day 1997, NYPD officer Michael Davitt, who in 14 years as a police officer had been involved in approximately eight shootings, shot and killed an unarmed Black man, Michael Whitfield (McFadden, 1997). Whitfield ran and hid when he saw police because he knew that there was a warrant out for his not having paid child support. He was following police instructions, coming out from behind a set of boxes with his arms outstretched in a grocery store, when Davitt shot and killed him. Davitt was not indicted.

These three cases are presented to suggest that there is no consistency throughout the country as to the criteria used to determine when a case of police brutality will be prosecuted. Moreover, as indicated earlier, charging decisions and prosecutorial effort tend to reflect the occupational ethos of win at any cost: the prosecutor's sociological baggage and mind-set (e.g., attitude about certain racial groups as well as crime and justice).

CONCLUSION

It appears that race and prosecution intersect. Most of the victims of police brutality are minorities, the officer who harms or kills is White, and the prosecutor who has discretion to pursue the matter is often White. So, it seems inappropriate for many Whites to assert that it is the police, as in "all police," versus minorities. There is not an epidemic problem in America of Black police officers, for example, engaging in racially discriminatory behavior toward Black people. In fact, many Black police associations have aligned themselves with Black citizens. The associations, comprised of Black police officers, are just as critical of police actions against Black people as are Black citizens and Black leaders (see Dulaney, 1996; Cooper, 2001a; Chivers, 2001; National Black Police Association [NBPA] **http://www.blackpolice.org**).

Cincinnati was engulfed in rioting in April 2001 because a White police officer shot and killed a Black male simply because he (the black male) refused to go to jail for minor violations. Many Whites were then and are now unwilling to accept that Black police officers in Cincinnati were just as outraged as the Black community. Black officers in Cincinnati held press conferences and denounced the shooting, yet many White people and some of the mainstream media (national and local) continually described the rioting in Cincinnati as resulting from a phenomenon of the Black citizens versus the police, rather than admitting that there was a problem of White police versus Black people in Cincinnati.

It behooves prosecutors to recognize that there are police officers who commit brutality out of racial animus. In a May 2001 article entitled "Racist Past Catches Up with Mayor," the mayor of York, Pennsylvania, Charlie Robertson, "conceded that he was a racist police officer in the summer of 1969 when three people died during 10 days of rioting" (Ellison, 2001). He has since been charged with the murder of one of those people, a young Black woman, Lillie Belle Allen, the mother of two small children at the time. Robertson admits to shouting "white power" at a rally the night before (Ellison, 2001). His accomplice explains that [on-duty] Officer Robertson told him: "Kill as many niggers as you can" (Ellison, 2001).

In the performance of many acts of racism today, the officer does not use a racial epithet or make an admission that he or she was behaving in a racially discriminatory manner. Such omissions should not be construed or interpreted by a prosecutor to mean that the officer "did not" behave in a racist manner. Once again, in the 21st century, the officer who polices in a racially discriminatory manner will do so with caution, making sure "not" to express his or her subjective state of mind vocally. Sadly, it is not comprehensible to the typical White liberal that racism still exists post–civil rights (movement). If there are racist people in the general population, there must be some in police work.

Lack of indictment for and acquittals of police officers in police brutality trials likely explain why even with the nationwide attention on police brutality and racial profiling in America, some officers are not the least bit deterred. Whether you believe that the officers who killed Amadou Diallo acted properly or improperly, one fact remains: his death has called national attention to how use of force by police can bring a police officer under intense scrutiny from both the media and the criminal justice system and, in rare cases, from an officer's own department. Knowing this, it seems logical that officers who have a propensity to abuse use of force policy would refrain out of fear of scrutiny or prosecution. But to the contrary, the many questionable shootings and physical confrontations in which police have used force, following the Diallo verdict, suggest otherwise. Rather, for many police officers, the acquittal of the officers has meant to them that they are freer than ever to act with impunity.

Successfully prosecuting police officers for police brutality represents formidable challenges. These challenges are not impenetrable. To borrow the words of an attorney commenting on whether a federal prosecution of the officers who killed Amadou Diallo would be successful, "I think that if you prosecute this case in the right way, convictions will be obtained" (Smith and Saltonstall, 2000). Although the attorney was not calling attention to arming oneself with knowledge of the Code, his remarks personify the Code's significance in prosecution of police brutality cases. Prosecutor attention to the secrets of the police subculture (some of which are on public display thanks to generous leaks in recent years) is an absolute necessity. Having a conceptual understanding of the policing subculture enables reasonably deducing what really happened on many scenes. Code knowledge generates needed suspicion and development of legal strategy by which to achieve a criminal conviction in police brutality cases.

Open-minded prosecutors are needed if prosecutions of police officers for police brutality are to occur and have a reasonable likelihood of success. Just as there is a problem with many individuals in society who are intolerant of racial and ethnic diversity, there too is a problem with prosecutors who do not prosecute because of their racial or ethnic animus or biases. Not any less problematic is the prosecutor who denies, because of privilege, naiveté, or even intentional disregard, the existence of the police brutality reported to him or her. There is something wrong with prosecutors automatically accepting the authoritative report of police officers without concern for a wealth of evidence and common sense that show how police reports can be—and often are—molded by officers to either mitigate the use of force or outright deny the occurrence of use of force. These phenomena coupled with the prosecutor's marginalization of the victim because of the person's social status, race, or ethnicity stand in the way of officers ever having to take responsibility for criminal wrongdoing because a police brutality case is never brought. No doubt, prosecutorial inattention to police brutality condones police brutality.

Finally, this piece has focused on the role of police officers and prosecutors in prosecuting brutality. These issues must be explored in other analyses, in more depth, to understand whether and how stereotypical perceptions of minorities lead prosecutors and judges to blame the police brutality on the victim. For example, in a presentation at the Alternatives to the Use of Lethal Force by Police Conference in June 2000, the Diallo case defense expert witness, Dr. James Fyfe, described the neighborhood where Amadou Diallo was killed as a "terrible" place, saying that the officers were not in a civilized community but on a battlefield (though this neighborhood was not then or now among New York City's most crime-ridden neighborhoods). Fyfe described Diallo as bearing responsibility for his own death for not following the instructions of officers. He went on to explain that the reason that the officers fired so many shots was because Diallo was so "strong" that he remained standing erect. Testimony of this sort and victim-blaming in general do not increase the probability that an officer will be convicted for an act constituting police brutality. Moreover, these xenophobic characterizations often fuel judge instructions to juries that are riddled with victim-blaming suppositions. What should be determined to have been a crime is then deduced to be a mistake or "terrible" happening that was avoidable had the victim not contorted his or her body "so" and had the victim not been recalcitrant, but simply submitted to the police inquiry without questioning authority.

Finally, the phrase "insufficient evidence" is commonly heard by minorities as to why a prosecutor will not seek charges against a police officer who engaged in police brutality. This chapter has demonstrated that whether or not evidence is deemed insufficient is often based on the color of the prosecutor's skin. After all, life experiences had by a prosecutor as well as the cultural and socialization processes that he or she has undergone determine in large part whether or not an act is perceived as police brutality or racist.

REFERENCES

American Friends Service Committee. (1999). **http://www.afsc**

Armstrong, K., & Possley, M. (1999, January 10). How prosecutors sacrifice justice to win: The verdict: Dishonor. *Chicago Tribune*, pp. 1, 8.

Baldus, D., Woodworth, G., & Pulaski, C. (1990). *Equal justice and the death penalty: A legal and empirical analysis.* Boston: Northeastern University Press.

Barkan, S., & Cohn, S. (1998). Racial prejudice and support by whites for police use of force. *Justice Quarterly, 15,* 743–753.

Barker, T. (1978). An empirical study of police deviance other than corruption. *Journal of Police Science and Administration, 6* (3), 264–272.

Barnes, A. (2000). *Say it loud: Middle-class Blacks talk about racism and what to do about it.* Cleveland, OH: The Pilgrim Press.

Barnicle, M. (2001, June 10). Black clergy must face up to AIDS menace. *New York Daily News,* p. 40.

Barry, D. (2000, February 27). Diallo legacy: Myriad questions about tactics for policing streets. *New York Times,* p. A1.

Barry, D., & Waldman, A. (2000, February 22). Erecting a blue wall of silence. *New York Times,* p. B1.

Bils, J., & Possley, M. (1995, November 4). Judge rules Cruz innocent: Nacarico case still open after 12 years. *Chicago Tribune,* p.1.

Birkbeck, C., & Gabaldon, L. (1996). Avoiding complaints: Venezuelan police officers' situational criteria for the use of force against citizens. *Policing & Society,* 6, 113–129.

Bowers, W., Stein, B., & Sandys, M. (2001). Symposium race, crime and the Constitution: Article, death sentencing in black and white: An empirical analysis of the role of jurors' race and jury racial composition. *University of Pennsylvania Journal of Constitutional Law,* 3, 171–273.

Boyer, B., & Gibbons, T. (2000, Novemeber 3). Ruling upholds officer's dismissal; Christopher DiPasquale killed an unarmed driver. The FOP was "extremely disappointed" by the ruling. *Philadelphia Inquirer,* p. B1.

Brennan, C. (2001, May 2). No love lost between campaigns. *Philadelphia Daily News,* p. 5.

Brunknow, A., & Spencer, K. (2000, September 2). No indictment in police shooting. *Omaha World Herald.* Retrieved September 2, 2000, from the World Wide Web: **http://www.omaha.com**

Caparella, K. (2000, May 10). DA hires top-gun Sprague. He'll handle fight over cop rulings. *Philadelphia Daily News,* p.31.

Cascio, W. (1977). Formal education and police officers performance. *Journal of Police Science & Administration,* 89–96.

Casimir, L., Fenner, A., & O'Shaughnessy, P. (1999, March 26). Blacks, Latinos: Cops harass us, young men call tactics offensive and degrading. *New York Daily News.* Retrieved from the World Wide Web on May 27, 2001: **http://www.nydailynews.com**

Castaneda, R. (2001, June 8). Jury rejects Laurel officers' account of arrest. *Washington Post,* p. B5.

Chevigny, P. (1969). *Police power: Police abuses in New York City.* New York: Vintage.

Chevigny, P. (1995). *Edge of the knife: Police violence in the Americas.* New York: New Press.

Chivers, C. (2000, July 28). Grand jury clears detective in killing of unarmed guard. *New York Times,* p. 1.

Chivers, C. (2001, April 3). Alienation is a partner for black officers. *New York Times,* p. A1.

Christopher, W. (1991). *Report of the Independent Commission on the Los Angeles Police Department.* Los Angeles: The Christopher Commission.

Cohen, A. (2000, March 6). Gangsta cops: As the LAPD scandal keeps growing, a city asks itself, how could the police have gone so bad? *Time Magazine,* 30–34.

Cohen, B., & Chaiken, J. (1972). *Police Background Characteristics & Performance.* New York: Rand.

Coke, T. (1994). Note: Lady justice may be blind, but is she a soul sister? Race-neutrality and the idea of representative juries. *New York University Law Review 69,* 327–386.

Colangelo, L., & Marzulli, J. (2000, October 6). Rudy hits racial profiling charge. *New York Daily News,* p. 43.

Cole, D. (1999). *No equal justice: Race and class in the American justice system.* New York: The New Press.

Cooper, C. (1995, October 6). The O. J. Simpson trial and rotten apples: Academics are to blame for the neglect of police racism unmasked by the O. J. Simpson trial. *Times Higher Education Supplement,* p. 12.

Cooper, C. (2000, July 21). Entrenched subculture is at root of police brutality and bias cases. *Philadelphia Inquirer,* p. A27.

Cooper, C. (2001a). An afro-centric perspective on policing. In G. Alpert and R. Dunham (Eds.), *Critical issues in policing* (pp. 376–400). Prospect Heights, IL: Waveland Press.

Cooper, C. (2001b, April). *The racism of white liberalism.* Paper presented at the meeting of the Midwest Sociological Society, St. Louis, Mo.

Crank, J. (1997). *Understanding police culture.* Cincinnati: Anderson Publishing.

Crank, J., Payne, B., & Jackson, S. (1993). Police belief—systems and attitudes regarding persistent police problems. *Criminal Justice and Behavior, 20-2,* 199–221.

Davis, M. (2000, January 30). Friendly fire victims haunt fellow police. *Providence Journal,* p. A1.

Death Penalty Information Center (2000). *The Death Penalty in 2000: Year end report. A watershed year of change: New revelations about death penalty reverse years of division.* Washington, DC.

Dirrane v. The Brookline Police Department, et al.; Commonwealth of Massachusetts; Norfolk County; Case no. 99-00484.

Dulaney, M. (1996). *Black police in America.* Bloomington: Indiana University Press.

Dunne, J. R. (1991, March 20). *Hearings before the subcommittee on Civil and Constitutional Rights, House of Representatives.* Washington, D.C., 102nd Congress, 1st Session, 348.

Dvorak, P. (1997, February 1). NOPD cop held as accessory to woman's murder, woman's body found after 3 weeks. *The Times-Picayune,* p. A1.

Egan, T. (1999, March 1). Soldiers of the drug war remain on duty. *New York Times,* p. A1.

Ellison, M. (2001, May 19). *Racist past catches up with the mayor.* Retrieved May 19, 2001, from the World Wide Web: **http://www.theage.com.au**

Fried, J. (1999, May 28). Prosecutors finish case against remaining officers in torture trial. *New York Times,* p. A14.

Fyfe, J. (Ed.). (1982). *Readings on police use of deadly force* Washington, DC: Police Foundation.

Fyfe, J. (1995). Training to reduce police-civilian violence. In W. Gellar and H. Toch (Eds.), *And justice for all: Understanding and controlling police abuse of force* (pp. 163–176). Washington, DC: Police Executive Research Forum.

Gearty, R., Siegel, J., & Marzulli. J. (1995, May 23). Wall of silence too high: Bratton. *New York Daily News,* p. 15.

Gifis, S. (1996). *Barron's law dictionary.* Hauppauge, NY: Barron's Educational Series.

Glaberson, W. (1989a, March 15). 2 New York City transit officers are guilty in false-arrest scheme. *New York Times,* p. A1.

Glaberson, W. (1989b, February 13). 2 women deny being victims of sex abuse. *New York Times,* p. B4.

Goldstein, J. (1960). Police discretion not to invoke the criminal process: Low visibility decisions in the administration of justice. *Yale Law Journal, 69,* 543–594.

Gonzalez, C., & Spencer, K. (2000, August 13). Handling of shooting called gutsy by some. *Omaha World-Herald,* p. 1A.

Gottlieb, R. (2000, March 14). Manslaughter; Guilty: In hushed courtroom, a historic verdict. *Hartford Courant,* p. A1.

Halbfinger, D. (1998, March 12). Officer cleared in kicking incident. *New York Times,* p. B4.

Harrison, E. (1992, December 19). 2 white policemen fired in beating of black colleague; Race relations: The clash continues to heat up tensions in Nashville. Some say such incidents are the norm. *Los Angeles Times,* p. A31.

Human Rights Watch. (1998). *Shielded from justice. Police brutality and accountability in the United States.* New York: Author.

Jo Patterson, M. J., & Roberts, R. (2001, May 3). Official says cop tormented his victim. *The Star-Ledger.* Retrieved May 3, 2001, from the World Wide Web: **http://www.nj.com/news**

Kappeler, V., Sluder, R., & Alpert, G. (1998). *Forces of deviance* (2nd ed.). Prospect Heights, IL: Waveland Press.

Kelling, G. (1997). Efforts to reduce police brutality should not interfere with effective crime control. In *Police brutality* (1999) (pp. 48–51). San Diego: Greenhaven Press.

Kertscher, T. (2000, November 2). Jones abused power, suit alleges: Officers say he ordered drugs planted in retaliation. *Journal Sentinel.* Retrieved June 12, 2001, from the World Wide Web: **http://www.jsonline.com**

Kidwell, David, & Tanfani, Joseph (September 8, 2001). Two ex-officers plead guilty, help prosecutors. Retrieved September 8, 2001 from the World Wide Web: **http://www.miami.com/herald**

Kifner, J. (1997, August 25). Nurse claims staff cover-up on Louima. *New York Times,* p. B1.

Knapp Commission Report on Police Corruption. (1973). New York: George Braziller.

Kriegel, M. (1998, March 11). Cop acquitted in maiming: Verdict stuns kin of man who can never father kids. *New York Daily News.* Retrieved on June 11, 2001, from World Wide Web: **http://www.nydailynews.com**

LaKamp, P. (1995, March 1). Troopers unpoliced. The *Post Standard,* pp. A1, 8, 9.

Levine, R., & Neuffer, E. (1987, November 24). 4 New York transit officers accused of unlawful arrests. *New York Times,* p. A1.

Lhotka, W., Hollinshed, D., Jonsson, G., & O'Connor, P. (2000, August 29). County grand jury declines to indict officers in killings; Shootings of two on restaurant lot sparked protests; Federal inquiry continues. *The St. Louis Post-Dispatch,* p. A1.

Maas, P. (1973). *Serpico.* New York: Viking Press.

MacDonald, H. (2001). The Myth of Racial Profiling. *City Journal, 11,* (2).

Maude Stout v. A.T. Gallemore, 138 Kan. 385; 26 P.2d 573; 1933 Kan. LEXIS 210. (1933).

McFadden, R. (1997, December 27). After man is slain by officer, anger and calls for patience. *New York Times,* p. B1.

McGriff, M. (1999, May 28). Officer on patrol awaiting disciplinary hearing. *Philadelphia Tribune,* p. 3A.

McKinnon, J. (2000, February 9). Cooperstein not guilty; Jurors say policeman acted within law in fatal shooting of motorist. *Pittsburgh Post-Gazette,* p. A1.

McPhee, M. (2000, June 17). Report slams NYPD: Accused of racial profiling by rights panel. *New York Daily News,* p. 2.

Mcquillan, A., & Garcilazo, M. (1997, April 8). Machete teen shot in back. *New York Daily News.* Retrieved June 11, 2001 from the World Wide Web: **http://www.nydailynews.com**

Medina, R., & Lucey, C. (2000, July 24). Cop rallies: Pro and con supporters and critics raise voices. *Philadelphia Daily News,* p.7.

Mollen Commission. (1994). *Commission Report: Commission to Investigate Allegations of Police Corruption and the Anti-Corruption Procedures of the Police Department.* New York: City of New York.

Mozingo, J. (2000, February 6). New Claremont chief had role in LAPD spying case. *Los Angeles Times,* p. B1.

National Black Police Association. Retrieved May 27, 2001, from World Wide Web: **http://www.blackpolice.org**

Rudy's toughest foe: In New York, the mayor may be his own worst enemy. *Newsweek 135* (14), 39. Retrieved June 1, 2001, from the World Wide Web: Missouri Education and Research Libraries Info Network, Expanded Academic ASAP, Article 60836048.

New York City Police Department. Patrol Guide, General Regulations, Procedure No. 203-12, 01/01/00 New York: Author.

Niederhoffer, A. (1969). *Behind the shield: The police in urban society.* Garden City, NY: Doubleday.

Nossiter, A. (December 19, 1994). Police in New Orleans: Film noir in real life. *New York Times,* p.14.

Nugent, D. (1994). Judicial Bias. *Clev. St. L. Rev.* 42, 1, 20.

O'Connor, A. (1999, September 2). Riverside force rife with racism, black officer says; Police: Complaint to state says he is on leave because of post-traumatic stress. Chief avows 'no tolerance' for bigotry. *Los Angeles Times,* p. A1.

Ousley, Y. (1999, July 9). Round 3 for ex-cop: Officials file motion to rearrest officer who shot and killed teen in car. *Philadelphia Daily News,* p. 4.

People of the State of New York v. Kenneth Boss, Sean Carroll, Edward McMellon and Richard Murphy; State of New York Bronx Supreme Court.

Perlstein, M. (1998, August 27). Ex-cop sentenced for cocaine ring: His testimony helped convict others. *The Times-Picayune,* p. B1.

Pierre-Pierre, G. (1995, June 10). Expect suspensions, even dismissals, Bratton warns. *New York Times,* p. A23.

Practising Law Institute. (2000). *How to handle unreasonable force litigation: Prosecution and defense strategies in police misconduct cases.* Practising Law Institute: New York.

Prial, F. (1987, February 27). Judge acquits Sullivan in shotgun slaying of Bumpurs. *New York Times,* p. B1.

Purdum, T. (1989, March 16). Prosecuting officers: False-arrest case shows it can take time and publicity to redress wrongs. *New York Times,* p. B3.

Quinnipiac College Polling Institute. (1999, June 17). *New York is safer, but police brutality is a problem.* Hamden, CT.

Raab, S. (1987, January 14). Civilian describes 'struggle' before shooting of Bumpurs. *New York Times,* Sec. B, p. 2.

Racher, D. (1999, May 27). Judge throws out request to rearrest cop in slaying. *Philadelphia Daily News,* p. 22.

————.(1999, June 18). Judge: Arrest them she orders 2 parole officers charged in Griffin slaying. *Philadelphia Daily News,* p. 6.

————. (2000, December 23). Private complaint in killing, dismissed attorney lacks standing to charge parole officers, court says. *Philadelphia Daily News,* p. 6.

Reuss-Ianni, E. (1982). *Two cultures of policing.* Englewood Cliffs, NJ: Transaction.

Schmitt, C. (1991, December 8). Plea bargaining favors Whites, as Blacks, Hispanics pay price. *San Jose Mercury News,* p. 1A.

Scott v. United States, (1978) 436 U.S. 128; 98 S. Ct. 1717; 56 L. Ed. 2d 168; 1978 U.S. LEXIS 89.

Scrutton, Lord Justice. (1921). The work of Commercial courts. *Cambridge,* 1, L.J.1, 8.

Sexton, J. (1995, March 3). Prosecutor is sympathetic, but officer is indicted. *New York Times,* p. A1.

Skolnick, J., & Fyfe, J. (1993). *Above the law: Police and the excessive use of force.* New York: Free Press.

Smith, G., & Saltonstall, D. (2000, February 27). Federal rights prosecution possible, suit is likely. *New York Daily News.* Retrieved May 27, 2001, from the World Wide Web: **http://www.nydailynews.com**

Smith, J. (2000, May 3) No federal charges in shootings. *Philadelphia Daily News,* p. 6.

Smothers, R. (December 18, 1992). 2 Nashville officers dismissed in beating. *New York Times,* p. A7.

Sontag, D., & Barry, D. (1997, September 17). Using settlements to gauge police abuse: The price of brutality. *New York Times,* p. A1.

Sounds of silence: Cop's federal trial in choke-hold death puts spotlight on "blue wall." (1998, September 15). *Law Enforcement News,* p. 7.

Stark, R. (1987). Deviant places: A theory of the ecology of crime. *Criminology, 25,* 893–909.

Stewart, S. A. (1993, March 16). Defense's turn in King case: "Educating the jury" is key for police officers on trial. *USA Today,* p. 2A.

Stoddard, E. (1968). The informal "code" of police deviancy: A group approach to "Blue Coat Crime." *The Journal of Criminal Law, Criminology and Police Science,* 59 (2), 201–213.

Taylor, L., & Mullen, S. (2001, April 26). Race in DA's race. *Philadelphia Daily News,* p. 7.

Tennessee v. Garner, 471 U.S. 1; 105 S. Ct. 1694; 85 L. Ed. 2d 1; 1985 U.S. LEXIS 195; 53 U.S.L.W. 4410.

Terry, D. (1995, August 28). Philadelphia shaken by criminal police officers. *New York Times,* p. A1.

They saw no evil. (1995, May 23). *New York Daily News,* p. 28.

Troutt, D. (1999). Screws, Koon, and routine aberrations: The use of fictional narratives in federal police brutality prosecutions. *New York University Law Review,* 74, (1) 18–122.

United States of America v. Stacey C. Koon, Laurence M. Powell, Timothy E. Wind and Theodore J. Briseno, 833 F. Supp. 769; 1993 U.S. Dist. LEXIS 17926; 93 Daily Journal DAR 10845.

United States Code Service. (2001). LEXIS Law Publishing.

United States Department of Justice (year not indicated). *Addressing police misconduct: Laws enforced by the United States Department of Justice.* Washington, DC.

U.S. Department of Justice, Bureau of Justice Statistics Law Enforcement Management and Administrative. (1999). *Statistics, 1999: Data for individual state and local agencies with 100 or more officers.* Washington, DC: Government Printing Office.

Waldman, A. (2000, February 28). The Diallo case: The trial; Too many in the court of public opinion, the prosecution is now the accused. *New York Times,* p. B5.

Waldman, A. (2001, June 6). Officer guilty in 1999 shooting of a teenager. *New York Times,* p. B1.

Warnick, M. (1999, March 23). Police homicide charges shake Pittsburgh: After three deaths, some see pattern of abuse by White officers against Black motorists. *Chicago Tribune,* p. 8.

Washington, L. (1999, May 21). Different standard of justice for police. *Philadelphia Tribune.* Retrieved June 17, 2001, from the World Wide Web: **http://www.phila-tribune.com**

————.(2000, April 11). A new weapon against police abuse. *Philadelphia Tribune.* Retrieved June 17, 2001, from the World Wide Web: **http://www.phila-tribune.com**

Weich, R., & Angulo, C. (2000). *Justice on trial: Racial disparities in the American criminal justice system.* Washington, DC: Leadership Conference on Civil Rights; Leadership Conference Education Fund.

Weiser, B. (1999, February 10). Some favor federal role in police shooting inquiry. *New York Times,* p. B6.

Weiss, M. (1995, June 7). "Wild bunch" witness: Lawman: I saw cops go crazy. *New York Daily News,* Editorial page.

Wilkinson, H., & McCain, M. (2001, May 8). Officer indicted on least serious charge. *Cincinnati Enquirer.* Retrieved May 8, 2001, from World Wide Web: **http://enquirer.com**

Williams, J. (2000). *How to handle unreasonable force litigation: Prosecution and defense strategies in police misconduct cases.* New York: Practising Law Institute.

Worden, R. (1995). The causes of police brutality: Theory and evidence on police use of force. In W. Gellar and H. Toch (Eds.), *And justice for all: Understanding and controlling police abuse of force* (pp. 31–60). Washington, DC: Police Executive Research Forum.

Wright, B. (1993). *Black robes, white justice.* Secaucus, NJ: Carol Publishing Group.

Zambroski, J., Shafer, S., & Tangonan, S. (2000, March 3). Louisville police chief fired. *The Courier Journal,* p. A1.

Zamora, J., & Hendricks, T. (1998, October 1). Witness account assert that officers 'shot even when safe.' *San Francisco Chronicle,* p. A1.

10

The Roads Not Taken

Improving the Use of Civilian Complaint Review Boards and Implementation of the Recommendations from Investigative Commissions

Karen J. Terry and Heath B. Grant

> *It is no coincidence that the only two times in the past twenty years that fighting corruption has been a priority in the Department was when an independent Commission publicly reviewed and disclosed the Department's failures to keep its own house in order. (Mollen, 1994, p. 6)*

In modern societies, the police "are the central institution concerned with maintaining order and enforcing the law. Beyond that, they are expected to be a symbol of order and of consensus about the existing order" (Morgan and Smith, 1989, p. 1). Individuals entering the profession of policing go through selection and training procedures that aim to exclude individuals who will not be capable of maintaining the law to the highest standards (Yuille, 1986; Spielberger, 1979; Niederhoffer, 1967). Nonetheless, some officers will abuse their legitimate powers. Those who are most often adversely affected by police abuse of power are minorities, according to much of the research on excessive use of force (Condon, 1986).

Throughout the history of policing in the United States, a myriad of investigative Commissions (e.g., Wickersham, Kerner, Knapp, Christopher) have been appointed to investigate allegations of police abuse of power. These Commissions have repeatedly offered recommendations for improving the accountability of the police, both hierarchically and democratically. Unfortunately, these recommendations are cyclical, with three main recurring recommendations continually reappearing: improve recruitment and training, improve police-community relations, and improve the existing police complaints system. However, given the reactionary and political nature of Commission formation, when the recommendations are implemented, approaches tend to lack the necessary long-term planning and understanding of underlying issues required to be truly effective.

Each of these recommendations is closely related; in order to improve relations between the police and the community, it is necessary to improve recruitment and training standards for officers, and offer outlets for citizens to voice their complaints in a manner that is perceived of as legitimate and fair. Since the riots of the 1960s, which resulted from strained relations between minority communities and the police, there has been a focus on the reasons why minorities are more often victims of police abuse of power than Whites. A number of explanations have been offered, including that minorities are more frequently involved in the violent and related crimes that result in increased interactions with the police, particularly in cities with aggressive zero-tolerance strategies in place to eradicate crime. Some, however, have refuted this overrepresentation in type of criminal offending. After taking into consideration varying crime rates, one such study shows that Blacks are still stopped 23% more often than Whites (Spitzer, 1999). Despite these everyday differences in police-community interactions, it is only after severe cases of excessive force or corruption against minorities and, often, media intervention that such abuses come to the public attention (Skolnick and McCoy, 1985).

Although the underlying rationale behind the Commission recommendations is clear, one has to recognize that the implementation of any departmental change policy or practice does not occur within a vacuum. Reaching the desired long-term outcome of sustained improvements in police-community relations does invariably require a reexamination of recruitment policies to increase minority representation in American law enforcement agencies. However, a department's ability to mobilize minority representation will be dependent on the perceived legitimacy of policing in the community; a fact that must be addressed with increased efforts to improve day-to-day interactions between the police and its communities. Similarly, where perceived abuses do occur a viable police complaints system must be in place to increase departmental accountability to the civil rights of its citizenry.

The aim of this chapter is to analyze the root of problems between the police and minorities within the context of the history of investigative Commissions in the United States. The cyclical nature of Commission recommendations, as well as the continued difficulties in reaching the desired long-term goal of improved police-community relations for many departments, is the product of a failure to truly address the full scope of the problems, even where reactive approaches (i.e., civilian oversight systems) are implemented with the best of intentions.

PROBLEMS ENCOUNTERED IN POLICING MINORITY COMMUNITIES

Understanding the Nature and Quality of Police-Community Interactions

If there is a question as to why relations are strained between the police and minority communities, particularly the African American community, one needs only to look at the nature of interactions between the two groups. One New York report indicates that the police stop both Blacks and Hispanics at a higher rate than White citizens (Spitzer, 1999). Nationwide statistics show that while Blacks represent only 12% of the population, they represent 30% of all arrests and are three times as likely to be shot by the police than Whites (Walker, Spohn, and DeLone, 1996). Though these statistics are representative of interactions in the 1990s, the overrepresentation of minorities in the criminal justice system was even more pervasive in the 1960s. Riots erupted throughout the country for the first five years of the decade, and the cause of the riots was almost uniformly negative interactions between the police and the African American community.

The Kerner Commission, appointed in 1965 by President Lyndon B. Johnson, asserted that the rioting was caused by the same problems that had been pervasive in the communities in the beginning of the century (e.g., police abuse of power, disproportionate focus on minority communities), and that nothing was done to address these problems. Yet the problems were not eliminated in the 1960s and resurfaced as a nationwide issue following the 1991 beating of Rodney King. This incident, which involved the beating of a Black man by four White officers after a car chase, would not have come to the attention of the public had a citizen not been videotaping the incident. This brought the issue to public attention, along with the realization that racial tensions had not completely subsided but were merely concealed.

The nature of police interactions makes prosecution for incidents such as the beating of Rodney King difficult, as the use of coercive force is necessary to maintain order and enforce the law (Bittner, 1974; Klockars, 1995; Reiss, 1971). Although policing involves tasks directed at maintaining a social order, the underlying tactics for this peacekeeping include the power to wield legal sanctions, and, ultimately, the use of reasonable force (Reiner, 1994). When the police use excessive force beyond that necessary to maintain order, a violation has occurred. However, the distinction between "reasonable" and "excessive" force is often ambiguous and may be interpreted differently according to subjective values.

Discretion as an Underlying Issue

Embedded in the controversy over reasonableness of force is the concept of discretion, or the individual interpretation of the law in enforcement decisions. "A constant inherent in police work" (Sherman, 1974, p. 12), discretion allows officers to be recognized as "street-level politicians" (Muir, 1977) who possess the broad powers of decision making that will determine the policies representative of the department. The level of discretion increases as one moves down the hierarchy within a police force (Wilson, 1968, p. 7). This means that patrol officers use discretion in nearly every situation that occurs, including situations that require use of coercive force. Discretion cannot be eliminated because every situation that an officer encounters cannot be predicted. The question then becomes, does an officer's discretion to act on the law differ between contact with White citizens and minority citizens?

Much attention is being given now to the police use of racial profiling to stop minorities who are either driving or walking in what is described as "pretextual" stops (e.g., *Whren v. United States*). Though no analyses currently provide accurate statistics on the degree to which racial profiling occurs—primarily because of the lack of reporting on all stops conducted—two reports were recently published citing that minority motorists, in particular African Americans, are more likely to be stopped than White motorists (Spitzer, 1999; Harris, 1997). Harris claims that the offense of "driving while black," or DWB, is a result of the war on drugs, though pretextual stops also serve as a vehicle to search for weapons. Pretextual stops and the frequency of them are newsworthy of late, but it is the use of deadly force on minorities that has previously been the focus of concern. In describing deadly force, one researcher claims that the police have two trigger fingers: one for Blacks and one for Whites (Fyfe, 1978). It is the deadly force incidents that prompt Commission investigations, though the daily interactions between the police and minority citizens and use of racial profiling are the primary cause of tension between the two populations (Condon, 1986; Walker, Spohn, and DeLone, 1996).

Though there are few objections to such findings of differential interactions across ethnic groups described above, the question remains: How much of this difference is fueled by differential involvement in crimes, and how much is the result of misunderstanding or bias on the part of officers? Given the tremendous role discretion invariably plays in determining the outcomes of police-community interactions, an inability to communicate effectively and subsequent misunderstandings between the police and community can lead to poor relations, poor relations may lead to more situations being inappropriately assessed, and more situations being inappropriately assessed may lead to improper use of force. The more pervasive such situations are in a community or city, the greater the wall that develops between police and the community. Even where people have received a negative outcome (i.e., traffic stop), the ultimate determination of its fairness can be determined by the degree of respect evidenced by the officer involved.

Cycle of Misunderstanding Leading to the Development of an "Us versus Them" Mentality for Both Police and the Community

The objective of policing is to maintain a social order, which refers to the balance between the rights of individuals versus the power that is delegated to the police. The status of this relationship is determined in part by public opinion of police accountability, which is influenced significantly by media coverage of negative incidents (Skolnick and McCoy, 1985). Because these negative incidents so commonly involve minority citizens, an "us versus them" view generates between the minority communities and the police alike, causing a polarization of the relationship between the two in a manner similar to the era of civil unrest in the 1960s (Bayley, 1991).

The Commissions investigating incidents of brutality often recognize the strained police-community relations as a problem, and they even go as far as to suggest reforms for improving these relations. The reforms generally include the modification of recruitment and training standards, getting to know the community that is being policed and the problems therein, and improving the system of civilian oversight. Yet these are long-range goals, requiring a complete overhaul of the system and corroboration between the police and the community.

THE CYCLICAL NATURE OF POLICING INVESTIGATIVE COMMISSIONS

There are a number of Commissions and investigative Task Forces that were influential throughout the 20th century in investigations of police abuse of power. The ones discussed here include the Wickersham Commission, Kerner Commission, Knapp Commission, New York State Deadly Force Task Force, Mollen Commission, and Christopher Commission. Though this list of Commissions is by no means exhaustive, it is representative of the various investigations conducted on police throughout the century. Table 1 summarizes the findings and results of these Commissions.

TABLE 1 Major Commission Findings and Recommendations

Commission/ Task Force	City/State/ Country	Incident	Underlying Problem	Recommendations
Wickersham	United States	Prohibition, increasing crime rate, need to reevaluate juvenile justice, evaluate the adult criminal justice process	Increasing crime rate, particularly organized crime, need for evaluation of governmental agencies and adequacy of the criminal justice process	• Social awareness of problems between police and minority communities • Establish a complaints system
Kerner	United States	Riots of the 1960s, complaints by minorities about police abuse of power	Police misconduct, lack of accountability to all citizens, no oversight of police procedures	• Better recruitment and training standards • Accountability to the community • Establish mechanisms for registering complaints
Knapp	New York	Widespread corruption and bribery, particularly amongst undercover units in New York City	Lack of oversight of police procedures, decreasing hierarchical accountability, identification of "blue wall of silence"	• Reorganize IAD • Civilian oversight of the police • Create post of State Special Prosecutor
Deadly Force	New York	Numerous cases of police use of deadly force, disproportionate against minorities	Deteriorating police-community relations, increasing crime rate and therefore increasing interaction between police and citizens	• Create a fair and impartial mechanism by which citizens can register complaints against the police • Enhanced police-community understanding • Expanded minority recruitment

Commission	City	Event	Problem	Recommendations
Christopher	Los Angeles	Excessive use of force by the police against a Black motorist, subsequent riots and inability of the LAPD to adequately control the situation	Lack of accountability, lack of repercussions for misconduct, concealment of brutality	• Implement structural changes in recruitment, selection, training, and evaluation • Establish a new system for handling complaints and improve civilian oversight • Implement a community-based policing model
Mollen	New York	Corruption scandal in specific undercover units, linking of corruption and brutality	Lack of accountability in under-cover units, concealment of corruption and brutality by officers and management	• Improve screening, recruitment, and training (for new and in-service officers) • Increase and improve supervision • Reform internal/external oversight • Enhance sanctions for brutality and corruption

The Foundation: The Wickersham Commission (1931)

I. Incident Prior to 1929, there were no external investigations of police departments or the actions of officers therein. Yet by the end of the 1920s President Herbert Hoover felt that there were a number of social issues that required investigation and thus established the Wickersham Commission. In particular, he was concerned about the effects of Prohibition on both the political agenda and law enforcement. There was also a concern at this time on the increasing crime rates, particularly in regard to the organized crime in cities such as Chicago. In total, the Commission produced 14 volumes of reports on crime, crime statistics, and the criminal justice process. One of the most important reports to surface from this investigation was the *Report on Lawlessness in Law Enforcement,* examining the problem of extracting coerced confessions through the technique of the "third degree" (National Commission on Law Observance and Enforcement, 1931). The three authors of this report— Zechariah Chafee Jr., Walter H. Pollak, and Carl S. Stern—were active in promoting civil rights; not a politically influential position at the time and considered radical (Walker, Spohn, & DeLone, 1996).

II. Recommendations For the first time, police misconduct became a national issue and leaders in the policing community—in particular, O. W. Wilson—began forming a system whereby citizens could register complaints against the police. Internal systems of investigating complaints were established with the development of Internal Affairs units. Although the main focus of the Wickersham Commission was on issues other than police abuses of power, it served as a precursor to future Commissions, most notably President Johnson's Commission formed in 1965—the Kerner Commission.

The Kerner Commission (1965)

I. Incident In the 1960s, relations between the police and the public were deteriorating, which was a contributing factor to the era of civil unrest in the United States. Political and minority groups began calling for professionalism and accountability amongst the police as well as an adequate system of redress for victims of police abuses. The majority of complaints about the police were in regards to the constitutional rights of individuals and the amount of power that the police were allowed to exercise. Police powers were limited for the first time with the ruling on several landmark civil rights cases, including *Mapp v. Ohio* (1961), *Escobedo v. Illinois* (1964), *Miranda v. Arizona* (1966), and *Terry v. Ohio* (1968). Most of the remaining complaints against the police that did not involve constitutional elements alleged police brutality or racial discrimination. Minority groups and political activists complained most vigorously about misconduct, which sparked the debate over control and review mechanisms of police practices. A political axiom surfaced at this time: when an obviously popular solution is not readily available, appoint a Commission (Kerstetter, 1995).

Several Commissions were formed to look at police misconduct, the first and most notable of which was the Kerner Commission, formed by the Johnson administration in 1965. The report found widespread and justified dissatisfaction with the internal review procedures of police practices that were in use (Morris and Hawking, 1970, p. 99). With the dissemination of the Commission's reports in 1967 and the Civil Rights movement as a powerful political force, the period was marked by a greater social awareness amongst all citizens, including the White population, about the need to combat racial injustices by the police.

II. Recommendations Though the Kerner Commission looked at a number of issues involving the minority community (e.g., the level of disorder in the communities, the administration of justice under emergency conditions, and media response to the disorder), a primary focus of the Commission was to recommend effective police reforms. The reforms suggested are many in number, and, if reworded, sound identical to the recommendations made by all other Commissions (Kerner Commission, 1968).

The first recommendation was to eliminate abusive (i.e., aggressive) policing tactics in urban areas, and to ensure protection of residents who live in these areas. They also recommended that "fair and effective mechanisms" be established so that citizens can register complaints, though they did not specify the need for external versus internal mechanisms. They also claim that minority recruitment for the police force is necessary, and that there must be some promotional policy in place so that minorities can proceed hierarchically in the force. In order to improve police-community relations, the Commission recommended that a "community service officer" program be established as well as "innovative programs" to create community support for law enforcement. Though some of these recommendations were implemented—for instance, minority recruitment increased slightly—there was no significant reduction of police brutality or corruption as a result.

In an effort to increase accountability to the community, the Kerner Commission recommended the institution of better recruitment and training standards. As with the Wickersham Commission before it, the establishment of effective mechanisms for registering complaints was also stressed in the Kerner Commission's findings.

The Knapp Commission (1972)

I. Incident In the 1970s, corruption scandals were widespread. Though corrupt practices existed before this time, officers were reluctant to testify against each other because of the alleged "Blue Wall of Silence" or the "Blue Curtain." It was Frank Serpico, a plainclothes officer in the Bronx division of the New York Police Department (NYPD), who originally exposed and testified about the widespread corruption within the NYPD. The allegations of corruption were investigated for two and a half years by the Knapp Commission, and their findings showed that the corruption existed at all levels of the department and in many forms. The main focus of the investigation was on corruption, bribery, and participation in illegal activities (e.g., gambling and prostitution), and two important reforms were proposed in the Commission report (Knapp, 1973).

II. Recommendations The committee recommended that the Internal Affairs Division (IAD) be reorganized and that a post be created to prosecute police officers for corruption. The purpose of both recommendations was to increase accountability of the police, the first hierarchically and the latter democratically. Although these recommendations were implemented, they proved to be largely ineffective. The post of State Special Prosecutor to prosecute officers for corruption dissolved in 1990, though this post never effectively prosecuted officers for cases of police brutality.

The New York State Deadly Force Task Force (1986)

I. Incident In the mid-1980s, at a time when violent crime and drug trafficking were increasing in New York City, NYPD officers committed several acts of deadly force upon citizens. Many of those subject to deadly force by the police were minorities, causing uproar in the community. The mayor, Mario Cuomo, assigned a task force to investigate the causes and, more importantly, the relationship between the police and minority communities. The findings were not surprising; it found that minorities were, in fact, the victims of deadly force disproportionately to White citizens. However, the report found that negative perceptions of the police by minority communities were not most directly a result of the alleged "disproportionality" of use of deadly force. Rather, it was the day-to-day interactions with the police that had the most significant influence, and repeated incidents of discourtesy, disrespect, and use of racially offensive language created the "us versus them" attitude of the communities.

II. Recommendations The task force claimed that these daily interactions "establish the framework within which minorities evaluate all police behavior" (Condon, 1986, p. 7). Though the task force recognized efforts that previously failed to improve relations between the police and minority communities, they suggested strikingly similar reforms: a fair and impartial mechanism by which citizens can register complaints against the police; enhanced police-community understanding; and expanded minority recruitment (Condon, 1986, p. 15). Some of these recommendations were implemented; most notably, the Citizens Complaint Review Board (CCRB) was revised so that it contained only private citizens and no police personnel. However, the changes implemented did not eliminate or even reduce police abuse of power, and soon the NYPD was involved in another corruption scandal.

The Mollen Commission (1994)

I. Incident Six NYPD officers were arrested on drug charges in Suffolk County in 1992, which led to a new inquiry about the department and the appointment of the Mollen Commission. The 1994 report by the Commission indicated that although the corruption charges were not as widespread as those investigated by the Knapp Commission, they were of a more serious nature and based on similar issues in the department. One question asked in the Mollen inquiry was how such serious corruption could have existed in the department for an extended period of time, and it was discovered again that the most significant influence was the code of silence amongst officers. Additionally, they found that everyone from the management to the rank-and-file officers were not adequately managed and charges of corruption were not sufficiently investigated. The crimes included protecting narcotics traffickers, conducting illegal searches and seizures, falsifying records, and committing felonious crimes (e.g., robberies, drug trafficking). An important finding from the Mollen Commission was that it linked corruption and brutality, particularly in areas with a high population of minority citizens (Mollen, 1994).

II. Recommendations The Mollen Commission, like the Knapp Commission, recommended a reform of the IAD and suggested new procedures for monitoring corruption and brutality. Scandals investigated by both the Mollen and the Knapp Commissions involved, on the most serious levels, officers who were involved in undercover or vice quads. Reforms implemented after both Commission reports were intended to improve supervision of officers, reduce corruption and brutality, and increase officer accountability. However, the report from the Mollen Commission noted that it would be challenging to maintain these reforms without independent oversight.

The Christopher Commission

I. Incident The Los Angeles Police Department was also subject to independent review in the early 1990s. The 1991 beating of Rodney King, a Black motorist, by four LAPD officers became a highly publicized case of police use of force when a civilian videotaped the officers beating King with their nightsticks. Despite attempts to register complaints against the police by both King's brother and the civilian who taped the incident, the police dissuaded both from doing so. A formal complaint was only registered after the civilian sent the tape to a national television station for coverage (Skolnick and Fyfe, 1993, pp. 2–3). The Christopher Commission, formed as a result of the King beating, found this type of dissuasion to be common in the department (Skolnick and Fyfe, 1993). The Commission also found widespread evidence of racism and bias within the LAPD and a lack of accountability hierarchically and to the community.

II. Recommendations The Commission recommended a number of reforms, from structural changes to recruitment, and, as with most other Commissions, the need to improve civilian oversight of the police (Christopher Commission, 1991). The report also noted that there was a need to improve community policing and involve the community in assessing which problems needed to be addressed by the police. Because complaints about excessive use of force were rarely reprimanded in the LAPD, the Commission found that management of the officers was inadequate and it was shortly after the publication of the report that Police Chief Darryl Gates stepped down from his position in the department.

The Commission reports have all cited poor police-community relations as an underlying factor in the cases they have investigated, and all have given recommendations on how to improve such relations (see Table 1 for a sample of Commission reports and recommendations).

OUTCOMES OF THE COMMISSIONS: IMPLEMENTING THE REFORMS TO IMPROVE POLICE-COMMUNITY RELATIONS

Improvements in Recruitment and Selection

There has been some, but not much, improvement in the recruitment and selection process; education standards in 1997 were approximately double what they were in 1990 (see Table 2), though less than one-quarter (23.8%) of all city, county, and state agencies require at least some college education. Although one study found that educational standards did not make a difference in the number of complaints filed against officers (Cao and Huang, 2000), others have found that officers with a higher level of education have fewer complaints against them relating to excessive use of force.

TABLE 2   Educational Requirements for New Officer Recruits in City, County, and State Agencies (Department of Justice, 1992; 1999)

	1990 (N = 584)	1997 (N = 651)
Four-year degree	3 (.51%)	13 (2.0%)
Two-year degree	29 (4.9%)	50 (7.7%)
Some college	41 (7.0%)	92 (14.1%)
Total	73 (12.5%)	155 (23.8%)

In addition to education requirements, some departments have residency requirements mandating that officers live within the jurisdiction in which they are policing. This is a recommendation that surfaced from many of the Commissions in the hopes that by living in the communities they police, officers will be better equipped to understand, and thereby interact with its citizenry.

Perhaps the greatest recruitment push resulting from investigative Commissions has been toward greater minority representation within the composition of law enforcement agencies. Recent LEMAS statistics demonstrate that although there has been some improvement in this area within the last 10 years, there is still proportionate ethnic representation in most police forces (Department of Justice, 1999). Racial and ethnic minorities represented 21.5% of local police departments in 1997, compared with just 14.8% in 1987 (Shusta, Levine, Harris, and Wong, 2002).

Improving Accountability Mechanisms: The Formation of Internal Review Processes

Before the 1960s, review of police complaints was an entirely internal process. This internal process of investigating citizen complaints began shortly after the publication of the Wickersham report, which proposed Internal Affairs units. These units operated so that citizens could make complaints in police departments and their complaints would then be investigated at a convenient time by a specialized unit—comprised of police officers. Most complainants were encouraged to withdraw their complaints, and those that were investigated were most often unsubstantiated or the officer was exonerated (Terrill, 1991). It was in the 1960s that various citizen groups began to demand some form of civilian review for complaints, contending that the existing means for seeking redress were ineffective (Goldstein, 1990, p. 158). These views peaked in the 1960s with the outbreaks of urban rioting in response to police misconduct. There were several attempts to form civilian review boards, the first of those being in Philadelphia. Though the board survived for nine years, it eventually disbanded.

Experiments with Civilian Oversight

One key concern of all Commission reports is accountability, both hierarchical and democratic. Hierarchical accountability and sound management practices are necessary in order to foster an environment in which individual officers model their own actions based on positive influences exhibited within the department. In order to achieve democratic accountability, most Commissions have cited the need for civilian oversight of the police. Nonetheless, by 1997 only 97 police departments had a system of civilian oversight in place and only 35 of those had a civilian review board with independent investigative authority with subpoena powers (Department of Justice, 1999, pp. 211–282). All civilian review boards vary, and none have higher rates of substantiation for complaints than internal investigative boards. Despite the need for improvement with some of these boards, it is important to retain methods of civilian oversight in order to preserve some form of democratic accountability over the police.

Various Commission reports have claimed that an adequate police complaints system is one of the most important ways for society to maintain a positive social order. Although such a system will not eliminate prejudicial discretion, it can eliminate the ability of an institution to gain an unrestricted power in society. A police complaints system, even if ideal, cannot hope to eliminate all abuses of police power; however, it is one method of maintaining a democratic supervision of the law. It is this system that will alert senior officers to potential problems with officers in the force, thus allowing for actions to be taken to deter future misconduct. It is also one system that can help to instill or revoke public confidence in the police, as those who register complaints are likely to consider the effectiveness of the police complaints system to be based on the way they are treated (Kerstetter, 1995) as well as the outcome of their cases. The paradox of this is that no matter how good the complaints system is it will still elicit negative responses from those involved with it. This is because of its inherent nature of being a system whereby individuals register *complaints,* to the people whom they are complaining about, and then allow for this same group of individuals to investigate their complaints. The only citizens involved with this system are those expressing negative feelings towards the police, and a low rate of substantiated complaints reinforces these negative feelings.

Nearly all Commission reports have suggested that a system of external oversight of the police would serve to reduce tension between the police and the community, particularly minority communities. Though the number of police departments with civilian review boards has increased since the 1960s, only 15% of police departments had implemented such a system. Additionally, all civilian review boards vary significantly in relation to their power to take complaints, investigate complaints, suggest an outcome and offer a reprimand. Unfortunately, there is no agreement as to what the best system of oversight is. While the public wants to have power to oversee the complaint process, complaints are more often substantiated when the police themselves conduct the investigations. Some review boards since the 1960s have achieved success at fulfilling the four goals of civilian oversight—to deter future misconduct, remove deviant officers, satisfy individual complainants, and maintain public confidence in the police. Others have suffered as a consequence of hasty implementation and lack of foresight into problems from previous boards. The bottom line is that the mere existence of a civilian review board will not eradicate tensions between the police and the community. The board must be created so that it is suitable for the community it is serving, and it must have adequate powers to make the process satisfactory to the citizens making the complaints.

Early Citizen Advisory Boards

In 1957, the Philadelphia branch of the ACLU called for the creation of the first civilian review board to reduce the increasing tension between the police and the public, especially amongst minorities. Mayor Richard Dilworth formed the Philadelphia Police Advisory Board, an entirely civilian body, in 1958 despite vehement opposition by the Philadelphia police union. It consisted of five citizens whose responsibilities were to assess complaints of police brutality, false arrest, discrimination charges, or any other wrongful conduct against citizens.

The first problem with the Board was the paradox of its origination: it was created on the premise of moving away from a centralized force of power (the police leading investigations against themselves), and yet it was formed by one authority figure (the mayor) who circumvented the votes of the city council with an executive order (Terrill, 1991). Another problem with the Board was that it lacked a sense of permanency, as the reason for its formation was based on the beliefs of one person. Because the Board was initiated by one executive order and could be rescinded by another, it was also deficient of any legal standing. In addition, there was no widespread political backing for the establishment, with the mayor having overshadowed the requests of the city council. While some minority groups such as the ACLU and the National Association for the Advancement of Colored People (NAACP), endorsed the idea of a civilian review board all citizens did not support it. The White community was at this time demanding more law and order, not less, and other minority groups saw the formation of the Board as a way to merely placate the Black community (Hudson, 1968). The most important reason for the failure of the Board, however, was the single-minded, fierce opposition to the Board by the police.

The primary reason the police were opposed to the initiation of civilian review boards was that they were offended by the notion that their actions would be judged by individuals removed from the situations which they encountered on a daily basis (Goldstein, 1990, p. 158). They considered the civilian review boards to be an "unwarranted political interference in police affairs" (Brown, 1983, p. 16), and they believed that such a model of review would eliminate a large percentage of the initiative, aggressiveness, and necessary discretion that is the basis of police work. Police saw the law as a double-edged sword: they were its enforcers, and at the same time subject to its judgment (Kerstetter, 1995, p. 260). It was feared that the people who made complaints (the "assholes," according to Van Maanen, 1978) would be considered more credible than officers when relating accounts of events, thereby undermining the role of the officers and their moral superiority. They felt that in order to understand the discretion that is crucial to the job and requires an officer to deviate from exact written rules of the law, one must have had experience in the job (Reiner, 1993).

The Ombudsman Model

With the cessation of the civilian review boards of the 1960s, individuals in the 1970s turned increasingly to the courts for restitution (Cheh, 1995). In turn, the government focused on eliminating the misconduct that led to complaints and limiting police malpractice. There was an increase in attempts to improve training programs and styles of police management in order to inculcate higher values in subordinates (Brown, 1983, p. 19). With regards to the complaint review process, the concept of an ombudsman was introduced for the first time. The ombudsman, patterned after that of the Scandinavian system, would be a neutral figure concerned with complaints against *all* public servants, not just the police. Patterns of organizational malpractice would be evaluated rather than just individual complaints, and the ombudsman's interest would lie in controlling misconduct rather than seeking redress through adversary proceedings, which had a tendency in the past to polarize relations between the police and the public (Cheh, 1995). Although the ombudsman concept showed promise, it was not fully implemented at this time. Instead, attempts were made to combine the functions of reviewing complaints and appeasing the public, the most notable of the decade being in Detroit, Chicago, Berkeley, and Kansas City (the first boards to survive through to the 1990s).

Combined Benefits: Linking Internal Review Processes with Civilian Review

The city of Detroit was the subject of many serious police riots in the 1960s, and by the 1970s the mayor, police commissioners, and city council all agreed that external control over the police was both inevitable and necessary. The Board of Police Commissioners (BPC), which was established in 1974 and consisted of five civilians appointed by the mayor and approved by city council, embodied many powers: It had the provisions to receive and resolve complaints about the operation of the city's police department; establish policy, rules, and regulations; review and approve the department's budget; act as final authority in reviewing and imposing discipline on officers; and finally, approve all promotions (Brown, 1983). An important aspect of the Detroit Board was its ability to hire its own investigation staff, which would have access to all departmental records and the authority to interrogate officers. Although the Board appeared to wield a great deal of power over the police, very few investigations were actually carried out by the Board alone. It was often the case that the Board would pass complaints on to the police or retain the use of the precinct's investigative staff. Unlike Boards in the past, Detroit's BPC had gained legal authority with its acceptance into the city charter, a factor essential for the viability of a civilian review board.

Another city with a reputable complaints system in the 1970s was Chicago. The publication of the *Metcalfe Report* in 1973, an account of police abuses in Chicago, prompted the 1974 formation of Chicago's Office of Professional Standards (OPS). A notable difference between Chicago and other cities that were organizing review boards was that Chicago instituted two boards. The Police Board, formed in 1961, had limited responsibilities: its only powers were to review and overturn, if necessary, the sanctions given by the superintendent. The OPS, on the other hand, was given investigation duties for cases of excessive force and the shooting of a civilian by an officer, along with receiving and recording all complaints against personnel. It consisted of nine civilians and, like Detroit, had legal standing because it was established in the Chicago Municipal Code and Illinois Revised Statutes. Like the Police Board, it also had the power to alter the sanctions imposed by the superintendent. A controversy arose, however, when a trend was observed of the originally suggested sanctions consistently being *lowered* by the OPS (Terrill, 1991). It was this ironic finding that initiated research into the severity of sanctions imposed by police compared to those imposed by civilians, and it was found that civilians regularly administered a lower level of disciplinary action than officers in internal review boards (Terrill, 1991).

Berkeley and Kansas City also formed review boards in the early 1970s; however, each of these boards was given less power of review than either Chicago or Detroit. Berkeley's Police

Review Commission (PRC) was allotted jurisdiction over appeals from the police department's complaint office (Brown, 1983), and was also able to review departmental policies, practice, and training with recommendations being made to the city manager (Terrill, 1991). Kansas City's Office of Citizen Complaints (OCC) was established in the mode of the Scandinavian ombudsman system. The most important task of the OCC was to alleviate the fears of the public as they registered complaints by providing a reception center. All investigations were carried out by the Internal Affairs Division of the police department, and an important distinction between this system and others was the significant rise in the number of registered complaints since the system's initiation: between 1970 and 1974, the number of complaints more than tripled from 174 to 600. Although the number of complaints has stabilized over time, the OCC has been successful in establishing rapport between the police and the public.

The 1980s brought about a politically conservative period in the United States, with a notable increase in support for law and order due to the increasing recognition of the problems associated with illicit drug use (Terrill, 1991; Harris, 1997). This conservative climate also saw the establishment of 15 lasting civilian oversight agencies (Petterson, 1991). Regardless of the increase in boards, there continued to be police opposition to civilian review. As a result, the police attempted to improve upon the accountability of their own internal systems, sparking a debate over the advantages of hierarchical accountability versus democratic accountability (Terrill, 1991). The main issue considered in the 1980s regarding civilian review was how much independence was necessary for the boards to function, while maintaining fairness to the police and the public alike. Independence required gaining political strength across the various groups that make up local communities, rather than the support of only restricted minority groups as was seen in the 1960s.

Other cities followed suit and established civilian review boards after highly publicized incidents of police use of force. For instance, the Independent Review Panel (IRP) was established in Dade County, Florida, in 1980 as a result of deadly force against a minority. In 1979, four White police officers beat Arthur McDuffie—a Black insurance salesman—to death following a high-speed car chase (Porter and Dunn, 1984). All of the officers involved had previous records of misconduct complaints against them (Terrill, 1991), and the media exposed the police's internal complaint system as inadequate and in need of supervision. In a similar fashion to the ombudsman system, the IRP was unique in that its jurisdiction covered complaints against all county employees. Because the police were not singled out for scrutiny by civilians, they were less resistant to this particular system of oversight. The Dade County system has experienced a high degree of success for this reason as well as its role as an *advisor* to the department for the appropriate methods of discipline or alterations in departmental policies. Although every system thus far has elicited some degree of negative feedback by the public and the police, the ombudsman systems of civilian oversight in Kansas City and Dade County have encountered the least resistance from each source.

Implementation of Civilian Review Boards Nationally

The number of civilian review boards in the United States increased substantially in the 1990s, with 97 agencies having some form of civilian oversight by 1997 (Department of Justice, 1999). These are not just in large cities, but also medium-sized cities and rural areas. Some civilian review boards that had already been in place were modified to incorporate changes suggested by Commission reports. For example, the CCRB in New York City was transformed into an all-civilian review board in July 1993. Prior to 1987, it had been composed solely of non-sworn police personnel (e.g., police dispatchers), and from 1987 to 1993 the board members consisted of both civilians and non-sworn police personnel. The change to a 13-member civilian board was a direct result of the Mollen Commission report, but the modification of this board still did not placate the community. Additionally, there was much opposition to it by the police because they felt that no one could understand the duties of a police officer other than someone who had been in their position as a police officer.

Outcomes of Civilian Review: Reasons for Continued Dissatisfaction

Relations between the police and minority communities are tense and strained, largely as a result of the zero-tolerance policing tactics adopted by many police agencies today. Aggressive policing styles, which lead to frequent interaction between the police and minorities, are not the issue of discussion here. Rather, it is how to use such tactics to reduce crime and not alienate members of minority communities. If citizens have complaints against the police, there should be a fair and systematic way to register those complaints and have them investigated. But many minorities lack confidence in the police or the system for registering complaints against them (Cashmore and McLaughlin, 1990; Skolnick and McCoy, 1985). An "ideal" police complaints system would accomplish the four goals listed previously—to deter future misconduct, remove deviant officers, satisfy individual complainants, and maintain public confidence in the police—though few complainants would agree that current systems of police oversight do so.

The primary ground of dissatisfaction with civilian review boards is the low number of substantiated complaints. The more serious the complaint is, the less likely it is to be substantiated. Table 3 shows the rates of fully investigated complaints that were substantiated in New York City in 1999 (Civilian Complaint Review Board, 2000).

This difficulty in substantiating complaints is due to several important factors. First, the charges must be proven "beyond a reasonable doubt," the same standard of proof required in criminal courts, and if the evidence does not meet this standard the charge is dismissed. In order to prove a charge beyond a reasonable doubt, there must be corroborating evidence. The majority of complainants cannot substantiate their statements because there are rarely witnesses to the officers' actions except perhaps other officers or friends of the complainant. Thus, the only statements that exist are those of the complainant and the officer, which often directly contradict each other. In such cases, the word of the officer is

TABLE 3   Substantiated complaints in New York City in 1999 that were fully investigated

	Force	Abuse	Discourtesy	Offensive Language	Total
Substantiated	98 (9.8%)	136 (16.9%)	36 (17.1%)	5 (23.8%)	275 (13.5%)
Total investigated	998	805	211	21	2,035

often believed over the complainant so as not to destroy the integrity of the officer in a case where the complaint was registered maliciously. Individuals registering complaints are usually unaware of the high standard of proof required and are subsequently disappointed in the results of the process.

In cases of serious complaints, the corroborating evidence is particularly important because of the potentially serious consequences if the results are substantiated. These allegations are important to substantiate if the charges are true, and they are also the most damaging to the officer's career if they are not. The use of coercive force is a tactic that the police use to maintain social order. There is a delicate balance between the amount of force that is legitimate and that which is excessive, and what may be excessive in one circumstance might be necessary in another. Complaints of assault and excessive force are most likely to come about in situations where danger is present and force was a necessary action to protect the officer, the public, or the suspected offender (Cheh, 1995). When officers are accused of assault or excessive force, their actions are generally understood—legally, though not to the person receiving force—to be a necessary aspect of their jobs since the police are allowed to use coercive force. Unfortunately, minorities are disproportionately affected by the use of force when it is excessive—in New York City in 1990, 44.8% of those filing complaints were African American but yet they only consisted of 28.7% of the population. Additionally, their complaints were substantiated less frequently than those of White citizens. This indicates a bias in the system against minorities in two places: the use of force by the police and the investigation of the complaint by the review board.

Another issue of concern to citizens about the police complaints process is that the police usually conduct investigations of the complaints—only 35 civilian oversight agencies in the country have the power to conduct investigations. Despite the existence of civilian boards that would supervise the investigations, the public is likely to be skeptical of investigative outcomes, especially those which are unsubstantiated and reached after police investigations. The duties of the civilian review boards are undermined by the fact that the police generally produce the information they review. Therefore, even though the civilian review board conducts an "external" review, it is not entirely external and the results are dependent upon police investigations (Police Complaints Authority, 1995). Unfortunately, the police *and* the public are not likely to be satisfied with any one complaint system; the public views police investigations as unfair, feeling that the police will protect each other (Reiner, 1993; Niederhoffer, 1967), and the police feel that civilian investigations are unfair because the word of the complainant might be accepted over that of the officer (Van Maanen, 1978). In the past, police have argued that the "inexperienced, politicized review of police conduct would seriously jeopardize public safety by creating an overly cautious police department more concerned with avoiding complaints than protecting the public" (Kerstetter, 1985, p. 160), despite the fact that nearly all Commission reports suggest that this is a necessary aspect policing in order to achieve democratic accountability.

Though the public is often dissatisfied with police investigations, the police have in the past proved to be the most thorough investigators. The police have access to more information necessary to conduct a thorough investigation. Investigative duties should be the responsibility of the agency that will fulfil the task to the highest standard, and in the past this has been the police. Boards that employed civilian investigators have almost universally collapsed, and those that still exist regularly utilize police investigators to conduct their investigations.

Best Practices for Complaint Review

Although some aspects of the police complaints system can be improved upon to better police and public relations, no severe structural changes should be made to the complaints systems at any one particular time—particularly in the aftermath of an emotionally charged case of excessive force. Kerstetter (1995) showed how major changes made in a system at a time of unrest are more likely to enhance problems than solve them. One example of this is the police protest against the sudden erection of civilian boards in New York in 1966; the demise of the board was the result of police believing it to be a political interference in their affairs, for which the public had neither the knowledge nor the right to impose their outside beliefs about proper police procedures. Nonetheless, some structural changes may help to achieve a greater social order between the police and the public. First, police departments should have both internal and external systems of review, as research indicates that the most effective police complaints departments utilize a combination of the two (Terrill, 1991; Kerstetter, 1985). Though civilian review boards do not have higher rates of substantiating complaints, they do appear to improve police-public relations. The civilian review board should consist of all nonpolice personnel—even boards with non-sworn police personnel create suspicion.

Second, the police should conduct the actual investigations, as these tend to be more exhaustive than civilian investigations of complaints. Some civilian review boards that have the power to conduct their own investigations (such as Detroit) continue to utilize the police to conduct more thorough investigations. Many police officers believe that to grant investigatory power to civilians would undermine their powers. They would resent the civilians who encroach upon the expertise, which has been developed throughout their careers. It has also been proposed that civilian investigations are less effective at deterring future misconduct than police investigations (Kerstetter, 1985, p. 164). By removing the power of investigative and disciplinary actions from the Chief of Police, there is no form of hierarchical responsibility of the chief over the "rank-and-file" officers. Rather, the superior officers encourage other officers to develop a "we-them" view of the board members who are conducting investigations. With police investigations, there exists a peer review over police actions that have in past studies shown to be more effective than civilian investigations (Kerstetter, 1985).

Though the police should conduct the investigations, civilians should be allowed to review the procedures to ensure that all applicable measures of investigation were utilized before a particular decision is reached. A combination of internal and external review would allow the police to secure a sense of hierarchical accountability and deter future misconduct, while the review process by civilians would allow for a greater democratic accountability to the public, thus creating more public confidence in the police. In order for a system of police complaints and discipline to work, both the police and the public must view the system as fair and impartial. Kerstetter (1995, p. 224) explains the existence of the "procedural justice" effect: if the process by which a decision in a dispute is reached is perceived as fair, even an unsuccessful party will have a more favorable attitude about the outcome. "The picture that seems to be emerging is of people much more concerned about the process of their interaction with the law and much less concerned with the outcome than one might have supposed" (Lind and Tyler, 1988, p. 92).

Another important consideration for civilian review is the legal standing of the board. As was seen from the first civilian review board in Philadelphia, a board without legal standing will cease to exist at the first instance of opposition. In order to survive, a board must establish permanency through democratic agreement about the terms of its existence. Boards cannot survive with an executive order alone. As an example of what may happen to a board without legal standing, the Oakland civilian review board should be observed. In a similar fashion to the first board created in Philadelphia, it was created through an executive order, had little power, and was subsequently ineffective because the city manager would not uphold any of the findings by the board (Skolnick and Bayley, 1986).

Another form of review that would be beneficial to adapt into more departments is the Early Warning System (EWS), which was introduced by Alpert and Dunham (1992). The EWS allows the department to keep track of all complaints registered against its individual officers, whether or not they are sustained, and identify behavior patterns that are potentially problematic. After an officer acquires a number of complaints, his or her entire record is reviewed and early assistance is provided to overcome the behavioral problems (Gaines et al., 1994). The allegations should not imply that the officer is guilty, but rather should alert to the officer's supervisor that there is a *potential* behavioral problem. This should be an internal procedure, providing a means of assistance rather than punishment. Officers will be more likely to respond positively to constructive criticism from their peers than an external review committee.

Another positive development in some larger police agencies are systems of alternative dispute resolution; namely, mediation. Sixteen agencies currently have such a system, which allows for the informal resolution of minor complaints (e.g., verbal abuse) to be resolved quickly and with preferred outcomes. Initial research (Corbett, 1991) shows that a higher percentage of individuals are satisfied with the process of informal resolution than with fully investigated complaints. Maguire and Corbett (1989) showed that for cases that have been informally resolved, over half of the complainants were at least fairly satisfied and 30% were very satisfied. This can be compared with only 10% of complainants for investigated cases being even fairly satisfied and 68% very dissatisfied.

The most important result of informal resolution may be the increased communication between the police and the community. Not all complaints can be resolved informally, though; complaints about use of force, racial epithets, and repeat allegations are not subject to mediation in most departments. Where the formal complaint process is used, the civilian oversight agency should increase levels of communication with the complainant because this is the only way that the complainants will understand that action is being taken to investigate their complaints thoroughly. This is especially important if there are time delays in the investigation of serious complaints. Increased levels of communication between the police and the community follow the primary reason for establishing a civilian board: individuals, especially those from minority communities, are often reluctant to deal with the police. Many such individuals would not file complaints because of their fears that the police would "be out to get them" (Pinkney, 1994). These individuals might respond more positively to the complaint process if they have access to civilian members of a complaints board than if they had to communicate only with the police. This would be especially true if the civilian board were comprised of a representative percentage of minority members of the community, following a quota composition to represent the community that it involves.

BREAKING THE CYCLE: MOVING BEYOND RECOMMENDATIONS ON THE ROAD TOWARD IMPROVED POLICE-COMMUNITY RELATIONS

Relations between the police and minority communities continue to be based on mutual distrust, suspicion, and resentment, similar to the era of upheaval in the 1960s (Cashmore, 1995). While this is partially related to the emotionally charged, high-profile cases such as the Rampart scandal and the brutalizing of Abner Louima, it is more directly the result of everyday police interactions in the community. Regardless of reason (both legitimate and illegitimate), officers stop, frisk, and question minorities more often than White members of the community, and as a result minorities are overrepresented in the use of force and related complaints.

The Commissions, almost universally formed in response to high-profile cases such as that of Rodney King, relate current problems in policing minority communities to poor recruitment, selection, training, and management. They recognize the need for increased accountability both hierarchically and democratically, and claim that a system of civilian oversight is necessary in order to achieve this. Despite the increase in civilian oversight agencies in the 1990s, most review boards take a long time to investigate the complaints and rarely substantiate them. Additionally, there is little communication between the complainant and the police throughout the process.

As has been explained by the procedural justice concept (Kerstetter, 1995), individuals who file complaints against the police are more likely to be content with the outcome if the process through which the outcome was derived can be viewed as fair and impartial. Maguire and Corbett (1991) and Brown (1987) showed that most individuals do not consider police investigations about police complaints to be fair and impartial because it is believed that the police exist within a closed institution and they will protect each other from the public. In order to allow a greater public confidence in the police and satisfaction from complainants, some form of external review over police actions is necessary. It is not enough for a Commission to be formed to investigate an act of police misconduct and, subsequently, suggest the implementation of civilian oversight.

The root of this issue remains that if police-community interactions themselves represented positive interactions based upon mutual respect, law enforcement would be viewed with a greater sense of legitimacy. In turn, fewer complaints would be filed, even when the citizen did not view the outcome as necessarily positive (i.e., receiving a ticket). Increasing the level of positive police-community interactions requires reforms much larger than simply instituting a fair complaints system, covering recruitment, deployment, and training practices. The investigative Commissions formed throughout history all too often present "quick fix options," without truly diagnosing the full array of issues and concerns that are contributing to current conditions. As such, although there have been significant improvements in terms of practices related to complaint processing and recruitment, the final long-term goal of corresponding improvements to police-community relations remains elusive.

CONCLUSION

The myriad Commissions have cited two issues at the core of police misconduct to be lack of hierarchical and democratic accountability. Without hierarchical accountability, it is unlikely that officers will be deterred from future misconduct. Without democratic accountability created through external review boards, it is unlikely that the public will have confidence in the complaints system and individual complainants are also unlikely to be satisfied. Research shows that systems combining internal and external forms of review produce the greatest level of satisfaction amongst the police and the public. Additionally, mediation appears to be a promising system of resolution and is accepted by both the community and the police for minor grievances. Because the nature of a complaints system is inherently negative, there will always be a significant level of dissatisfaction with the process which is increased because of the low level of sustained complaints. The key is not only to employ an adequate police complaints system and increase communication between the police and the community, but to reduce the number of complaints to begin with. Rather than focus on high-profile brutality and deadly force cases, the focus should be on everyday interaction between the police and the citizens they are policing. The aim must be to prevent abuses against minorities by improving recruitment, selection, training, and management, rather than to reprimand those who get caught in the system.

REFERENCES

Alpert, G. P., & Dunham, R. C. (1992). *Policing urban America.* (2nd ed.). Prospect Heights, IL: Waveland Press.

Bayley, D. H. (1991). Preface. In A. J. Goldsmith (Ed.), *Complaints against the police: The trend to external review.* Oxford: Clarendon Press.

Bittner, E. (1974). Florence Nightingale in pursuit of Willie Sutton: A theory of the police. In H. Jacobs (Ed.), *The potential for reform of criminal justice.* Beverly Hills: Sage.

Brown, D. C. (1983). *Civilian review of complaints against the police: A survey of the United States literature.* Home Office Research and Planning Unit. London: H.M.S.O.

Brown, D. C. (1987). The police complaints procedure: A survey of complainants' views. *Home Office Research Study No. 93.* London: H.M.S.O.

Cao, L., & Huang, B. (2000). Determinants of citizen complaints against police abuse of power. *Journal of Criminal Justice, 28,* 203–213.

Cashmore, E. (1995). *Dictionary of race and ethnic relations,* (3rd ed.). London: Routledge.

Cashmore, E. and McLaughlin, E. (Eds.) (1990). *Out of order? Policing black people.* London: Routledge.

Cheh, M. M. (1995). Are lawsuits an answer to police brutality? In W. A. Geller and H. Toch (Eds.) *And justice for all: Understanding and controlling police abuse of force.* Washington, DC: Police Executive Research Forum.

Christopher Commission. (1991). *Report of the Independent Commission on The Los Angeles Police Department.* Los Angeles.

Civilian Complaint Review Board (2000). *Status Report January–December 1999.* New York.

Condon, R. J. (1986). *Police use of deadly force in New York State: A report to Governor Mario Cuomo.* Albany, NY: Division of Criminal Justice Services.

Corbett, C. (1991). Complaints against the police: The new procedure of informal resolution. *Policing and Society, 2,* 47–60.

Department of Justice (1999) Law enforcement management and administrative statistics, 1997. Washington, DC: U.S. Department of Justice.

Escobedo v. Illinois, 378 U.S. 478 (1964).

Fyfe, J. J. (1978). Reducing the use of deadly force: The New York experience. In U.S. Department of Justice, *Police Use of Deadly Force*. Washington, DC: U.S. Government Printing Office.

Gaines, L. K., Kappeler, V. E., & Vaughn, J. B. (1994). *Policing in America*. Cincinnati, OH: Anderson Publishing Company.

Gilroy, P. (1987). *There ain't no black in the union jack: The cultural politics of race and nation*. London: Century Hutchinson.

Goldstein, H. (1990). *Problem-oriented policing*. New York: McGraw-Hill.

Harris, D. A. (1997). "Driving while black" and all other traffic offenses: The Supreme Court and pretextual traffic stops. *Journal of Criminal Law and Criminology, 87*, 544–582.

Hudson, J. R. (1968). The civilian review board issues as illuminated by the Philadelphia Experience. *Criminology, 6*, 16–29.

Kerstetter, W. A. (1985). Who disciplines the police? Who should? In W. A. Geller (Ed.) *Police leadership in America: Crisis and opportunity*. Chicago, IL: American Bar Association.

Kerstetter, W. A. (1995). A 'procedural justice' perspective on police and citizen satisfaction with investigations of police use of force: Finding a common ground of fairness. In W. A. Geller and H. Toch (Eds.) *And justice for all: Understanding and controlling police abuse of force*. Washington, D.C.: Police Executive Research Forum.

Kerner Commission (1968). *Report of the National Advisory Commission on Civil Disorders*. New York: Bantam.

Klockars, C. B. (1995). A theory of excessive force and its control. In W. A. Geller and H. Toch (Eds.), *And justice for all: Understanding and controlling police abuse of force*. Washington, DC: Police Executive Research Forum.

Knapp Commission (1973). *The Knapp Commission Report on Police Corruption*. New York.

Lind, E. A., & Tyler, T. R. (1988). *The social psychology of procedural justice*. New York: Anchor Press.

Maguire, M., & Corbett, C. (1989). Patterns and profiles of complaint against the police. In R. Morgan and D. J. Smith (Eds.), *Coming to terms with policing: Perspectives on policy*. London and New York: Routledge.

Mapp v. Ohio, 368 U.S. 871 (1961).

Miranda v. Arizona, 384 U.S. 436 (1966).

Mollen Commission (1994). *Commission to investigate allegations of police corruption and the anti-corruption procedures of the police department*. New York.

Morgan, R., & Smith, D. J. (Eds.), (1989). *Coming to terms with policing: Perspectives on policy*. London and New York: Routledge.

Morris, N., & Hawking, G. (1970). *The honest politicians guide to crime control*. Chicago: University of Chicago Press.

Muir, W. K., Jr. (1977). *Police: Streetcorner politicians*. Chicago: University of Chicago Press.

National Commission on Law Observance and Enforcement (1931). *Report on lawlessness in law enforcement*. Washington, DC

Niederhoffer, A. (1967). *Behind the shield: The police in urban society*. Garden City, NY: Doubleday and Company, Inc.

Petterson, W. E. (1991). Police accountability and civilian oversight of policing: An American perspective. In A. J. Goldsmith (Ed.), *Complaints against the police: The trend to external review*. Oxford: Clarendon Press.

Pinkney, A. (1994). *Lest we forget: White hate crimes. Howard Beach and other racial atrocities*. Chicago: Third World Press.

Police Complaints Authority (1995). *Police complaints authority: The first ten years*. London: HMSD.

Porter, B., & Dunn, M. (1984). *The Miami riot of 1980: Crossing the bounds*. Lexington, MA: Lexington Books.

Reiner, R. (1993). *The politics of the police* (2nd ed.). Sussex: Wheatsheat Books Ltd.

Reiner, R. (1994). Policing and the police. In M. Maguire, R. Morgan, & R. Reiner (Eds.), *The Oxford handbook of criminology.* Oxford: Oxford University Press.

Reiss, A. J., Jr. (1971). *The police and the public.* New Haven: Yale University Press.

Sherman, L. W. (1974). *Police corruption: A sociological perspective.* Garden City, NY: Anchor Press.

Shusta, R. M., Levine, O. R., Harris, P. R., & Wong (2002). *Multicultural law enforcement: Strategies for peacekeeping in a diverse society.* Upper Saddle River, NJ: Prentice Hall.

Skolnick, J. H. & Fyfe, J. J. (1993). *Above the law: Police and the excessive use of force.* New York: Free Press.

Skolnick, J. H. & Bayley, D. H. (1986). *The new blue line: Police innovation in six American cities.* New York: Free Press.

Skolnick, J. H. & McCoy, C. C. (1985). Police accountability and the media. In W. A. Geller (Ed.) *Police leadership in America: Crisis and opportunity.* Chicago, Ill.: American Bar Association.

Spielberger, C. D. (Ed.) (1979). *Police selection and evaluation: Issues and techniques.* Washington, DC: Hemisphere Publishing Corporation.

Spitzer, E. (1999). *"Stop and frisk" practices: A report to the people of the State of New York from the office of the attorney general.* New York: Civil Rights Bureau.

Terrill, R. J. (1991). Civilian oversight of the police complaints process in the United States: Concerns, developments and more concerns. In A. J. Goldsmith (Ed.), *Complaints against the police: The trend to external review.* Oxford: Clarendon Press.

Terry v. Ohio, 392 U.S. 1 (1968).

Van Maanen, J. (1978). The Asshole. In P. Manning & J. Van Maanen (Eds.), *Policing: a view from the street.* New York: Random House.

Walker, S., Spohn, C., and DeLone, M. (1996). *The color of justice: Race, ethnicity and crime in America.* Belmont, CA: Wadsworth.

Whren v. United States, 517 U.S. 806 (1996).

Wilson, J. Q. (1968). *Varieties of police behavior.* Cambridge, MA: Harvard University Press.

Yuille, J. C. (Ed.) (1986). *Police selection and training: The role of psychology.* Dordrecht: Martinus Nijhoff Publishers.

11

Policing a Diverse Community

A Case Study

Eli B. Silverman and James E. McCabe

Providing effective and respectful policing to diverse multicultural communities is policing's most critical challenge. This is particularly pertinent in New York City today where the New York City Police Department (NYPD) is the nation's largest.

From 1993 through 2000, New York City experienced a 57% decline in index crime. While scholars and the media debate various explanations, many agree that the city's police deserve a notable portion of the credit (Blumstein, 2000; Karmen, 2001; Silverman, 1999). In addition, the New York crime decline has greatly contributed to the widespread discussion of specific police strategies that work best under particular conditions. Situational crime prevention, problem solving, crime analysis, computerized crime mapping, community policing, "hot spot" policing and "intelligence based policing" are now more carefully examined (Sherman, 1998).

As valuable as the focus on effective policing has been, it only recently has addressed the vital concomitant question of "at what price to public confidence and trust?" On the one hand, there is international interest in approaches that champion police strategies to prevent low-level disorder such as public drunkenness, gambling, and prostitution from escalating into fights, robberies, and shootings. On the other hand, some observers believe, however, that sustained police efforts (sometimes labeled "zero-tolerance policing") designed to curtail spiraling disorder inevitably generate police harassment and a rise in citizen complaints, particularly from the minority community (Alderson, 1979; Burke, 1998; Greene, 1999). Recent events dramatically underscore the prominent issues of justice and due process. Controversy erupted in August 1997 when four NYPD officers were charged with torturing, sodomizing, and brutalizing Abner Louima, a Haitian immigrant, inside a police precinct, where a wooden stick was shoved in his rectum and then his mouth. Subsequently, four officers were convicted and sentenced to severe prison sentences ranging from 5 to 30 years.[1] Passions were further inflamed after the February 1999 killing of an unarmed West African street peddler in the vestibule of his Bronx apartment building. Four members of the New York City Police Department's elite Street Crime Unit (SCU) fired 41 times, with 19 bullets striking Amadou Diallo, who arrived from Guinea almost three years ago and had no criminal record.

Outrage rekindled numerous protests against police racism and brutality and triggered demonstrations outside City Hall and Diallo's Bronx residence. Protestors claimed the four White street crime officers judged Mr. Diallo a criminal because of the color of his skin. Columnist Jack Newfield (1999, p. 6) represented this view: "There has always been a famine of justice in communities like Soundview in the Bronx. Nobody I've spoken to can name a case where cops killed an unarmed, innocent white person." To compound racial sensitivities, an appeals court transferred the trial of the four officers from the Bronx's predominately minority population to the upstate city of Albany, with its majority White population. The court maintained that sustained adverse publicity emanating from widespread media coverage prevented the officers from receiving a fair trial. A racially mixed jury found the officers not guilty.

Supporters of the NYPD laud the SCU, which has expanded threefold since 1997 to over 400 officers, as key to the confiscation of guns from New York City's streets. Yet, in the eyes of some critics, this "elite force quells crime, but at a cost" (Roane, 1999, p. 6). The NYPD later announced improved training of all members and decentralization of the SCU, while others called for its disbanding.

Investigations of these New York episodes indicate that the police are clinging to the "blue wall of silence" as a protective device. Unbridled policing is rightly criticized when peacekeeping and minority rights are downgraded and subordinated to the primacy of law enforcement. These issues are of vital concern because even under the best of circumstances, as John Alderson states, there may be a "permanent state of conflict" between order maintenance and citizen confidence (Alderson, 1998).

This chapter seeks to explore one precinct's efforts to simultaneously focus on crime reduction and order maintenance while gaining citizens' confidence in the police department. First we provide the context of New York City policing.

TENSIONS IN NEW YORK CITY POLICING

In New York City, the tension between order maintenance and the security of all its citizens has entered center stage. Public confidence in the NYPD's ability to protect minority rights while addressing crime is under intense scrutiny (*Fordham Urban Law Journal,* 2000).

Determining the level of public confidence in the police is often fraught with difficulties and controversy. Clarity and consensus are difficult to unearth. This is perhaps no more applicable than in New York City, where reports are often conflicting and subject to numerous interpretations. There is sufficient data, however, to strongly suggest a widening chasm between police and citizens, particularly the minority community.

---

[1] Convictions against two of the officers were subsequently reversed on appeal. Those convictions did not stem from the torture itself, but from charges that they lied to cover up the incident.

Polls

A 1999 *New York 1* television poll found that the vast majority of African Americans and Latinos believed that police misconduct was a serious problem. A *New York Times* poll in March 1999, conducted just weeks after the Diallo killing, found that 72% of Blacks, 62% of Hispanics, and 33% of Whites polled believed that most officers use excessive force.

A Quinnipiac College poll surveyed over a thousand city voters from June 8 to June 14, 1999, in the midst of intense publicity about the police torture of Abner Louima, for which two officers were convicted and three acquitted.[2] The poll found 84% believed police brutality was a "very serious" or "somewhat serious" problem. Among Whites, 25% believed police brutality was very serious compared with 81% of Blacks and 59% of Hispanics. While a large majority believed the city has become safer, 45% said governmental policies have led to an increase in police brutality, an opinion held by 28% of White voters, 70% of Black voters, and 51% of Hispanic voters. At the same time citizens approved "of the jobs the cops in their community are doing and approve of the way their mayor is handling crime, but they turn thumbs down on the current police commissioner."

On the other hand, a poll commissioned by the NYPD at the end of 1999 to measure the effectiveness of a recent advertising campaign found that most residents respect the police, including a solid majority of the Blacks and Hispanics interviewed. Seventy-three percent of Blacks and 83% of Hispanics agreed with the statement "I respect the New York City Police Department and its officers." The proportion of Whites that agreed was 83%. Yet Black and Hispanic support for the police dropped off when they were asked whether the police were trying to improve their relationship with members of minorities. Fifty-one percent of Blacks and 58% of Hispanics believed the police were making an effort. At the minimum, there is enough evidence to urge the NYPD to strive for stronger community relations.

Civilian Complaints

The record of civilian complaints against the police also divulges a murky and disturbing view of public trust. Amnesty International, for example, released a report in June 1996 that raised questions regarding the department's use of force and the rise in complaints against NYPD officers for the use of force (Amnesty International, June 1996). In 1997 the New York Civil Liberties Union contended that only 1% of 16,327 police officers charged with complaints were disciplined. Another review at the same time found the department cleared or dropped 70% of the police officers charged with brutality by the Civilian Complaint Review Board. One year later, in June 1998, the Human Rights Watch Organization's report found a steady rise in civilian complaints since the NYPD began its heightened drive on quality of life offenses. In November of the same year, an American Civil Liberties' report condemned the police commissioner for failing to act on a substantial number of civilian complaints. These charges were echoed the following year, in September 1999, in a report

---

[2] Officers Justin Volpe and Charles Schwarz were implicated in having actually participated in the act of torture. Officers Thomas Weise and Thomas Bruder were acquitted of involvement in the torture, but were subsequently convicted of giving false statements regarding the incident. Those convictions were later reversed, while their Sgt. Michael Bellomo was acquitted at trial of lying to cover up the incident.

by the Office of the New York City's Public Advocate. The Public Advocate's preliminary report claimed that the police commissioner handled cases in a disciplinary manner in only one-third of the cases when the CCRB substantiated citizen charges of police abuse (Office of the New York City Public Advocate, September 15, 1999).

The evidence regarding civilian complaints, however, is also fraught with contradictory findings. In 1997, for example, Mayor Giuliani reported that civilian complaints dropped 21% compared with the same period the previous year. This decline followed a more modest 0.4% decline in 1996 compared with 1995. At the end of 1999, Commissioner Safir noted that the number of civilian complaints of excessive police force fell 12% from the previous year—culminating four consecutive years of decline. This decline occurred at the same time the number of police-citizen contacts swelled as the size of the police force increased from just over 30,000 in 1996 to almost 40,000 in 1999. A spokesman for the CCRB, however, challenged these figures as inconclusive since they did not include the last four days of the year.

Regardless of the level of downturn in civilian complaints from 1994 to 1999, these findings contrast with the earlier years of 1993 to 1995 when, according to the CCRB's semiannual report, there was a 57% increase in civilian complaints (Civilian Complaint Review Board, May 2000).

At the same time, particular minority communities experienced a rise in civilian complaints. Complaints rose 11.8% in the predominately minority Bronx for the first six months of 1999. In the Bronx's minority community of Soundview, where street peddler Amadou Diallo was killed by police officers in February, there was a doubling of citizen complaints during the month of June 1999 when the trial was attracting much attention.

Similarly, when Police Commissioner Safir announced the 68 fewer citizen-lodged complaints concerning police abuse discourtesy in 1999 compared with 1998, the NYCLU director responded that the Commissioner used selective numbers.

THE COMMUNITY IN POLICING

Not only do some critics depict the New York Model as inherently repressive, but they also characterize it as the antithesis of community-based policing. One well-respected journalist commented in April 1999, two months after the Diallo shooting: "A question many law enforcement officials around the country are asking is how much of this was self-inflicted after Mayor Giuliani and Police Commissioner Safir abandoned efforts by their predecessors to establish community policing, scorning it as social work. . . Whether police officers can do it all by themselves is at the center of the debate between New York City's approach—which relies on the massive use of officers to suppress crime—and the strategy of community policing and a related approach called problem solving policing" (Butterfield, April 4, 1999, p. 4).

Community policing in New York has been sporadic (McElroy et al., 1993). Its greatest expansion occurred in the early 1990s under Mayor David Dinkins and Commissioner Lee Brown. Though it met with mixed responses, there were audiences for whom it had genuine appeal (Silverman, 1999). For many, just the promise of more police generated favorable responses. Those concerned about crime, regardless of neighborhood or class, typically seek additional patrol officers. The notion of returning to the image of the friendly corner cop was inviting, if not nostalgic, and police officials took advantage of this. Beginning in October 1991, the NYPD used posters, radio spots, awards, and vans aggressively to market the slogan "The Beat Cop is Back."

The 1994 advent of a new Mayor (Giuliani) and Commissioner (Bratton) activated a redefined, refashioned community policing. The old way was denounced as too social service–oriented and ineffective in combating crime. The community policing concept was less prominently proclaimed, and the number of officers serving in community policing units was greatly reduced, although community policing watchwords—partnership, proactive, and problem solving—were frequently mentioned.

THE 110TH PRECINCT

What is actually happening on the ground level? What is the nature of police-community interaction? Has New York City, as Butterfield maintains, abandoned a community policing–problem solving approach? It is difficult to generalize because the NYPD consists of 76 precincts, each with its own history and particular brand of police-community interchange. This chapter focuses on one specific police precinct that is located in an exceedingly diverse community.

The community and its precinct are not intended to be either representative or nonrepresentative of other city areas. Rather, we seek to examine some indices of police-community interaction. This is an area that is receiving increasing attention from scholars and the National Institute of Justice (Duffee et al., 2001). The focus is on the manner in which the police and community interact to improve neighborhood space, construct community social capacity, solve problems, and encourage citizen participation and efforts.

Regardless of the time period, the vitality and efficacy of police-community interaction is closely linked to community activities and the level of police commitment to the public's quality of life. These vital building blocks have historically fluctuated throughout the city including the 110th Precinct—our area of research.

Demographics

The 110th Precinct encompasses the Elmhurst-Corona section of Queens. Its current position as perhaps the most diverse community in the city of New York began as the 1960s and 1970s ushered in a period of majority-minority transition. The White population fell from 84,000 to 47,000 as African Americans and Latin American and Asian immigrants became the new Elmhurst-Corona majority. The neighborhood's White population fell from 98% in 1960 to 67% in 1970, 34% in 1980, and 18% in 1990. During these decades, individuals from a variety of ethnic backgrounds arrived in sizeable numbers, and by 1990 Elmhurst-Corona was 45% Latin American, 26% Asian, and 10% Black. Among these newcomers were the established residents of German, Irish, Polish, Italian, Jewish, and other European ancestries.

In 1990, Elmhurst-Corona's 28,000 Whites were a mix of European ancestries (in descending order: Italian, Irish, Germans, Polish, English, French, Russians, Austrian Czechs, Hungarian, Yugoslavs, Ukrainians, Romanians, Portuguese, Lithuanians, Scots, Dutch, Swedes, Slovaks, and Norwegians). Its Asian residents included 16,300 Chinese, 8,900 Koreans, 7,600 Indians, 4,000 Filipinos, and smaller number of Thais, Vietnamese, Pakistanis, and Guyanese of Indian ancestry. The Latin American population comprised 13,600 Colombians, 12,000 Dominicans, 6,800 Ecuadorians, 6,500 Puerto Ricans, 2,900 Cubans, 2,700 Mexicans,

2,700 Peruvians, and other South and Central Americans. Black immigrants included 3,900 West Indians (including 1,200 Haitians) and 1,850 Africans (Sanjek, 1998).

In 1992, New York's Department of City Planning called Elmhurst-Corona "perhaps the most ethnically mixed community in the world" (Sanjek, 1998, p. 1). This diverse mix is concentrated within an area of approximately 2.2 square miles and has an official population of 137,000. The true population is likely to be twice that in size due to underreporting of unregistered immigrants.

The shifting population mix is reflected in the composition of community churches and schools that brought Whites into contact with the immigrant newcomers. Latin Americans, for example, revived the declining Our Lady of Sorrows Roman Catholic Parish and by the 1970s Dominicans and South Americans made up half of the population. Between 1960 and 1976, the five community primary schools' White population fell from 89% to 28% of the student body, while the Hispanic population grew to 50%, Asians to 12%, and Blacks to 10%.

In 1990, where three-quarters of the community's 4,000 Newton High School students don't speak English at home and the star of "Annie" was from Afghanistan, there are bilingual or English as a Second Language classes for children speaking 46 languages. At the City Hospital Center in Elmhurst—where seven women were in labor at the same time recently, all from different countries—a bank of volunteer translators is on call (Polsky, 1990).

Elmhurst-Corona is officially known as Community District 4 (CD4), one of the city's 59 community districts designated by the city government. In 1990 CD4's median household income was $30,100, nearly the same as the $29,800 figure for the city overall. In addition, average household incomes by race in CD4 were closer than anywhere else in Queens. In 1990 they stood at $36,000 for Asians, slightly over $35,000 for Blacks, $35,000 for Whites, and $33,000 for Hispanics.

In Elmhurst-Corona diverse people and languages run into each other in a "mix never seen before"; people are involved in "countless scenes and encounters where cultures flow into one another" (Sanjek, 1998, p. 9). By most accounts, Elmhurst-Corona has surpassed most neighborhoods in its ability to absorb such a rapid influx of diverse groups "with relatively little overt conflict" (Sanjek, 1998, p. 8). What role has the community and the local precinct played in this process? Much of the tale revolves around community interests and the extent to which the police have actively attended to community quality of life concerns and issues.

QUALITY OF LIFE AND THE POLICE

Like all city inhabitants, Elmhurst-Corona's residents seek to live in a safe, secure, healthy and enriching environment. These neighborhood concerns are frequently labeled "quality of life" issues. They may take several forms but they all speak to residents' everyday sense of well-being for themselves and their families. These concerns include crowded and understaffed schools, inadequate youth programs, congested streets and subways, unsafe homes and workplaces, insufficient beat police officers, lack of inspection of unsafe homes and workplaces, drug dealing, housing code violations, unruly street peddlers, prostitution, panhandlers, and gambling.

The nature of police-community relations in the 110th Precinct, as in other city areas, is largely tied to community action and its confidence in the police's willingness and ability to address the needs of the community. This theme repeatedly emerges among the diverse groups residing in Elmhurst-Corona. Their concerns are primarily articulated through organized groups which, when they fully emerge, generally reflect the aspirations of newly arrived residents.

Hayddee Zambrana, for example, was born in Puerto Rico, moved to Jamaica Queens during her teens and moved to Elmhurst in 1978, where she met other Latin Americans, including Puerto Ricans, Colombians, Ecuadorians, and Argentineans, also concerned about underrepresentation in Queens politics and inadequate social services for Spanish speakers. In 1980, while working nights as a civilian employee at the 110th Precinct, she organized Ciudadano Conscientes de Queens—Concerned Citizens of Queens (CCQ).

In addition to traditional group political activity and lobbying for improved services and increased Hispanic representation in community boards, Zambrana and Clara Salas, another Latino activist, joined Community Board 4, and later Latin American membership doubled to six in 1984. Like other active community groups, Zambrana and CCQ reported on quality of life issues, including drug selling on Roosevelt Avenue, conditions in Linden Park, and problems with car service. CCQ subsequently became more vigorous and met with Corona Plaza merchants—Colombian, Dominican, Cuban, Korean, Arab, Greek, Jewish—and "conveyed their complaints to the 110th precinct's commanding officer" through repeated meetings (Sanjek, 1998, p. 294).

In the highly residential borough of Queens, complaints often focus on the heavy traffic and parking congestion aggravated by new houses of worship and additional housing construction with parking provided for only two-thirds of these dwelling units. This perennial Queens problem has stirred numerous groups to work in concert with the local 110th Precinct. In 1987, for example, when the city's car services were required to register with the Taxi and Limousine Commission, there were 40,000 livery cabs. Some radio cars transported prostitutes, drugs, and drug money. The CB4 district manager, "Rose Rothschild and 110 precinct officers testified against two companies whose drivers had been arrested on these counts, and local suspicions about car services were reinforced in 1994 when police found $150,000 in cash in a livery car . . . " (Sanjek, 1998, p. 187).

Two years later, precinct community meeting participants complained to the precinct commander about inadequate precinct police response and coverage in drug dealing areas. The commanding officer noted the shortage of personnel due to retirements and insufficient replacements. A broad coalition including the Lefrak City Tenants Association (LCTA), the organization formed by Edna Baskin (a Black resident and leader), Concerned Community Adults (CCA), local merchants, and local officials' liaisons fashioned a plan and agreed to write to the mayor and the borough police commander requesting greater police presence. Within two weeks the Tactical Narcotics Team returned and made several drug arrests.

Over the next year, communications among those who had attended the meeting increased. What began as a response to a specific problem developed into a broad coalition whereby the merchants helped revive a 57th Avenue merchants' association; the group's Dominican president, a supermarket owner, and several Korean members paid for Christmas street decorations and donated meals and snacks to Baskin's summer youth area cleanup; and two LCTA officers joined CB4 (Sanjek, 1998, p. 249).

Baskin's CCA cleanup activity received a great deal of community attention. For example, a dinner hosted by a local Korean restaurant owner and a subsequent celebration dinner included a wide spectrum of community leaders, the 110th Precinct community affairs officers (generally two to a precinct, community affairs officers are responsible for forging close ties with the community), and the youngsters involved in the cleanup.

The community gauges police commitment to quality of life by its activities to address these concerns (Interviews, 2000). When residents consider police activities and/or capacity insufficient, they lobby for more energetic and extra precinct police officers. For example, when crime rates swelled in the late 1980s, the Elmhurst-Corona neighborhood lobbied for more beat cops and its share of the NYPD's Community Patrol Officer Program, which, by the mid-1990s, restored the citywide and local police force to its pre-1975 fiscal crisis levels (McElroy et al., 1993).

In the final analysis, effective community quality of life pursuits rest on the shoulders of vigorous community group leaders. These leaders assemble ethnically based organizations that insist on community and police respect for their rights. Enhanced community activity and interaction with the precinct often accompanies the coming of age of specific ethnic groups.

COMMUNITY GROUPS

Elmhurst-Corona's Korean community is one of many such examples. In 1985, 200 Koreans assembled outside the 110th Precinct protesting two recent arrests. The Ad-Hoc Korean Committee against Police Brutality claimed that police intervention in a dispute between a Korean Elmhurst boutique owner and a customer led to officers addressing the storeowner in racist terms, beating him at the precinct house, and charging him with disorderly conduct and resisting arrest. The committee also maintained that a Korean taxi driver, stopped for speeding, had been addressed in racist terms and then beaten and held for three days at the precinct. The police denied these contentions.

These and other incidents led to the formation of the Korean American Association of Mid-Queens (KAAMQ), which enrolled local Korean businesses in the 110th Precinct area and surrounding communities, forged alliances with other community groups, and registered over 2,000 Korean voters in 1995–1996. As they became better organized, they linked up with the police in securing enhanced protection for their constituency. They donated a bicycle to the precinct, addressed precinct officers about Korean culture and attitudes toward the police, and provided the police with translators when a problem involving Koreans arose (Sanjek, 1998, pp. 296–298).

In addition to single ethnic groups, geographically based associations, encompassing many ethnic groups in Elmhurst-Corona, have been vital forces in addressing community quality of life issues. They tackle a wide range of issues, including public safety. In this capacity, these groups maintain close contact with the 110th Precinct. In fact, one such group, the Coalition of United Residents for a Safer Community, virtually owes its origin to a proposal, 14 years ago, to move the precinct from its present location. Lucy Schilero, a beautician who grew up on 43rd Avenue (across from the precinct house), returned in 1977, with her husband, to her grandmother's house on the same block. (This block is home to Ecuadorians, Greeks, Hungarians, Brazilians, Bangladeshis, Dominicans, Chinese, and Irish.)

At first dismayed by inadequate street parking, Schilero assembled a small group of local residents to petition for added parking space. In 1986 the plan to relocate the 110th Precinct enabled Schilero to enlist larger numbers in her recently formed Coalition of United Residents for a Safer Community. The Coalition not only collected over 4,000 signatures in the successful petition to retain the precinct's location, it reached out to numerous ethnic groups, newly arrived residents, tenants' associations, CB4, and other civic groups. The Coalition's membership is based on members' residences not background. Its diversity induced Schilero to get three-way calling on her telephone so translators could help her talk to neighbors and plan civic events. "We are too mixed for bigotry," asserts Schilero, who, like other community leaders, shares membership in other community groups. She is a member of Community Board 4 and the 110th Precinct's community council, which has been in existence for over 20 years and consists of precinct and community members.

Like other community efforts, quality of life issues take center stage in the Coalition's activities. They include combating illegal occupancy and rent increases, absentee landlords and evictions, drug selling along Roosevelt Avenue, waging rent strikes and court suits against deteriorating services, and maintaining adequate police, jobs, recreational programs, and other local support. "The one thing that draws New Yorkers together," Schilero says, "is their fear of crime. We go after the landlords who rent to drug dealers and prostitutes and, of course, they hate us" (Duggan, 1998).

The Coalition has continued to work closely with the precinct. At a 1993 Coalition meeting held at the 110th Precinct house, for example, top police brass defended the withdrawal of the NYPD Tactical Narcotics Task Force from the area in the face of escalating drug activity along Roosevelt Avenue. After the meeting, new police antidrug efforts were introduced in the area (Kile, 1993). Drug activity is a recurrent community concern. In 1997, the 110th Precinct's commanding officer reported to 500 Coalition meeting attendees that newly assigned precinct rookie police officers would assist members of the Roosevelt Avenue Task Force (a combination of officers from the 110th and neighboring 115th Precinct devoted to concentrated criminal activity on Roosevelt Avenue in combating drugs and prostitution (Persaud, 1997).

What the police administration previously designated as minor irritations now receives public attention as quality of life offenses. For example, in 1995 when New York State almost removed adjudication of city violations from criminal court, the Coalition and many other groups objected on the grounds that this threatened to emasculate police enforcement of quality of life rules banning public drinking and urination. To the "standing room only crowd" at the 110th Precinct community room, Schilero declared "We are worth our tax money, we are worth our vote, we are worth being listened to" (Anderson, 1995, p. 6).

The coalition has over 2,000 members from numerous local immigrant groups. "When you join this organization," Schilero asserts, "you had better be ready to go to work. We definitely need people to work with us on the quality of life issues that are facing us all" (McAteer, 1996, p. 3). Coalition meetings frequently award those who have contributed to the community including 110th Precinct members such as commanding officers, community police officers, and community affairs officers.

RECASTING COMMUNITY POLICING IN THE 110TH PRECINCT

The Coalition is part of the broad band of local groups who not only insist on better quality of life policing, but also claim their share of a larger community-oriented police force (as described above). The NYPD's 1990s expansion in numbers has always received attention among the residents of the precinct. In 1993, in the midst of this growth, the 110th Precinct's commanding officer reported to a Coalition meeting that the precinct recently received 30 new officers who would be placed on community policing foot patrol duty. This group constituted approximately half of the full total of 55 officers slated for the precinct (Mitchell, 1993).

For the community, however, the issue of adequate patrol staffing is a relentless topic. Even though the NYPD has expanded approximately 30% in the last decade, the bulk of this growth, since 1994, has been assigned to units that either do not report to precinct commanders or are directed either by headquarters or the boroughs. Consequently, local communities have less input into the placement and activities of these units (New York City Council, 2000).

The large growth of borough narcotics officers is symptomatic of this expansion of specialized nonuniform units. Narcotics officers have increased from 2,138 in April 1997 to 3,284 in January 1999. On the other hand, according to the New York City Council, the number of uniformed officers assigned to neighborhood precincts between 1997 and 1999 declined from 17,619 to 16,575 in January 1999 despite the fact that the total number of uniformed officers grew by more than 2,000 (New York City Council, 2000).

The shrinkage of precinct community policing and other officers first received community attention after post-1994 NYPD shifts in personnel. In 1995, the district manager Rose Rothschild (previously supportive of the quality and quantity of beat officers) confronted the new 110th Precinct commander: "This administration is not committed to community policing. It looks like it is dying out." He responded, "The department philosophy is that everybody is doing community policing. In the 110, the Community Policing Unit is intact, downsized a bit." "I want more cops walking the beat," Rothschild replied. "When criminals see the patrol officers they know you're there, and they go somewhere else" (Sanjek, 1998, pp. 158, 163). Nevertheless, by 1996 there were only eight 110th Precinct community policing officers left, whereas there had been 15 beat officers in 1993 (Sanjek, 1998).

The precinct's total patrol strength also fluctuated over the years. According to Mayor Dinkins's community policing Safe Streets Plan, the 110th would grow from 187 to 265 officers. "Patrol strength steadily increased from 1992 until 1994. By 1997, however, the 110th's total officer complement stood at 233, not the 265 promised by the Safe Streets, Safe City Program . . . and [patrol strength] numbered 188—just one more than the pre-Safe Streets, Safe City level" (Sanjek, 1998, pp. 163–164). In 1999 there were 235 total officers in the precinct, which increased to 260 in 2000.

In this era of heightened public scrutiny and concern for proficient and equitable policing of diverse communities, precinct commanders face enormous challenges. How do they sustain and advance the crime decline while shoring up community confidence in the police? In operational terms, can a commander increase a neighborhood's sense of security through additional beat cops and not diminish other precinct crime fighting efforts (which, in the last few years, have been primarily based on specialized, nonuniform units such as anticrime and narcotics)?

RECENT DEVELOPMENTS

How to best use precinct resources claimed the attention of Captain James McCabe when he was assigned his first command, Elmhurst-Corona's 110th Precinct, in 1999. For the previous 10 months, McCabe had served as executive officer of a nearby precinct in Queens, the 113th. As the number two person in that precinct, he had been aware of the conflicting demands placed on precinct commanders. On the one hand, neighborhoods were frequently concerned about quality of life offenses and securing adequate police presence while headquarters, on the other hand, applied pressure to continue the downward trend in crime statistics.

When McCabe assumed command, crime was on the rise in the precinct. Compared with the year before, serious crime was up 1.3% and increasing fast (NYPD Compstat Report, July 18, 1999). In June, a Corona man, Ivan Collado, was arrested for the fatal stabbing of a former Flushing High School basketball star over an argument dating back to junior high school (*Newsday,* June 9, 1999, p. 44). The precinct recorded three murders the week just prior to McCabe's arrival, and robbery and serious assault were plaguing the community.

Organized community groups and local civic leaders took the opportunity to stake their claim for more police patrols and greater attention to neighborhood quality of life issues. During McCabe's first week at the precinct he met with organized groups representing the Korean Americans of Mid-Queens, Corona-Hispanic Merchants, and the African National Congress, as well as civic associations representing the communities of Maspeth, Elmhurst, Lefrak City, Corona Heights, and Newtown, all staking their claim to police services and all representing scores of different ethnic enclaves in the precinct. Most common among these demands was greater attention to neighborhood quality of life concerns, particularly along the "Roosevelt Avenue Corridor," which is one of the unique characteristics of the 110th Precinct. Roosevelt Avenue is the northern border of the 110th Precinct and a major thoroughfare in the borough of Queens. Roosevelt Avenue is a main shopping area during the day and the site of the #7 train, which carries 100,000 daily commuters into Manhattan. At night Roosevelt Avenue becomes a haven for nightlife. Bars and clubs line the avenue attracting people from all parts of Queens. The nightlife also attracts a seedier side, making Roosevelt Avenue a location known for prostitution, drugs, and other illegal activities. The characteristics of Roosevelt Avenue also make it a haven for serious index crime. In fact, more than 25% of the precinct's index crime is committed along Roosevelt Avenue. So much attention is paid to Roosevelt Avenue that the precinct specifically tracks incidents that occur on the avenue and one block south for the entire stretch of the precinct. This area is called the "corridor." Controlling this small area is key to controlling crime in the precinct.

Nevertheless, the needs and demands of the rest of the precinct compete with the demands of the corridor. With the simultaneous rise in other area and corridor crime, the balance of the precinct felt underserved. During McCabe's initial meetings with civic associations, community groups, block associations, school principals, and elected officials, the constant refrain was more police patrols. Every community organization sang the same song "When is our Beat Cop Coming Back" (Interviews, 2000).

The precinct's supervising command, Patrol Borough Queens North, further complicated the competing demands for Elmhurst-Corona's precinct resources. In New York City, each of the department's 76 precincts falls under one of the NYPD's eight major geographic organizational units—the Patrol Borough. The 110th Precinct falls under the jurisdiction of Patrol Borough Queens North. In April of 1999, Queens North mandated that at least 50% of the police officers assigned in each of its precincts be assigned to patrol squads in order to handle 911 calls for service. With ever-present 911 demands for service in Queens and equally increasing police response times, mandating specific manning levels ensured the Borough Command sufficient resources available to answer these calls.

In order to address crime and quality of life concerns in their precincts, Commanding Officers are usually given wide latitude in assigning personnel. Generally, a balance must be struck between providing a sufficient amount of officers to respond to 911 calls for service, 24 hours a day, seven days per week, and retaining a fair amount of officers to address specific concerns, thus relieving them from the direct responsibility of responding to

911 calls for service. Plainclothes officers, Community Policing Officers, Narcotics Officers, Peddler Enforcement, Traffic Safety, and so on all fall into the second group. The reassignment of even one of these officers to the patrol unit often means a loss of direct attention to a precinct condition in favor of 911 responses.

While seemingly benign, this borough mandate required a significant reshuffling of precinct personnel. Crime reduction strategies, which often call for specialized people to perform specialized functions and hence the creation of specialized precinct units, drew manpower away from patrol strength. When the 50% rule was implemented the spring of 1999, one of the hardest hit specialized units was the Community Policing Unit (CPU). In order to fulfill the requirement, five officers were reassigned out of the CPU into patrol squads. This reshuffling reduced the CPU from 15 to 10 officers.

Thus, in July of 1999 the 110th Precinct's 10-person CPU covered 10 beats. Despite the fact that the 50% rule had been in effect for several months, CPU officers were also pulled to cover other assignments in the precinct. For example, when patrol cars were short, or prisoners needed to be guarded, the CPU officers were the first ones to be used to backfill. The result was that while CPU officers were officially assigned full time on paper, in actuality they patrolled their beats less than half the time. The community was aware of this problem and wanted to get their fair share of the precinct's resources. Citizens and community leaders experienced this diminished presence of beat officers and communicated their concerns to the precinct (Interviews, 2000).

RESUSCITATING COMMUNITY INTERACTION

While community policing in the 110th Precinct was not dead, it was on life support. McCabe's challenge was to increase both the crime fighting and the community service efforts of the entire command.

The nature of police-community relations in the 110th Precinct, as in most areas of the city, is largely tied to community confidence in the willingness of the police to address their quality of life concerns. This theme repeatedly emerges among the diverse groups residing in Elmhurst and Corona. The dynamic between the police and the community is intensified in areas like Elmhurst-Corona because of its diversity. The diversity is not a stumbling block in police-community relations; rather it becomes a catalyst for organization and a means of access for immigrant communities into the valuable services the police can provide. What is common to each stage of development, both on the police and community side, is a willingness to work with each other toward improving the residents' quality of life.

McCabe thought that the command should be fashioned to meet the natural needs of an enormously diverse community, rather than structured only to handle 911 calls for service or addressing specific conditions. The key was to create an organizational structure that was capable of identifying community-police problems, formulating a solution acceptable to the community, implementing these solutions, and following up with the community to see if their concerns were addressed. This system also needed to be compatible with problems present in the Hispanic, Asian, African American, and the dozens of other ethnic groups found in the Elmhurst-Corona area. This entailed placing the right officers in the right positions and opening up the lines of communication between precinct personnel and community businesses, churches, schools, homes, and so forth. A dedicated effort was made to ensure that citizens believed they were heard, their problems were considered important, and their concerns would be addressed until they, regardless of color, culture, or creed, were satisfied.

The key to this entire process was the reorganization of the CPU. Revitalizing the community policing program meant providing it with a new mission, direction, and life. This entailed changes in precinct organization, supervision, operational policy, and personnel deployment. Essentially, the precinct needed to shift paradigms to see CPU as not merely foot patrol but as aggressive crime fighters who are community minded and attuned to their beat problems. This was crucial, because the residential beats are the heart of the diverse community. The beat officers would become the link between the community and their quality of life concerns, regardless of national origin, and the precinct and the department at large.

The linkage, however, was not based primarily on the traditional textbook approach to community policing in which the officer, in partnership with the community, creates innovative ways of addressing common neighborhood problems (Trojanowicz et al., 2001). The linkage would be based upon a different principle. It would be established on presence, responsiveness, and a willingness to participate vigorously in the amelioration of quality of life and crime conditions that were brought to the attention of the officers in particular and the precinct in general. By demonstrating the ability to be available for community concerns, by providing the access to the precinct commander and all members of the command, and by actively addressing community complaints, residents of the precinct were provided with a solution to their problems, tailor-made to their unique needs. The delivery of police service would become not "in partnership with" the community under the "old" Community Policing (Trojanowicz et al., 2001), but "on behalf of" the community as defined by community concerns.

The first task in this transformation was to reduce specialization within the precinct. While it is necessary to have officers specially trained to do critical functions, the full-time assignment of officers to some of these positions was inefficient (as determined by the precinct commander). The precinct, for example, fielded three squads of officers, called "conditions" units. These three squads, comprising roughly 20 officers assigned to steady hours, were responsible for addressing various precinct conditions during their tour of duty. For example, the day-tour conditions unit was responsible for detaining truant kids and returning them to school.

But what is the best use of precinct resources for truancy enforcement? While not directed to gather truants, precinct patrol officers are traditionally expected to do so if they see truants gathering. Cumbersome administrative procedures, however, impede the process of securing truants and returning them to their school or a "catchment" location. Due to these burdens, patrol officers generally shy away from this activity. If left exclusively to the patrol officers, truancy enforcement would not be conducted to the extent necessary to meet precinct crime reduction goals. Therefore, conditions units were established in all precincts for this truancy enforcement function. The 110th Precinct conditions unit, for example, generally gathered about 50 truants per week (Compstat Report, December 31, 2000). A conditions unit of five police officers familiar with the truancy process can return several times more truant kids per day than an officer assigned to routine patrol.

While specialization is necessary to address conditions, problems can arise. In the truancy example, for instance, what were conditions unit officers doing before the school kids became truant, what were they doing after they processed the kids for being truant, and, most importantly, what did they do to tie in the truancy enforcement with the needs of the community? Essentially, the conditions officers, as assessed by their supervisors, were underutilized during their periods of "nonenforcement" and had no contact with members of the community outside their enforcement role. In the 110th Precinct, McCabe assumed perhaps that the answer to the double-edged question of crime reduction and meeting minority community relations might lie in the elimination of condition-based operations and the creation of geographic-based operations where the beat officer would be the primary focus.

The switch to geographic-based operations required elimination of all the precinct conditions units, spawning an equal increase in the size of the community-policing unit. This shift in philosophy placed a greater burden on the CPU supervisors and beat officers, requiring revised thinking about the way policing was done in the 110th Precinct. The crime reduction initiatives were not being abandoned since crime was on the rise. To the contrary, these efforts were being increased. Officers' assignments, however, were not geared to a specific condition, but to a specific area to be covered. The crime reduction operations were to be performed by the CPU using beat officers for the time necessary. When the operation was completed, beat officers not required to process paperwork or arrests were returned to their community beats to perform the balance of their tour. Their time on patrol, visibility in the community, and attention to community concerns all increased while also enhancing the entire precinct's crime fighting functions.

The difference in this approach was that the activities of the beat officers were grounded in the information received from the community. The enforcement operations were designed to address the complaints raised by community members. The beat officers, with knowledge of the local needs of the businesses and residents, conducted their operations accordingly. The method of obtaining the information and the manner in which it was disseminated was unique to this area of Queens. How was this specifically accomplished?

Communications

One of the most important tools in policing a diverse community is the management of information. An open channel of communication between the police and the community is essential in identifying and addressing police problems. The free flow of information in minority communities, however, may sometimes by restricted due to tensions in police-community relations. Captain McCabe seized an opportunity to provide access and open and expand a channel of communication in order to promote the free exchange of information between the 110th Precinct and the Elmhurst-Corona community.

What would come to be named the "Community Notification Worksheet" was used by McCabe to disseminate important information to principal members of the various community organizations. McCabe and his community affairs officers chose the representatives after examining the precinct demographics and ensuring that all political, religious, educational, and ethnic groups would receive fair representation. The concept was simple. Whenever something unusual would happen in the precinct, McCabe, one of the CPU supervisors, or one of the community affairs officers would contact each member listed on the "Community Notification Worksheet" and tell them about the incident (the incidents, the person notifying the community, and the method of notification, e.g., phone or personal contact, were selected by McCabe after a careful review of the circumstances). The incidents could be serious such as murders or patterns of rapes or robberies, or they could be minor such as upcoming events involving street fairs or crime prevention initiatives.

The notifications not only provided valuable information about happenings in the community but also opened up a dialogue between the two groups. Once the phone call was made, it offered the community member being contacted an opportunity to lodge a complaint about a quality of life or crime condition in the community. Also, and most importantly, the community member in question was given a direct line of communication with the precinct and could vent the complaints of members of their constituency. The elected officials, school principals, block association presidents, ethnic community leaders, merchant association presidents, and clergy leaders no longer had to be in the dark about police services. The police empowered them with information about their communities; they in turn used this information to educate their groups, and the people in their groups would pass along valuable information about neighborhood conditions to their representatives and this would in turn go to the precinct.

A community group called COMET, which stood for Communities of Maspeth and Elmhurst Together, was active in the 110th Precinct. COMET represented an enormously diverse group of White, Black, Asian, and Hispanic residents and businesses. In July of 2000 a person was committing strong-armed robberies of young Asian women as they returned home from the subway. The robber struck six times in a matter of two weeks and Captain McCabe alerted COMET, through its president, about these crimes. The call went out to the entire community that a robber was preying on young Asian women. The Asian residents in the area were successful in contacting the four Asian newspapers in the area. The papers ran stories about the attacks, and within a few days the entire community was informed of the situation. On his seventh try the robber was caught in the act as he tried to rob a 30-year-old woman of Filipino descent on an Elmhurst street. Two members of the community interrupted the robber during the act as they sat on their stoop. The community members happened to be two sons of a member of COMET who had told her family to be watchful of the bandit (*Queens Ledger,* September 29, 2000).

Access to Precinct Resources

An added benefit of the "Community Notification Worksheet" was that it encouraged open communication between diverse groups and the precinct and almost immediate access to the Precinct Commander to resolve neighborhood problems. An incident within the homosexual community highlights the benefit such access has in dealing with problems.

As discussed, prostitution was one of the chronic conditions within the 110th Precinct. Not only were there female prostitutes to accommodate heterosexual patrons, but there were also male prostitutes to handle homosexual patrons. The 110th Precinct regularly conducts Operation "Losing Proposition," an NYPD tactic that addresses street prostitution. This operation calls for an undercover officer to stand in an area known for prostitution activity and wait for a "john" to solicit them with money in exchange for sex. Once the offer is made, the "john" is arrested for patronizing a prostitute.

On one evening in October of 2000, the 110th Precinct deployed a male officer to act as a prostitute to solicit male johns (records of the NYPD Vice Enforcement Unit indicate that complaints of male prostitution in the Roosevelt Avenue Corridor are as frequent as complaints of female prostitution). During this particular "Losing Proposition" several gay men were arrested for propositioning the male undercover officer with sex for money.

One defendant in particular complained to a prominent member of the gay community that his arrest was unlawful and that the police mistreated him. Having a preexisting relationship with the 110th Precinct, the member of the gay community complained strenuously to Captain McCabe and demanded an immediate remedy to this situation. A meeting was held at the precinct between several members of the gay community, local elected officials, and members of the 110th Precinct, including the supervisors who conducted the operation.

The community had cause for concern, and the precinct had equal cause to rectify this situation to root out mistreatment and provide fair and equitable treatment to all community residents. Essentially, Captain McCabe opened up the doors of the precinct to the gay community. They were invited to join the precinct on "Losing Proposition" operations to observe the way they are conducted. They were offered access to the 110th Precinct training session to lecture officers on the needs of the gay community and the responsibility of the police to provide fair and impartial treatment. And they were offered the opportunity to lodge a formal complaint against the command and the officer involved in the alleged conduct. All of these options were explored. The gay community received an opportunity to educate the police on their needs and remedy actions taken against one of their members. The 110th Precinct was able to reassure the gay community that they were being afforded police services equitably. The open and continual line of communication between the police and this minority community was forged at this meeting.

Precinct Newsletter

In order to strengthen linkages with the community, the CPU developed a monthly newsletter to distribute to the community. This short periodical provided crime information, crime prevention tips, and most importantly served as a means of reaching and forging close communication with the public. The newsletter was developed in collaboration between Captain McCabe, the community policing unit, and the community. Each month the newsletter was distributed to every person listed on any form of community organization known to the 110th Precinct. The content of the newsletter was created almost exclusively by the precinct, but one-half of the four-page journal was devoted to the submissions of the community. Often times this section would include letters written to the precinct about commendable actions by a member of the precinct, but also the section fielded information sent by the civic, ethnic, and religious groups alerting the precinct to crime or quality of life conditions, or announcing upcoming events. All groups were encouraged to participate, although the content was mainly created by the precinct.

Community Input

To further the precinct's outreach efforts a Precinct Management Team (PMT) was reestablished. While not new in concept, the PMT had been nonexistent for many years and was re-created to give the community input into precinct operations again. The PMT is made up of representatives from the local City Council Districts, the Precinct Community Council President, and four prominent members of the community selected by Captain McCabe. Together with the precinct's executive staff and PBA (the patrol union) delegates, the group meets monthly to discuss precinct policy, the needs of the community, and the needs of the police officers. The informal meetings have proven to be a useful tool in providing the community greater access to the police and allowing the police officers, through their union representatives, to see the community as an entity requiring their service.

Similarly, a Precinct Clergy Council was established. The 110th Precinct's community affairs officers combed the precinct and identified every religious institution within its boundaries. With over 60 institutions identified, the 110th Precinct sent notices to the religious leaders of these institutions inviting them into the precinct for a luncheon meeting to discuss matters of mutual concern. Captain McCabe believed that access to diverse members of all religious represented in the community, who were ordinarily either too busy or too fearful of the police, could be accomplished through their religious leaders.

Presumably there was a large segment of the community that needed police services but never availed themselves to these services. The local clergy was considered an excellent conduit to reach this population. The meetings were held every other month inside the precinct station house with lunch provided by the NYPD. The sessions provided an opportunity for the local clergy to get to know the precinct commander and many members of the precinct in order to air their concerns and enhance citizen trust of the police. The clergy, in turn, activated some of their membership to become more engaged in police-community issues.

PRECINCT REORGANIZATION: THE TEAM CONCEPT AND SUPERVISION

The clergy and other community leaders made it increasingly clear that they wanted greater uniform beat presence on the precinct's streets. There were many obstacles, however, in accomplishing more CPU-community contact. CPU beat officers, for example, were being pulled in several contrary directions. Beat officers were permitted to set their own hours, which presumably coincided with their beat conditions, resulting in their reporting for work at odd hours. The variability of reporting, often without their specific supervisors present at the time, led them to be easy prey for odd jobs around the station house. If the precinct found itself short a sector car, the Desk Officer in charge found the appearance of a newly reporting CPU beat officer as an able replacement. So while beat officers were supposed to be assigned to their beats, they were often used for other purposes.

The first policy to rectify this was to require the CPU to be organized into teams consisting of one sergeant and six beat officers. The dissolution of the conditions units (discussed previously) smoothed the quick buildup of CPU teams. In order to protect them from being assigned to nonbeat duties, the CPU teams were required to report to work at the same time. With the supervisor reporting at the same time, the beat officers are afforded greater protection and are less frequently assigned to other duties. And McCabe's directive barring their assignment to non-CPU functions also tied beat officers closer to their beats.

Enhanced Community Operations

Part of the reorganization entailed a shift in operations. No longer were CPU beat officers deployed without specific goals and objectives. Under the new system, beat officers took on additional responsibilities that not only extended their community outreach but also gave them a more prominent role in precinct crime reduction strategies. These activities endowed the officers with enhanced importance in the eyes of the community and also their fellow non-CPU officers. Some examples follow.

Burglary, Auto Theft, and Stolen Auto Recovery Recanvass Sheets During the initial report of a crime the responding officer is required to shift through the general area to see if anyone saw or heard the incident occurring. In police jargon, this process is called a "canvass." Every day the CPU officers were provided with copies of the crime complaints for occurrences on their beats. The complaints were originally provided to inform the beat officers of crimes on their beats. They also offer, however, an excellent opportunity to meet members of the community. Called the "CPU Recanvass," beat officers receiving crime complaints of burglary, auto theft, and the recovery of a stolen vehicle on their beats are now required to go back to the scene of the crime a few days later and perform a "recanvass" of the area.

The recanvass performs many valuable community outreach functions. First, it serves as an opportunity to reinterview victims and neighbors to elicit information about the crime and the local criminals. Second, it serves as a means of introducing the CPU officer to residents of his or her beat. Third, it reassures crime victims that the police department is interested in their victimization and responsive to their needs. Fourth, it gives the police department an opportunity to offer crime prevention services to prevent future occurrences. And fifth, it shows the "bad guys" that the police are watching. The simple act of returning to the scene of a burglary or auto theft offered reassurance to the crime victims—particularly those in the minority community who felt ignored or rejected—that the police were interested in their problem and willing to assist in whatever way possible.

School/Church Crossings Under the new systems, beat officers are now required to be present at all school and church dismissals on their beat. At first, many residents were skeptical at the sight of a uniformed police officer at Sunday services. But after a while the residents offered praise and began to rave about the police attention they were receiving. Furthermore, the presence of officers during school dismissals was successful at ending some afterschool violence before it even started (Interviews, 2000).

Rush Hour Subway Posts The use of public transportation is a daily routine in the 110th Precinct as in other New York communities. In addition to their other assignments, beat officers were required to spend 30 minutes per day posted at local bus stops or subway stations. Once again, the purpose was high visibility. For a few minutes a day the officers could be seen by hundreds of people either going to work or coming home.

COORDINATION

With the increase in CPU personnel and responsibility, it was necessary to coordinate operations and to increase communication both within the precinct and with the community. The following mechanisms evolved as ways of improving operations.

CPU Conditions Worksheet and Log

To better track CPU activities, Captain McCabe created a worksheet and a logbook. He began using the worksheets as a means of tracking complaints given to him by members of the community at various meetings, events, and so on. What began as an informal method of keeping track of complaints evolved into a system of communication between the precinct and the community. McCabe would fill out a worksheet and send it to the CPU to handle.

Ten months later, in May 2000, the CPU also started recording community complaints in worksheets and the logbook as the worksheets became a useful tool for the beat officers themselves to utilize to document complaints on their beats. Not only did the worksheets document what the officers were doing on their beats, but they also gave the CPU supervisors an understanding of beat conditions so the supervisors could deploy all the officers in the unit to address problem areas. Community members repeatedly referred to the worksheets and logbooks as important elements in the precinct's outreach network.

At the present time, the complaints generally come from members of the community at community meetings open to all members of the public or when they call the CPU Office. The information ranges from graffiti problems and abandoned cars to noise conditions, drug sales, and reports of domestic violence. All members of the command are permitted to prepare the worksheets, but so far they have only been used by Captain McCabe and the CPU officers. The worksheets are logged in by the CPU office coordinator and distributed to the beat officer concerned and all the supervisors in the unit. This procedure ensured that complaints were being documented, daily activities (including scheduled hours) were justifiable, and permitted follow-up and evaluation of work performed. Each week Captain McCabe and the Special Operations Lieutenant, Kevin Keenan, reviewed the complaints and conditions called into the office and personally visited the locations and contacted the resident making the complaint. Not only were conditions being addressed but also residents and business owners felt the police were responsive and interested in their community.

Precinct Meetings

Each week Captain McCabe holds a meeting with the Special Operations Lieutenant and all the CPU sergeants. The purpose of the meeting is to discuss any conditions called into the office, the plan of attack for the coming week, the success of last week's work, and any logistical or personnel concerns. In addition to general crime trends, the CPU worksheet-logbook is a source of discussion. As previously mentioned, the logbook is the mechanism used to catalogue complaints coming into the office.

CONCLUSION

Advancing firmer police-minority community cooperation through community policing in the 110th Precinct is not dead; it is alive and well. But community policing in the 110th Precinct is not simply traditional foot patrol and community organizing. It is enforcement-oriented, community-oriented, and responsive. Community policing has evolved into a true service-oriented approach, addressing seminal questions. What are the pressing crime, disorder, public relations, and community outreach problems? What is the best way for the precinct to organize in order to respond to those problems? The answer to these questions is the same: create a unit attentive to the needs of the community while at the same time keeping an eye on the bottom-line of serious criminal offending. By providing visibility in highly traveled areas, by responding back to the crime scenes, by aggressively attacking disorder and crime conditions, by listening to the needs of the community and responding immediately, and by working closely with both precinct and community members, community relations and crime fighting can both improve.

REFERENCES

Alderson, J. (1979). *Policing freedom.* Plymouth: Macdonald and Evans.

Alderson, J. (1998). *Principled policing.* Winchester: Waterside Press.

Amnesty International. (1996, June). *Police brutality and excessive force in the New York City Police Department.*

Anderson, R. (1995, November 1). Coalition calls for quality of life rules, *Jackson Heights News,* p. 6.

Blumstein, A. (Ed.) (2000). *The Crime Drop in America.* Cambridge: Cambridge University Press.

Burke, R. (Ed.) (1998). *Zero tolerance policing.* Leicester: Perpetuity Press.

Butterfield, F. (1999, April 4). Ideas and trends: Citizens as allies: Rethinking the strong arm of the law, *New York Times,* p. 4.

Civilian Complaint Review Board, New York (May 2000). *Semiannual status report, January–December 1999,* Vol. VII, No. 2.

Compstat Report, NYPD, July 18, 1999; December 31, 2000.

Duffee, D., et al. (2001). *Police-community interaction and sustained community capacity: Results from a survey of neighborhood leaders.* Washington DC: National Institute of Justice.

Duggan, D. (1998, May 12). A nudge who makes news, *Newsday,* p. 2.

Fordham Urban Law Journal (2000, December). Special issue: The challenge of urban policing Vol. XXVIII, No. 29.

Greene, J. (1999). Zero tolerance: A case study of police policies and practices in New York City, *Crime and Delinquency, 45,* 172–187.

Interviews with community leaders and members, January through December 2000.

Karmen, A. (2001). *New York murder mystery.* New York: New York University Press.

Kile, L. (1994, June 24). Coalition wants more police to fight drugs, *Times Newsweekly,* p. 7.

McAteer, Shane (1996, July 18). Concern for community prompts growth of coalition, *Queens Gazette,* p. 3.

McElroy, J. et al. (1993). *Community policing: The CPOP in New York.* Newbury Park: Sage.

Mitchell, B. (1993, April 8). Residents Coalition Meeting Draws Full House to Hear Guest Speakers, *Times Newsweekly,* p. 5.

Newfield, J. (1999, February 12). Starving for justice from police, *New York Post,* p. 6.

Newsday, (1999, June 9), p. 44, Corona Man Charged in Fatal Stabbing.

New York City Council. (2000, June). Report from the Public Safety Committee. New York.

Office of the New York City Public Advocate, New York (1999, September 15). *Investigation of the New York City Police Department's response to civilian complaints of police misconduct, interim report.*

Persaud, F. (1997, September 28). Elmhurst residents voice concern over narcotics, homeless in area, *Queens Gazette,* p. 9.

Polsky, C. (1990, July 4). The United Nations of Elmhurst, *Newsday,* p. 6.

Queens Ledger, (2000, September 29).

Roane, K. (1999, February 6). Elite force quells crime, but at a cost, critics say, *New York Times.*

Sanjek, R. (1998). *The future of us all.* Ithaca: Cornell University Press.

Sherman, L. (1998). *Preventing crime.* Washington, DC: National Institute of Justice.

Silverman, E. B. (1999). *NYPD battles crime: Innovative strategies in policing.* Boston: Northeastern University Press.

Trojanowicz, R., et al. (2001). *Community policing: A contemporary perspective.* Cincinnati, OH: Anderson.

Epilogue

Changing the Image of the "Symbolic Assailant"

Delores D. Jones-Brown

On January 28, 2000, police sergeant Cornel Young, Jr. (age 29), son of Providence Rhode Island's highest-ranking African American law enforcement officer, was shot to death by two fellow officers, one of whom had attended the police academy with him. Off duty and in plainclothes, his colleagues had failed to recognize Sgt. Young when he came to their assistance in an altercation involving a suspect with a gun. The original suspect survived the police encounter, while Sgt. Young was shot three times in the mistaken belief that he was an accomplice to the original perpetrator.

The Cornel Young shooting was not the first incident of "friendly fire" where police officers had mistaken "one of their own" for a perpetrator when in plainclothes and armed with a gun. Several such incidents led to the merging of New York City's Transit Police and NYPD into one integrated unit in 1995. As noted by Christopher Cooper in Chapter 9, a consistent pattern with such shootings has been that the officers on the receiving end of the "friendly fire" have overwhelmingly been officers of color, particularly African Americans.

There are, however, several aspects of the Young "friendly fire" shooting that are particularly troubling to the prospect of improving police and minority community relations. In contrast to the incidents that have involved large metropolitan police forces with personnel numbering into the thousands, the shooting takes place within a relatively small force and involves a victim who, for at least two reasons, should have been known to the shooters. Sgt. Young's father, Major Cornel Young, Sr., was, at that time, the supervisor of the community police division (Rockoff, 2000). One of the shooters, Officer Saraiva, had attended the same academy class as Young and, consequently, had been serving on the force with Young for three years. In addition, the shooting takes place at an all-night diner where, like Young, several police officers were known regulars (Rockoff, 2000). Given these facts, how could Cornel Young, Jr. have been mistaken for a perpetrator?

In 1966, in his book *Justice Without Trial,* Jerome Skolnick introduced the term "symbolic assailant" to describe the view that the police in his research had of certain individuals. He notes that:

> The policeman . . . develops a perceptual shorthand to identify certain kinds of people as **symbolic assailants** [emphasis added], that is, as persons who use gesture, language, and attire that the policeman has come to recognize as a prelude to violence. . . the policeman responds to the vague indication of danger suggested by appearance. (p. 45)

Skolnick conducted his research in a location to which he gives the fictitious name of West-ville. He goes on to note that: "The patrolman in Westville, **and probably most communities,** has come to identify the black man with danger" (Skolnick, 1966, p. 49)[emphasis added].

As noted by Anthony Harriott in Chapter 3, more than 35 years after Skolnick's original research, policing in America is still plagued by "presumed criminality" based on race. It may be argued, however, that "presumed dangerousness" rather than mere "criminality," is a greater threat to the relationship between police and minority group members because the unwarranted presumption of dangerousness leads to results that are irreversible.

Both the Diallo shooting and the death of Cornel Young, Jr. emphasize the vulnerability of Black racial minorities and males, in particular, to a *perception* of them as dangerous. However, the Young shooting goes one step further in demonstrating how race may become the overriding cue in a police encounter, blocking out the effects of other factors.

In an interview with the *Providence Journal,* Suffolk University Law professor Michael Avery provides a framework in which to examine the death of Cornel Young that might also be applied to other cases. He notes that there are two essential questions that need to be addressed:

1. Was it reasonable for these officers to think that Officer Young posed a threat to the life or safety of another person;

and

2. Was it reasonable for them not to know that he was a fellow police officer?

He noted further that:

> there's [also] a big question of whether race played a factor; **and,** was the officers' perception that Officer Young posed a danger influenced by race?
>
> If so, how much?. . . [Were] the officers assuming a person is more dangerous because he's black?; **and,** [was] this a conscious or unconscious assumption? (Breton, 2000) [emphasis added]

The Avery analysis demonstrates the complexity of issues surrounding police encounters with minority populations. Chapter 1 of this book touches upon the historical background against which the two groups must work in order to see each other as individuals entitled to fair treatment. In Chapter 2, Robert McNamara provides substantive information that confirms that despite some effort there continues to be an imbalance in the quantity and quality of how different groups are policed. In Chapter 4, Mary Gibbons discusses the intricacies of profiling as a policing tool, concluding that "profiling" itself is a valid and valuable tool. But, the extent to which race should dictate any policing practice is highly questionable and grates against the constitution. However, it is noted that recent Supreme Court decisions have left unclear the extent to which police may lawfully consider race or ethnicity in exercising their duties.

While the analysis proposed by Avery may seem quite complex, it is the kind of analysis that must be pursued within police departments and courts when innocent civilians die at the hands of the police. Typically, the analysis ends with the first question posed by Avery (i.e., was it reasonable for these officers to think that Officer Young posed a threat to the life or safety of another person) and, as noted by Cooper in Chapter 9, often officers can give an explanation, even if that explanation is not true. Whether truthful or not, such explanations are frequently accepted by legal authorities, and warranted or not, the deaths go unpunished as "tragic mistakes." (Tables 1 and 2 contain a summary of 17 incidents from the 1990s and 2000 that led to protests and/or riots because they were perceived as unlawful use of force against a minority "suspect.") These repetitive scenarios wear on the patience of minority group members, particularly in cases that involve completely innocent victims or where the police version of the facts is viewed as highly questionable. In Chapter 8, Roger Dunham and Geoffrey Alpert note that both minority and nonminority officers may be guilty of engaging in the "presumption of dangerousness" and therefore using fatal or excessive force during encounters with minority citizens. Ultimately, the advice of John Kleinig in Chapter 5 may be the most important for practicing police officers. They must develop a professional ethic that recognizes the uniqueness and importance of their profession.

In recent years, officer survival training has become an integral part of police training. There are allegations that during officer survival classes police officers are being taught that "the most important thing is to go home at the end of the shift." Indeed, Officer Solitro, the rookie officer involved in the Cornel Young shooting, is quoted as having made a similar statement during an interview after the shooting. If this is indeed the police mantra rather than the popular "To protect and serve," then all ordinary citizens are at risk. However, given the substantial evidence that minority males are most likely to be viewed as "symbolic assailants," it is clear that they are at greatest risk of death or serious bodily injury from this mind-set.

If there is not a collective effort to change the image of the "symbolic assailant" within police departments and the society at large, there is little hope to improve police-community relations by recruiting a greater number of minorities as suggested in Chapter 10. The Young shooting emphasizes the unprotected status of minorities. In addition, research such as that conducted by Dunham and Alpert in Chapter 8 will have very little value because police encounters will continue to be influenced not merely by actual criminality but by officers' perceptions of who are "suspects," and those same perceptions may influence their view of whether and how much "resistance" is being engaged in by the "suspect." (See the 1995 death of Jonny Gammage by Brentwood, Pennsylvania, police. [Jones-Brown, 2000])

The greatest hope for improved police-community relations with minority groups is for each acting police officer in each police encounter to ask himself or herself the questions in the Avery analysis. As unrealistic as this may seem during those times that split-second decisions must be made in an aura of intense fear, the hesitation may save an innocent civilian life. Chapter 11 provides proof that a good working relationship can exist between police and minority communities. Chapters 6 and 7 discuss at length the consequences of failing to address issues raised by the Avery analysis. If an officer is not willing

TABLE 1   Questionable Use of Deadly Force in Police/Minority Encounters (Select Cases Pre- and Post-Diallo)*

Post-Diallo

10/28/2000	**Anthony Dwaine Lee,** 39-year-old movie actor, shot by police five times holding a toy gun at a Hollywood, CA, mansion, Halloween costume party.
9/1/2000	**Prince Jones,** 25-year-old unarmed Howard University graduate student; son of a Philadelphia doctor, shot by a Prince Georges County, MD police officer more than 5 times in mistaken belief that he was a wanted criminal.
3/16/2000	**Patrick Dorismond,** 26-year-old security guard/bouncer shot by New York City police in an unwarranted buy/bust attempt.
1/28/2000	**Cornel Young, Jr.,** 29-year-old police sergeant and son of highest ranking Black Providence, RI, police official, shot 3 times by fellow officers, including one who had attended the police academy with him, when, in plainclothes, he attempted to assist in the arrest of another man with a gun.
11/27/1999	**Gary Hopkins,** 19-year-old, unarmed student, shot and killed by a Prince Georges County, MD, police officer after attending a school-related dance at a local fire hall.
7/24/1999	**A. Demetrius Dubose,** 28-year-old Notre Dame graduate and former professional football player, shot by San Diego, CA, police 12 times during the investigation of a criminal trespass.
5/21/1999	**Margaret Mitchell,** 55-year-old former bank teller and mother of one son shot by the police (Los Angeles) during the investigation of an alleged stolen shopping cart.
2/4/1999	**Amadou Diallo,** 22-year-old street vendor, shot 19 times in mistaken belief that he was holding a gun. (Total bullets fired, 41).

Pre-Diallo

1999 (January)	**Irvin Landrum, Jr.,** 18-year-old motorist, shot 3 times by two Claremont, CA, police officers during a stop for speeding. The officers say Landrum shot at them first, but a Los Angeles County Sheriff's Department examination of the gun that Landrum is alleged to have held found that the gun had not been fired and contained no fingerprints.
1998	**Tyisha Miller,** 19-year-old motorist, shot 12 times by Riverside, CA, police (4) who had been called by her family to render assistance because she appeared to be unconscious in her locked car. (Total shots fired, 24).
1998	**Four unarmed teenage minority males** (3 Black, 1 Latino), were shot at 11 times by New Jersey State troopers during a stop for speeding.**
1997	**Abner Louima,** attacked with a wooden stick by NYPD officer Justin Volpe following a bar fight.**

(continued)

TABLE 1 *(continued)*

1996	**Tyron Lewis,** 18-year-old unarmed, suspected car thief, shot by St. Petersburg, FL, police.
1996	**Carolyn Adams**, alleged prostitute shot by New Brunswick, NJ, police officer for biting him.
1996	**Richard Brown,** 72-year-old suspected drug dealer, was shot at 123 times by Miami Police Department's SWAT team but no drugs or drug paraphernalia were found in his home.
1995	**Jonny Gammage**, killed by Brentwood, PA, police when stopped for speeding, death by asphyxiation. (Five officers kneeled on his back crushing his chest against the asphalt).
1994	**Anthony Baez,** killed by NYPD officer who applied a chokehold during a verbal altercation about a football hitting a patrol car.

*See chapter 9 by Christopher Cooper for additional details of these and similar cases.
**Incident did not involve fatalities.
Note: In the 1985 United States Supreme Court decision, *Tennessee v. Garner,* police use of deadly force was limited to *felons* reasonably believed to present a risk of serious bodily injury or death to the officer or the public.

TABLE 2   Case Outcomes and Race of Officer(s)

Victim	Case Outcome	Race of Officer(s)
Anthony Dwaine Lee	no indictment	Black
Prince Jones	not presented to grand jury	Black
Patrick Dorismond	no indictment	Latino
Cornel Young, Jr.	no indictment	White/Portuguese
Gary Hopkins	manslaughter indictment	White
A. Demetrius Dubose	no indictment	White
Margaret Mitchell	no indictment	unspecified
Amadou Diallo	not guilty–jury verdict	White
Irvin Landrum, Jr.	no indictment	White
Tyisha Miller	no indictment	White/Latino
Four Teens	guilty pleas to false reporting ($250 fine each)	White
Abner Louima	guilty–jury verdict	White
Tyron Lewis	no indictment	White
Carolyn Adams	no indictment	White
Richard Brown	federal indictment for obstructing justice	Latino
Jonny Gammage	not guilty–jury verdict	White
Anthony Baez	not guilty–bench trial (state)	White

to absorb the risk to his or her own life, inherent in confirming that he or she is responding to the objective evidence rather than to a particular civilian based on stereotypes about the group to which that civilian belongs, it may be time to consider a new profession.

REFERENCES

Breton, T. (2000, February 8). Experts: Criminal charges against officers unlikely. *Providence Journal*, p. A8.

Jones-Brown, D. (2000). *Race, crime and punishment.* Philadelphia, PA: Chelsea House.

Rockoff, J. (2000, February 3). How it all happened: A diner fight escalates, an officer is killed. *Providence Journal*, p. A1.

Skolnick, J. (1966). *Justice without trial: Law enforcement in democratic society.* New York: John Wiley & Sons.